1979-

Arthur Frommer's Guide to

BOSTON

by
FAYE HAMMEL
assisted by
RITA POLLAK

Published by
THE FROMMER/PASMANTIER PUBLISHING CORPORATION
380 Madison Avenue
New York, New York 10017

Distributed by
SIMON & SCHUSTER
A GULF+WESTERN COMPANY
1230 Avenue of the Americas
New York, New York 10020
0-671-24906-1

Distributed outside the U.S.A. and Canada by
FLEETBOOKS
c/o Feffer and Simons, Inc.
100 Park Avenue
New York, New York 10017

Distributed in Canada by
P J PAPERBACKS LTD.
330 Steelcase Road East
Markham, Ontario L3R2M1

Motif drawings by Paul Berkow

NOTE: Although every effort was made to insure the accuracy of price information appearing in this book, it should be kept in mind that prices can and do fluctuate in the course of time.

Manufactured in the United States of America

CONTENTS

MAPS

Chapter I

AN INTRODUCTION TO BOSTON

MORE THAN ANYTHING ELSE, it is the lure of history that draws visitors to Boston. From all over the country—and the world—they come, to follow the path of Paul Revere, to visit the shrines where long-haired radicals like John Hancock and Samuel Adams incited the colonists to revolution, to pay homage to the one city that is, more than any other, the birthplace of these United States.

But there is a lot more about Boston to enchant and excite the visitor than the memories and monuments of the past, important as they are. Boston is very much a metropolis of the '70s, a unique town that combines big city excitement and sophistication with a pace that is positively relaxing. Boston has long prided itself on being the "Athens of America" (America's Florence rather than its Rome, its Leningrad rather than its Moscow), and the cultural vibrations are strong; Bostonians are inordinately proud of the great Boston Symphony Orchestra, the superb Boston Museum of Fine Arts, Harvard University, and the Massachusetts Institute of Technology. There are schools, colleges, and medical centers, research and cultural institutions wherever one looks. Boston is the big city which draws bright young people from all over the New England area—and far beyond—to live and work here. In fact, employment recruiters for New York and other big-city firms often get flat refusals from Ivy League college grads; they all want to move to Boston instead!

Boston is a modern city where the old still lives and is cherished. Centuries-old meeting houses sit almost side by side with some of the most modern architecture and grandiose civic projects in the world, all part of contemporary "New Boston." Boston has some of the best hotels in America (the Ritz-Carlton, for one, is on a level with the grand hotels of Europe); scores of exciting restaurants, both old-world and daringly new, serving perhaps the best seafood in the the country; a host of attractions and amusements for children; a vast complex of museums, parks, zoos, an aquarium, flower gardens; and a shopping scene that is irresistible. Boston has its Back Bay Brahmins and its counter-culture seekers, the Old Money of Louisburg Square and the blacks and Puerto Ricans of Roxbury and the South End. Its population is a fascinating mix of *Mayflower* settlers, old fami-lies, vast quantities of Italians and Eastern European Jews who came to work in its factories and mills around the turn of the century, and, most prominently, the Irish—the Curleys and Kennedys and Fitzgeralds and Cushings—who have given Bos-ton a full share of both raffish history and glory.

Boston itself has a population of less than 650,000, but as the hub of the Greater Boston area, which numbers some 2¾ mil-lion people spread out in 76 smaller cities, its importance is far-reaching. The most prosperous city in New England, with eletronic equipment, computers, machinery, fishing, and shoes all big business, it has big-city know-how plus small-town charm. It is a particularly pleasant city for walking and ambling about. Fruit and flower stands can be found on occasional corners, especially in the downtown banking area and around Copley Square. Newbury and Boylston Streets abound with inviting shops and galleries and, in the '30s, Winston Churchill once walked the entire length of Commonwealth Avenue and de-clared it to be one of the most beautiful boulevards in the world.

Best of all for the traveler, Boston is ideally situated as the starting point for all sorts of New England holidays. Even if you just stay in Massachusetts you can, within an hour, drive to the beachy, boaty North Shore resort towns of Salem, Marblehead, Gloucester, and Rockport, each filled with more than its share of historical and contemporary interest. Head south, and within 90 minutes you're at Plymouth, where it all began, and in anoth-er hour you're on that fabled peninsula called Cape Cod, one of the best summer vacation areas in the world. Fly, train, or drive to Boston to start your holiday; rent a car there and explore the state of Massachusetts. That is, if you can bear to leave the absorbing sights of the city.

Boston's History

Boston's history and American history practically started together. Settled ten years after the Pilgrims landed in Plymouth, the marsh-covered Shawmut Peninsula (later to be named Boston) quickly became an important shipbuilding center and fishing port, and, very early in the game, the British began pressing for laws to restrict the trading activities of the colonies which were cutting into their own profits. By the middle of the 18th century, "taxation without representation is tyranny" had already become a battle cry for revolution, and after the Boston Massacre of 1770, in which five men were killed by British soldiers after a petty row, the colony was ripe for action. The famous Boston Tea Party started it. Paul Revere's ride took place on April 18, 1775, the Battle of Bunker Hill on June 17 of that year, and by the fall Boston was a military garrison, with General George Washington taking charge of the colonial army. The British were sent scurrying home and the city was free.

By the close of the century, trade was picking up; the population was pushing 25,000; Charles Bulfinch's architecture was gaining an international reputation; and many of the fine houses of Beacon Hill (which are still lived in today) were being built. In the 19th century, Boston became a shipbuilding and manufacturing center as well as an important stop on the "underground railway" via which the Abolitionists smuggled slaves into Canada. The city continued to expand and has done so until the present. Not only has the population swollen, but much of the marsh area has been filled in. The original Back Bay behind the tiny Shawmut Peninsula is now the midtown area (although still called Back Bay); all of South Boston, with its docks and marine park, is on land reclaimed from the bay; and what had been Noddle Island, across from the bay, is now the vast Logan International Airport, also built on landfill. Either from here or from one of the fine highways that lead into the city you begin your explorations of the "Hub of New England"—Boston.

Chapter II

FINDING YOUR WAY AROUND BOSTON

BOSTON IS AN EASY CITY to find your way around, once you get the "lay of the land." Contrary to the general impression, Boston's streets were not built on existing cattle paths. The settlers carefully copied the procedures used in old England for laying out streets (which, come to think of it, were probably based on following cattle paths). We'll orient you with some views from the top, then show you how to get about on ground level. Let's start at Logan International Airport in East Boston.

Arrival

Boston's Logan Airport may be the most accessible of any in the country, situated just across the bay, only three miles from the downtown area; from it, taxis ($3 to $5), limousines ($2.25), and even the subway run into the heart of the city. Cabs charge 80¢ for the first third of a mile, 10¢ for each additional ninth of a mile, plus a handling charge of 50¢ for trunks, and one-way toll charges for the tunnel, turnpike, or bridges. If your destination is not Boston or Cambridge, you can share a cab with other passengers headed in the same direction; check the Share-A-Cab stand at each terminal. Limousines circle the airport every 20 minutes, and there is also limo or bus service north, south, and west of the city. If your luggage is not too heavy, try the subway. A shuttle bus (25¢) takes you to the MBTA's (Massachusetts Bay Transport Authority) Airport Station which borders the terminal, and, for another 25¢, you get to downtown Boston in seven minutes. For specific information, check the subway kiosks at all the airline terminals. (More details on the "T" later.)

THE VIEW FROM THE TOP: Our favorite way to survey any new city is from the top, and Boston obliges with three skyscraping observation points: the John Hancock Tower, the Prudential Skywalk, and the Air-Traffic Control Tower at Logan Airport. If you've come by jet, try the **Logan Tower** for your first look at the city, the harbor, and the beaches you'll be touring later. Take the elevator in the parking garage to the 16th floor where you can listen to piped-in control-tower talk at the snackbar while you enjoy the view. There's no admission fee and it's open from 10 a.m. to 9 p.m. Or try the picture-windowed lounge, one floor up, where you can watch the planes, the ships, and the city traffic from 11:30 a.m. to 2 a.m.

The newest high point in Boston is the **John Hancock Tower** (of the famous "popping glass" walls, now rebuilt with tempered safety glass). Take the "T" to Copley Station, walk one block to the Tower, where elevators whiz 60 floors in 30 seconds. Try to time your visit to just before sunset. The view can be spectacular, and it's always fun to watch the city light up at night. Admission is $1.50 (75¢ for children aged 5 to 15, and senior citizens), and includes a 15-minute sound-and-light show focused on a diorama of 1775–76 Boston, a filmed helicopter ride of present-day Boston, a taped description of the city by the late historian Walter Muir Whitehill, and a display of color slides of Boston and New England. There are free adult and kid-sized "fun-scopes" to focus on Boston landmarks, and telescopes (10¢) that can zoom you in on objects 740 feet below or miles cross-town. Hours are 9 a.m. to 10:15 p.m., Monday through Saturday; 10 a.m. to 10:15 p.m., Sunday, during the months from May to October, and noon to 10:15 p.m. November through April. Open daily with the exception of Thanksgiving and Christmas.

You can get the same view from the **Skywalk** on the 50th floor of the Prudential Tower (one of the most exciting examples of the "New Boston" architecture) just a few blocks away. Admission for adults is $1.50; 75¢ for children aged 5 to 15 and for senior citizens. The "Pru" is open Monday through Thursday from 9 a.m. to 11 p.m.; Friday and Saturday, 9 a.m. to midnight; and Sunday, from 10 a.m. to 11 p.m. From its glassed-in walk, a 360-degree panorama of Boston spreads out before you, and on a clear day you can see for miles, even as far as the mountaintops of southern New Hampshire with the help of one of the coin-fed telescopes. "Here's Boston," a built-in recorded tour, is available. (And on the 52nd floor the view comes with food and drink at the Top of the Hub Restaurant and Lounge.)

(One of our favorite viewing spots, the Custom House Tower, at State Street on Boston's waterfront, is closed for remodeling for the next two years. But check it out anyway just in case the project is finished early.)

From either of these towers you can get the general layout of Boston, below.

Face the ocean and you'll see the wharves from which Boston's fishing fleet and merchant ships sailed. They still bear names such as India Wharf and Commercial Wharf, and are now being renovated for luxury apartments, marinas, hotels, restaurants, and urban-renewal projects. In front of you is the Aquarium, which you must visit later, and across the harbor, the airport and the North Shore beaches. As you turn counterclockwise, you see the Mystic River Bridge leading out of the city to the north. (The original town is on a peninsula, and is connected by bridges and tunnels to surrounding areas.) To the left of the bridge is Bunker Hill Monument; and to the right, the site of the Charlestown Navy Yard (now decommissioned) where the U.S.S. *Constitution ("Old Ironsides")* is docked. Now, look across the panorama of Boston—the Old State House, wedged in between the skyscrapers of the banks and insurance companies; the beautiful new Waterfront Park; the Quincy Marketplace and Faneuil Hall; the new City Hall; and in the distance, the golden dome of the State House. In the center is a long stretch of green (in season) which marks Boston Common, the Public Garden, and the tree-shaded expanse of Commonwealth Avenue. To the right of Commonwealth Avenue is the Charles River, which separates Boston from Cambridge. The park area bordering it is the Esplanade, where the young sunbathe and jog and the Boston Pops and other orchestras and dance groups perform at the Hatch Memorial Shell. To the left is the vast complex of apartments, hotels, smart shops, and restaurants known as the Prudential Center. And in between is Back Bay, with the art galleries and boutiques of Newbury Street, the Boston Public Library, the Romanesque Trinity Church, and Old South Church at Copley Square. Beyond is the Christian Science Center, with its beautiful reflecting pool, Kenmore Square, Fenway Park; and in the distance, the Blue Hills (where there is winter skiing), the road to Cape Cod, and on a clear day, the White Mountains of New Hampshire.

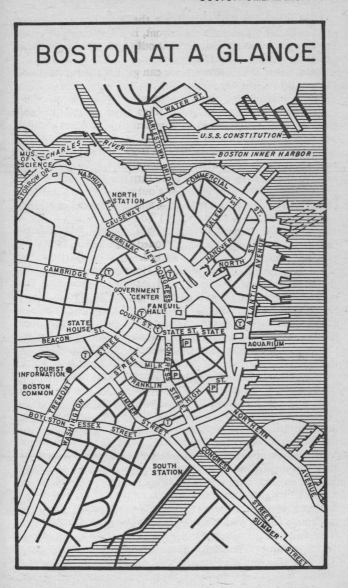

BOSTON AT A GLANCE

YOUR WALKING TOUR BEGINS: Now come down to earth, and we'll give you instructions on how to reach the places you've just seen. Let's go to the **Boston Common** first. This is the oldest people's park in the United States, dating back to the 1630s. (The pigeons came later.) It was from here that the British redcoats marched to Lexington, and it is here that Freedom Trail starts. And so will we.

Begin at the **Visitor's Information Center** on the Common. You're standing on Tremont Street, a busy shopping center. Across the Common is Beacon Street with the gold-domed State House designed by Charles Bulfinch. This is also the start of Beacon Hill, with Louisburg Square, the last outpost of the Proper Bostonians, at the top; and Charles Street, the new "Left Bank," at the bottom. Between them are rows of steep little streets, stretching back toward the Massachusetts General Hospital.

Park Street forms the right-hand side of the Common (the Park Street subway is here), and then gives way to the rest of Tremont Street, which leads to Government Center, Faneuil Hall, Quincy Marketplace, and the waterfront. Beyond that area is the North End. Boylston Street runs along the left side of the Common and leads to the Public Garden, the Back Bay area, the Prudential Center, John B. Hynes Civic Auditorium, and the Christian Science Center. Massachusetts Avenue, behind the Auditorium, divides this area from the cultural and educational zone on the other side, which includes Symphony Hall, the Museum of Fine Arts, the Gardner Museum, Northeastern University, and Simmons College. Boston University is beyond Kenmore Square.

If you're still standing at the Information Center, behind you is the shopping district, Washington Street, Filene's department store with its famous basement, and Chinatown. (See our sightseeing section for more complete descriptions.)

Remember, there is no real pattern to Boston's streets. They just happened. Just be aware of the general arrangement. And if you get lost, well, sometimes you find the most interesting shops and restaurants that way.

And if you wonder what happened to Scollay Square with its burlesque houses and tattoo parlors, be advised that it is alive and well, and functioning under the name of the Combat Zone in the vicinity of Washington and Essex Streets. (Government Center took over the former location, and the new City Hall stands close to the spot where the generations of Harvard boys watched burlesque at the Old Howard.) Bookstores in the Combat Zone carry as sleazy a line of erotica as can be found anywhere, and some of the lounges feature topless shows. Gone is the Boston that banned the books and had a "Watch and Ward Society" to protect the morality of its citizens.

BOSTON'S WEATHER: New England has never been known for ideal weather. Winters can get cold, very cold, with snow on the ground for months. Summers can be hot and sticky, with temperatures soaring into the 80s and 90s during July and August. Spring is usually mild and beautiful; fall, crisp and clear, with the kind of Octobers that the poets used to write about. But it can be hot in fall and breezy in summer and cool in spring, so when you pack for your visit to Boston, be prepared for anything. But Boston is "on" whenever you arrive. Winter is high season for theater, symphony, and the like (and you can get off to the mountains and ski for the weekend); and a summer vacation is fun because you can always mix an afternoon at a nearby beach into your sightseeing. Besides, so many of the locals will be "down the Cape" for the summer that the city will be much less crowded than usual. (After a few days you can head down the Cape yourself, about which more later.)

To get the weather report, dial 936-1234.

ABOUT THAT BOSTON ACCENT: Yes, it's true. In Boston, they don't have horses, they have "hosses"; they love to drink "watah"; every dad hopes his son or daughter will qualify for "Hahvahd"; and they all love to hop down for the weekend to "New Yok." So strong, in fact, is the Boston accent that it takes natives about ten years of living away from town to overcome it. But don't worry, you'll catch on to the dialect quickly, and when you get back home, your own accent may sound awfully hahsh (we mean harsh) to the eardrums.

Getting Around

The subways and your feet are your most practical means of transporatation in Boston.

TAXIS: They're expensive and not always easy to find. Sometimes, even if you do find a hack, you'll get stalled indefinitely in traffic. However, at other times and on certain days, such as

Boston: Average Monthly Temperatures			
January	29.9	July	73.7
February	30.3	August	71.7
March	37.7	September	65.3
April	47.9	October	55.0
May	58.8	November	44.9
June	67.8	December	33.3

Sundays, Boston will seem almost deserted.

Boston's taxi drivers are, in our experience, remarkably safe drivers and they may be among the most literate in the country. Many students work their way through college by cabbing, and you can even find Ph.D.s, unable to find a job, piloting a taxi. Most of the cabbies, no matter what their backgrounds, are full of opinions, ranging from critiques on politics to hotels, restaurants, the architecture of the "New Boston," and "the syndicate." A good way to get informed.

THE MBTA: These code letters stand for the Massachusetts Bay Transport Authority, "T" for short, which runs both the subways and the trolley buses. It's the oldest subway system in the country, and some commuters feel they're riding the original 1895 trains. But the system is being remodeled, and some showpiece trains run on the Cambridge-Ashmont-Quincy line which has leather-cushioned seats and music. If you avoid the rush hours, a subway ride is not at all traumatic and it's then that you can get a look at the murals adorning the station walls in the historic districts. They're not as good as Moscow's subway art, but it's a start; the scenes are both of Boston's past and of the parks and buildings you'll see when you emerge to the surface. And, if above the roar of the trains you think you're hearing music, don't panic, that's just what you are hearing. Entertainment is now provided along with the subway crush. Local musicians perform on the station platforms 7 a.m. to 10 a.m., and 4 p.m. to 7 p.m. Helps make the commute a bit more pleasant!

Free route maps of the MBTA are available at the Park Street subway station (under the Common) which is the center of the system. Each line is shown on the subway map in color—Blue,

Red, Green, and Orange. For quick reference: the Red line goes to Cambridge, Ashmont, and Quincy; the Blue, to Government Center, Aquarium, Airport, Revere Beach, and Wonderland; the Green, from Science Park and North Station through downtown Boston to Prudential Center, Symphony, Kenmore, Brookline, Brighton, and Newton (you'll probably use this line the most). The Orange line runs from Malden and Charlestown, through downtown Boston to Forest Hills. "Park Street Under" is on the Red line; Fenway Park, on the Green.

Note on transfers: Don't try to switch from an inbound to an outbound car—or outbound to inbound at Copley. There's no pedestrian walkway joining the two. Make the transfer at Arlington.

Fare is 25¢ for the rapid transit lines (underground) and 25¢ for the surface lines. You pay an extra 25¢ for the Quincy extension of the Red Line and the Oak Grove extension of the Orange Line. If you stay on the Green Line when it surfaces beyond Kenmore Square, you pay an extra 20¢. For specific information on the subway system, call 722-3200, Monday through Friday, 7 a.m. to 6 p.m. Transfers between lines and for suburban buses can be made at various stations. Exact fares are required on the trolleys and connecting buses, and change can be made in the stations. All of the "T" lines close down by 1:00 a.m.—some earlier—so be sure to check time schedules so you won't be stranded.

Note: Elevators are being installed in all new and remodeled stations, a boon to the elderly, handicapped, parents with baby strollers, and shoppers with heavy bundles. Park Street station's elevator will be at the corner of Winter and Tremont streets, and others will be at State Street and suburban terminals, 21 in all.

DRIVING AND PARKING: If you're a motorist staying in one of the motels on the outskirts of town, it may be easier to leave the car in the lot and come into town by public transportation. Driving can be confusing since the streets have no logical numerical or alphabetical order, and one-way streets and construction sites pop up at you unexpectedly. Also, parking is expensive and inadequate. The two largest garages are hidden underground: at the **Prudential Center** and **Boston Common.** The garage at the Pru charges $1 for the first hour and 50¢ for each additional hour. At the Boston Common garage, it's 75¢ for the first hour, $1.50 for two hours, $2.00 for three hours, and $2.25 for four hours. For $2.50 you can park from 7 a.m. to 7 p.m.; and for $3.50 you can stay 24 hours. And that entitles you to free bus service to the other side of the Common and back to the garage. From 6 p.m. to midnight the fee is $1. At the high-rise garage near **Government Center** you can park from 7 a.m. to 7 p.m. for a $2 maximum while you explore the North End, the Haymarket (the famous pushcart market), and the Faneuil/Quincy Marketplaces. There are other multilevel garages near the **John Hancock Building** and **Symphony Hall,** and many city-owned garages, private garages, and parking lots where buildings used to be. (However, to change the trend, some new buildings are replacing parking lots.)

Rates often depend on location, hour of the day (shopping facilities charge more during the day; those near theaters and clubs, more in the evening), demands for space, and what the traffic will bear. The **waterfront garage** near the Aquarium can demand $1 each hour for the first two hours and $2.75 for three hours because on-street parking is very limited and tow trucks are very busy; while the **Shopper's Garage,** 14-40 Beach Street (near Chinatown and Washington Street shopping area) gives you a full day from 6 a.m. to 6 p.m. for $2.25. And it's only $3.25 for a full 24 hours. Hotels such as **Howard Johnson's** at Park Square and the **Colonnade** have public garages. **The Woolworth Building,** at Franklin and Washington streets (opposite Filene's), has a garage on the top floors.

City facilities are the best buy. For example, the City of Boston garage on **Berkeley Street** (near the posh shopping areas) charges $1 the first hour and another $1 each additional hour to a maximum of $3.50 between 7 a.m. and 6 p.m. Evening rates are the same with a maximum of $3. Many restaurants provide free parking at nearby facilities. Check when you call for reservations. And some places are so cavernous that you can easily get lost trying to find your car when you return. Be sure and check all markings and entrances before you leave.

And pay attention to all the signs if you miraculously find a metered space and park on the street. Violate one of the numerous rules and you'll be fined an exorbitant fee and perhaps be towed away. In some areas (near the Public Garden, for example) you must feed the meter 25¢ a half hour. In other sections it's 10¢ for an hour. Sometimes there is a different fee or time limit on each side of the street. Read the signs, study the hieroglyphics on the meters, or, better still, take the "T".

Note: And you can bike *around* Boston, too. Not in the downtown area, but along a Greenbelt Bikeway that covers the area from Boston Common to Franklin Park. It's about seven miles and you can ride it in about an hour. Interesting spots along the Bikeway are the Fens, the Arboretum, Larz Anderson Museum of Transportation, and the Children's Museum. There's also an MDC bike path along the Charles River Esplanade; an East Coast Bicycle Trail that starts at the State House and goes all the way to Richmond, Virginia. You can get a free set of bicycle maps showing routes in and around the Greater Boston area by writing or visiting the Department of Environmental Management of Forests and Parks, Saltonstall Building, 100 Cambridge Street, Boston, MA 02202.

RENTING CARS: When the time comes for those out-of-town excursions, you can find offices of all the major car-rental firms both in Boston and at Logan Airport. A very convenient place to rent a car is Econo-Car of Boston, 7 Eliot Street (tel. 542-9800).

BUSES: Boston's major bus terminals are the **Greyhound Terminal** at 10 St. James Street (tel. 423-5510) and the **Continental Trailways** station at 10 Park Square (tel. 482-6620). **Almeida Bus Lines** (tel. 642-7580) goes to the Cape; **Bonanza Bus Lines** (tel. 423-5810) runs to southeastern Massachusetts and Rhode Island; **Peter Pan Bus Lines** (tel. 482-6620) travels to western Massachusetts; and **Michaud Bus Lines** (262-3100), to New Hampshire.

RAILROADS: Three major lines serve Boston and they're all accessible by MBTA. **Amtrak** (tel. 523-5720) has arrival and departure points at South Station on Atlantic Avenue and Back Bay Station, 145 Dartmouth Street; the **Boston and Maine** (tel. 227-5070), otherwise known as the B&M, is handy for day trips north of the city and has a terminal at North Station on Causeway Street; and **Conrail** (tel. 482-4400) is the commuter line from South Station.

Chapter III

HOTELS IN BOSTON AND CAMBRIDGE

WHERE TO STAY in Boston? That depends on your taste and the style in which you're accustomed to traveling. For a city of its size, Boston offers an excellent range of accommodations, from a *grande dame* on a par with the Ritz of Paris to luxury hotels in both the gracious style of "Old Boston" and the sleek modernity of "New Boston" to moderately priced motels and inns, and budget lodgings. After the lean years for Boston hotels, new giants like the Colonnade and Howard Johnson's 57, the Sheraton Boston at Prudential Center, and the beautiful Hyatt Regency in Cambridge have signaled a renaissance. And the suburbs offer charming inns and guest houses, while some of the major highways, such as Route 1 North, could well be renamed Motel Row.

Even in the key vacation months of July and August, you should have no trouble getting a room, but it's always advisable to reserve ahead. (Area code is 617.) And it's imperative in spring and fall, when conventions descend upon the city. Most of the hotels do not charge for children sharing rooms with their parents, and some offer special rates for students with ID cards and senior citizens with AARP or NRTA cards (these are noted in our listings). Parking is available at most hotels and motels, and others have arrangements with nearby garages. If you must leave your key with the car, check on the liability of the hotel and garage in case of theft. Better yet, find a place where you can lock the car and keep your key.

And, oh yes, there is a tax of 5.7% on all hotel bills which must be added to the price. Sorry.

To help you in making your own choice of a Boston hotel, we've divided our recommendations into four general categories: Deluxe Hotels (those charging from $45 to $75 per night, double); First-class (from $38 to $54 double); Moderate to Budget (from $24 to $36 double); and Hotels in Cambridge. (Note: Less expensive hotels are listed under "A Student's Guide to Boston.") We've concentrated on those hotels that are convenient to historic areas and transportation, that offer special touches of luxury of service, or just plain good value for the money. Our listings are mainly for Boston and Cambridge and some of the suburbs on the rim of the city. Accommodations on the North and South Shores and on the "Paul Revere Trail" (Lexington and Concord) are listed in the sections further on describing those areas. Rates are subject to change if operating costs rise.

So now, let's begin, in the heart of the hub, with . . .

Deluxe Hotels
(Doubles, $45 to $75)

Boston's newest "grand hotel," **The Colonnade**, 120 Huntington Avenue (tel. 261-2800), immediately created its own aura of stylish elegance (President Ford stayed here when he visited Boston.) The derby-hatted doorman who greets you at the entrance sets the mood at once, and so does the plush orange-and-gold lobby with its potted palms and comfortable sitting areas, all dominated by an exquisite crystal chandelier. The location is perfect, across from the Prudential Complex, adjacent to the Massachusetts Turnpike extension and the Prudential subway station.

The guest rooms all have an L-shaped floor plan with distinct sleeping, sitting, and dressing areas; they are big, bright, attractively decorated and furnished, with color TV, a large dressing table and makeup mirror, soft carpeting, and even tinted windows to prevent sun glare.

Each room has at least one double bed. Singles are $56 to $64. Doubles are $64 to $72. Mini-suites (or honeymoon suites) with a large sitting-dining area overlooking the Prudential Center are $66 for a single and $74 double. Children under 12 stay free. An additional person in the room is $10 extra. Babysitters are available through the hotel's concierge service. And the staff can cater to you in 18 languages!

If you can bear to leave your room, head for the "intown resort" on the roof, with its pool, putting green, shuffleboard, snackbar, and occasional afternoon and evening entertainment. On the lower level, you can sizzle in the sauna, then have a

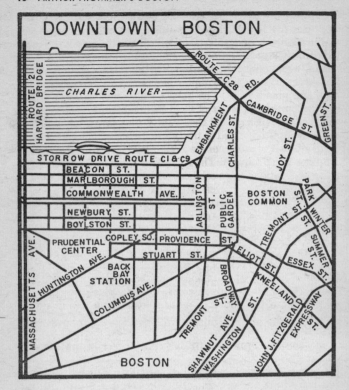

massage, or patronize the barbershop or beauty parlor. And there is parking in the hotel's garage with complimentary "in and out" privileges.

Hungry? Room service is available 24 hours a day. Or try one of the hotel's restaurants, The Zachary—expensive and elegant —or the Promenade Cafe, an attractive restaurant and sidewalk cafe serving breakfast, lunch, and dinner from 7 a.m. to 11:30 p.m.

The Copley Plaza, 138 St. James Avenue (tel. 267-5300), has been synonymous with Boston elegance since it opened in 1912 as a sister hotel to New York's famed Plaza Hotel. Now the mosaic floors, rich wood paneling, and original works of art on the walls (such as the trompe l'oeil Italian Renaissance scenes in the Venetian Room) have been restored by master craftsmen to the splendor that attracted Caruso, Churchill, and scores of political, royal, and entertainment celebrities over the years. Gilded ceilings, Waterford crystal chandeliers, marble-topped tables, and antique furniture grace the lobbies and function rooms (home to so many diplomatic receptions, debutante parties, and grand balls). The gracious ambience extends to the guest rooms with the use of quilted floral bedspreads, mirrored triple closets, plush velvet chairs, thick rugs, and marble-topped night tables. And to add to the charm, potted palms and Boston ferns are part of the decor (two full-time employees care for the Copley's 1,200 plants). The suites are decorated individually, some with antique china cabinets (with the china), Oriental wallpaper, fireplaces, or even a replica of a French Provincial mahogany and ormulu cabinet, custom-designed for the Copley to house the color TV. And if you really wish to be pampered, try the Hancock Suite or the Presidential Suite (you don't have to be president), either one available at $300 a day. Other suites are available from $125. Singles are $47 to $64 (depending on the view), $55 to $72 for doubles. Children or an extra person under 18 are free, and a rollaway bed with a full mattress is $7 extra. All rooms have color TV and touchtone telephones. Parking is available at the nearby John Hancock Garage for $2 a day (a 60% discount on the regular price). And there is room service from 7 a.m. to 11 p.m.

The Copley features outstanding dining and drinking facilities; the gourmet Cafe Plaza, Copley's, a turn-of-the-century restaurant; Copley's Bar, where the "beautiful people" meet; the Plaza Bar; and Copley Court, for authentic English set tea among the palms.

The undisputed *grande dame* of Boston's hotels, of course, is the **Ritz-Carlton**, 15 Arlington Street (tel. 536-5700), at the corner of the Boston Public Garden, one of the last bastions of proper Bostonianism, where understated elegance, conservatism, and a proud adherence to tradition are the order of the day. Comparing favorably with the Ritz in Paris and the Ritz in London, and attracting the same kind of celebrated guests, the Ritz-Carlton prides itself on its highly individualized service, its meticulous attention to every whim and wish of its clients (kitchens are maintained and waiters assigned to each floor, to provide speedy room service; barbers will cut your hair in your room, if you wish), and its courtly European readiness to be helpful. Considering that these qualities are not overly in abundance wherever one goes, it is no surprise that the Ritz charges the highest rates in town for its rooms, which are large and handsomely done in traditional decor. They rent from $70 to $75 a day for single occupancy, from $70 to $80 for double. Suites range from $100 to $210. Each room is equipped with combination television-FM radio, and all of the suites have woodburning fireplaces. Reservations may be made through Preferred Reservations, 800/323-7500.

As might be expected, every shop and service one needs—including the Ritz-Carlton Beauty Salon—is on the premises. The pleasant second-floor lounge, with its white-and-gilt Adam paneling and provincial furnishings is fine for afternoon tea and cocktails. A cafe is open for all meals and, of course, the Ritz Bar is well known, opening off the street-floor lobby. And the Ritz Dining Room (also described in our restaurant chapter) is elegant, expensive, and world-renowned for gourmet food and service.

A prime example of the architecture of the "New Boston," the **Sheraton Boston,** Prudential Center (tel. 236-2000), is the town's most stunning modern hotel, a veritable city within a city, its 1,431 rooms joined by a covered passageway to the 52-story Prudential Tower. The Sheraton is a skyscraper in its own right, with a wall of glass in each room providing spectacular views of Boston. It's a busy, exciting place, with a covered swimming pool open year round from 10 a.m. to 8 p.m., shops, boutiques, restaurants, lounges, and summer concerts.

All public areas are decorated in red, white, and blue, and guest room decor is mostly contemporary. Single rooms range from $35 to $63; doubles from $57 to $75. Suites begin at $75 in the main hotel and $115 in the Sheraton Towers crowning the hotel. There is no charge for children under 17 in the same room with their parents. Extra cots are $7. Students, faculty, and retired persons with appropriate IDs receive a 25% discount when rooms are available. Parking is available at an adjacent garage; $3.50 for 24 hours with unlimited access.

Dining or drinking here is an adventure, a trip around the world. The Falstaff Room features beef and lobster and the best Sunday brunch in town in an Old English atmosphere, and Kon-Tiki Ports sails the Pacific, especially at the popular lunchtime buffet. The New Doubles, the Mermaid Lounge (built with boards removed from a century-old New Bedford fisherman's shack), and Shelley's Upstairs Pub are all popular for drinks and dancing. The Pavillion Cafe serves from 7 a.m. to midnight and the Mermaid Restaurant, open for lunch and dinner, features traditional New England seafood.

Located right on the historic Freedom Trail, the **Parker House,** 60 School Street, (tel. 227-8600) is regarded as the oldest operating hotel in America. However, there is nothing antiquated about this member of the Dunfey Hotel chain. Guest rooms are decorated in brown and gold tones or blue and white prints, with velvet chairs, thick carpeting, furniture with imported marble tops, and beds with elegant spreads and dust ruffles. Bathrooms are nicely appointed with large vanity mirrors, although the old wing has only showers (if you wish a tub, request the new wing). All modern amenities are available—color TV, vending machines for soft drinks and ice on every floor—alongside crystal chandeliers and views of Old City Hall and the new Government Center from rooms on the School Street side.

Rates are $39 to $48 for singles (deluxe singles, $60 to $65); $47 to $56 for doubles. Mini-suites are $68 to $73; larger suites, $95 to $210. Overnight parking is free from 8 p.m. to 8 a.m.; but you must pay $3 for daytime parking. No charge for children under 16 sharing a room with their parents, otherwise there is a $5 charge for an extra person. Room service is available from 7 a.m. to midnight. Hospitality hostesses are available to answer questions on local tours and attractions. The Parker House also offers mini-vacation rates. Ask for the mini-vacation desk when you call.

The eating and drinking facilities are outstanding. The gourmet Parker's Restaurant serves lunch, dinner, and Sunday brunch. Cocktails and lunch are served at Parker's Bar, site of the "Saturday Club" of 1860s fame where Emerson, Longfellow, Oliver Wendell Holmes, Whittier, and James Russell Lowell met. The Last Hurrah is a turn-of-the-century-type room serving lunch, dinner, and drinks against a backdrop of pictures of politicians, sports and show-biz figures. Breakfast and lunch are served in the Revere Room Coffeeshop, with the famous Parker House rolls and a popular buffet.

Don't let the utilitarian Howard Johnson name fool you. The **57 Park Plaza Hotel–Howard Johnson,** 200 Stuart Street at Park Square (tel. 482-1800), may not sound glamorous, but its 350 rooms are on a par with those of luxury hotels. The hotel is centrally located downtown, within walking distance of theaters, shops, the Public Gardens, and Boston Commons; and it's about a 15-minute drive from Logan Airport.

Now for those rooms. Each has its own private balcony with

a commanding city view, one or two double beds, a sitting area, shower-bath combination, full-length mirror, attractive furniture, color TV, climate control, and a wakeup alarm and message center system. The bedrooms are newly redecorated in soft, comfortable earth tones. Also available are mini-suites with one double bed and a parlor area with sofa, round table, and chairs.

You can swim year round in the seventh-floor pool, take a free sauna bath, enjoy the playgrass putting green at the pool, and take advantage of tennis privileges at the Boston Harbour Tennis Club.

The hotel is part of a new complex that includes the renowned 57 Restaurant—you guessed it—a Howard Johnson's Restaurant and two cinemas. Rates are $42 to $47 for singles and $50 to $55 for doubles, the price increasing with the view. Mini-suite rates are $47 single and $55 double. There's no charge for children under 18 with their parents, or for cribs, but there is a $5 tab for extra cots. And, joy of joys, there's free indoor parking with direct access to your room in the hotel's 1,000 car garage. The Howard Johnson toll-free number is 800/654-2000.

The **Midtown Motor Inn,** 220 Huntington Avenue (tel. 262-1000), is located in the midst of Boston's cultural belt. Stay here and you'll be within easy walking distance of Symphony Hall, the Museum of Fine Arts, the Christian Science Center, and the Prudential Center. The rooms are modern and attractive, all 161 of them equipped with air conditioning and TV. Rates go from $42 to $50 for singles, $46 to $54 for doubles. Children under 18 are free with parents; an extra person in the room is $8 additional. Senior citizens may take 10% off the tab with an AARP card, and government employees are offered a discount, subject to availability. There is free covered parking and 24-hour room service. The Colony Room Restaurant and the Coffee Shop, open 7 a.m. to 10 p.m. are more plus features.

Although the **Logan Airport Hilton** (tel. 569-9300) is right at the airport, many visitors find it a convenient headquarters for their stay in Boston. It's about ten minutes by car or taxi to downtown Boston, depending on the traffic situation, and subway and bus connections are available as well.

The 559 newly decorated rooms have soundproofed picture windows and are furnished in a modified modern style. Some open into an inner courtyard with a swimming pool and lawn. Singles rent from $37 to $45, and doubles, from $47 to $55. Especially nice if you'd like to rest between planes is the fact that one or two persons can book a room for half a day at $25.

Guests gather in the attractive Down One Saloon or in the Waterfront Lounge for drinks.

Nestled at the base of Beacon Hill, near the Charles River, and convenient to the huge Massachusetts General Hospital, **Holiday Inn,** 5 Blossom Street (tel. 742-7630), is a splendidly modern new hotel. Its 300 rooms are spread across 14 floors, with an attractive top-floor dining room and cocktail lounge, and an appealing lobby with a winding staircase. The Inn is part of a plaza complex—itself a part of the massive Boston urban renaissance—that includes a movie theater and a garage with free parking for hotel guests.

As you would expect, the rooms are streamlined in style, each with a picture-window view of the city, tubs as well as showers and TV. They rent for $42 single and $47 double, and for those seeking additional luxury, two "glamor rooms" are available, complete with sunken tub, for $100. Children under 18 are free in their parents' room; there is a charge of $5 for an extra person in the room. Senior citizens with AARP cards get a 10% discount; and in season an outdoor pool is open from 10 a.m. to 9 p.m.

Eating is fun here, too. The Garden Room Coffeeshop is open 7 a.m. to 9 p.m. for breakfast, lunch, and dinner; and in summer the sidewalk cafe serves from 11:30 a.m. to 5 p.m. Our favorite, however, is the Flying Machine on the top floor, a dining room-lounge themed after the early days of aviation, and featuring steaks and seafood served up with a view of Beacon Hill, the Charles River, and Government Center. And disco and entertainment, too. Restaurant is open from 5 p.m. to 11 p.m., and the cocktail lounge from 5 p.m. until 2 a.m.

First-Class Hotels
(Doubles $38 to $54)

Located on the busy corner between the Boston Public Library and Lord & Taylor's, **The Lenox Hotel and Motor Inn,** 710 Boylston Street (tel. 536-5300 or 800/225-7676) housing Diamond Jim's Piano Bar, the Victorian Delmonico's Restaurant, and Ye Olde London Pub and Grille, hardly gives the outward impression of being family-oriented. Yet it's the only place we know of in Boston where children, no matter what age, can stay free in the same room with parents. They are also given special attention in the dining rooms, and the management will help plan sightseeing tours geared to young taste.

While most of the 225 rooms are furnished with reproductions of Ethan Allen Early American pieces, there are 45 rooms newly decorated with Oriental furnishings, Chinese prints and wallpaper, and even bamboo swivel rocking chairs. Rockers are found in the other rooms, too, but they are Boston rockers to blend with the colonial mode and paneled corner fireplaces that are found in some of the suites. In addition to color TV, AM-FM radio, and air conditioning, the Lenox offers some homey personal touches, such as sewing kits and coffee-makers in each room, and mirrors angled so you can see how you look from the back as well as from the front. The management also reimburses guests for airport limousine service ($2.25) for one person or cab fare for a group. (You need a receipt to collect.)

There's free overnight parking ("park and lock") in the adjoining Prudential garage from 6 p.m. to 10 a.m. Soft-drink machines and ice machines are located on alternating floors. Rates go from $32 to $44 for singles, from $45 to $52 for twins, and $110 for suites.

Ramada Inns are comfortable wherever one goes, and the **Ramada Inn** in East Boston, 225 McClellan Highway (Route 1-A), is also conveninetly located just a few miles north of Logan Airport (by courtesy car) and handy to Suffolk Downs and Wonderland Racetracks and the North Shore beaches as well as Boston. The 203 rooms are nicely decorated in motel-modern, featuring double and king-size beds, color TV, individual heat and air-conditioning control. There's a glass-enclosed year-round pool adjoining the hotel through a connecting passageway, also a health club and sauna baths.

Rates range from $38 in a single to $45 in a double. Suites with a king-size bed are $65. No charge for children under 18 in the same room with parents. Cribs are free, and a cot is $5 extra.

The coffeeshop opens at 6 a.m. and the Captain's Table is a popular dining spot with a nightly floor show.

Practically on the Boston University campus, the **Howard Johnson's Motor Lodge,** at Kenmore Square (tel. 267-3100), is a great choice if you need to be near the colleges. (There is a shortage of hotels near Boston's colleges, since so many have been taken over by the schools for their own use.) Even if you don't, the location is excellent, near Fenway Park and a few subway stops away from downtown. You can spot it easily by the glass-enclosed outdoor elevator which goes to the new Up and Up Lounge (open 4 p.m. to 2 a.m.) and gives you a good view of the area.

An attractive orange-carpeted stairway winds down to the lobby from the bedrooms, which are furnished in a contemporary decor. Air conditioning, TV, radio, and direct-dial phones are provided. For a single you'll pay $32.50 to $34.50, and for a double, $38.50 to $44.50. Suites start at $36. Children under 18 stay free with their parents, and extra cots are $4.

Especially nice is the year-round enclosed swimming pool on the roof, open 11 a.m. to 7 p.m. And your car is garaged free.

Just a few giant steps away from the Public Garden at Park Square, near the Greyhound bus station, is the 800-room **Park Plaza Hotel** (tel. 426-2000 or 800/225-2008). Formerly the Statler Hilton, it has been renovated and given a new image. Still primarily a convention-hotel, its easy access to most of Boston's attractions also makes it a good choice for visitors who come just to see the town. The excellent location puts you within walking distance of Beacon Hill, Boston Common, the Esplanade, theaters and concert halls, and two of Boston's most delightful boutique-laden streets: Boylston and Newbury. Light, cheerful colors predominate in the guest rooms, all of which have air conditioning, direct-dial phones, TV, and radio. Rates for singles are $32 to $42; doubles $38 to $50. All rooms have showers and baths.

You can get a good breakfast and a basic lunch or dinner at the Hungry Pilgrim, and quench your thirst with scotch on the rocks at the Captain's Piano Lounge. Continental breakfast and light lunch are served in the Garden Lounge in the lobby.

Moderate to Budget Hotels
(Doubles $24 to $36)

Although it's an older, unprepossessing hotel in an area of glamorous neighbors—the Prudential Center, Lord & Taylor's, Saks Fifth Avenue—the **Copley Square Hotel** (tel. 536-9000), at the entrance to the Massachusetts Turnpike, offers excellent values. The rooms have recently been renovated and are large, yet cozy, with thick brown shag rugs and a yellow, beige, and brown color scheme. The drapes and bedspreads are coordinated with the brown-print wallpaper and the overall effect is restful and pleasant. The unusual shape of the building gives a bonus of uniquely shaped guest rooms, including a series of hexagonal corner rooms with six windows to catch the sun and the view of the Prudential Center. Some of these corner rooms have king-size beds and bathrooms with their own small closets. And if you hate to wait for your turn in the shower, try a room with two separate showers, sinks, and commodes. Singles are $28 to $34; doubles and twins, $34 to $40; triples, $42. Family suites, $60 for four persons, have two bedrooms with two doubles beds each and a bathroom between the rooms. There is no charge for children under 14 sharing a room with their parents. There is free overnight parking from 6 p.m. to 10 a.m. in the adjoining Prudential Center Garage, and in most of the rooms you get free coffee as well. A coffeeshop and sports saloon in the lobby provide food and drink. And in the lower lobby is one of the finest restaurants in Boston, the Hungarian Cafe Budapest.

Red Sox fans take note: There's no hotel in Boston closer to Fenway Park than the **Fenway Motor Hotel,** 1271 Boylston Street (tel. 267-8300). Besides being adjacent to the park (you might even catch a home-run ball hit over the right-field wall) this hotel is also convenient to the Back Bay colleges and to the Museum of Fine Arts and the Gardner Museum. And it's a quick subway ride to downtown Boston, which makes it a big favorite with visiting businessmen. Its 94 rooms are modern, air-conditioned, and have color TV. Room rates are $23.50 to $31.50 single; and $32.50 to $39.50 double. Some rooms have a steam bath. Children under 18 can stay free with their parents, otherwise an extra person is $4 additional. After the game—or whatever—you can relax in the swimming pool, open 11 a.m. to 7 p.m., or dine at Bumpers, a restaurant and lounge, open 7 a.m. to 2:30 a.m. There is 24-hour room service, and parking is free.

How many plays have been whipped into shape and polished for Broadway while the company stayed at the **Hotel Bradford** must be a matter for the theater archives. For generations, the Bradford, located as it is adjacent to the Schubert Theater, at 275 Tremont Street near the Kneeland Street exit of the Mass. Turnpike (tel. 426-1400), was headquarters of traveling theatrical groups. Though the stardust is gone from the lobby, the location is ideal for visitors. It's across the street from the New England Medical Center, near Boston Common and the downtown shopping areas. Economy rates are $26 for singles and $32 for doubles. All 350 rooms are air-conditioned and have TV sets. Overnight parking is free in a parking garage across the street.

Back in the days when they built new hotels near the railroad station rather than near the airport, the **Hotel Essex** was put up near South Station at 695 Atlantic Avenue (tel. 482-9000). Now South Station is being phased out and there will be a huge transportation complex in the area, which is at the very end of the Mass. Turnpike. But the Essex is still a well-run and comfortable hotel under the management of the Carter Hotel people. If you don't mind being in a neighborhood that's undergoing rehabilitation, you'll find 400 rooms here, with private bath, TV, radio, and air conditioning.

Rates are $19 for singles and $25 and up for doubles. Student groups of 20 or more get special rates upon arrangement with the management. Children under 14 are free in the same room with parents. There is free parking from 4:00 p.m. to 9 a.m. at a nearby public garage. Special "no frills" weekly rates on request.

A quiet, residential hotel or an international inn? The **Hotel Eliot,** 370 Commonwealth Avenue (tel. 267-1607), near Kenmore Square, answers both descriptions. The only hotel right in Boston renting suites with kitchens, it attracts visitors who prefer to prepare their own meals as well as permanent residents who like the cheerful, attractive rooms and its proximity to subway transportation, the Prudential Center, Symphony Hall, and the Charles River. Some international visitors have included 20 Russian art experts who were in Boston to supervise an exhibit at the Museum of Fine Arts and wanted a place where they could cook their own borscht, Japanese marathon runners who found the beds too comfortable and slept on the floor, and Korean students.

Singles rent from $26 to $28; doubles, $32 to $38. If you're staying in Boston for at least two weeks, consider renting one of the one- or two-bedroom kitchen suites, $145 to $250 a week. (Also available at $445 to $675 monthly for a minimum of two months.) Nearby garages are available for parking. And for an unusual dining experience try the Medieval Manor located in the hotel. There you eat (using your fingers), drink, and carouse with the "lords and ladies" of the manor. The Eliot Lounge is the favorite watering spot of Boston Marathon runners, including champion Bill Rodgers.

Despite its intriguing name, **The Children's Inn,** 342 Longwood Avenue, Boston (tel. 731-4700) on the Brookline line, is not one of those Swiss-style hotels where you can leave the youngsters for a vacation of their own. The name comes, instead, from its association with the famed Children's Hospital, and it was built primarily to house visitors calling on patients. But this attractive, modern motel, a portion of a building complex combining a swimming pool, a handsome plaza, and shops, is open to the public as well. It makes an excellent Boston base, as it's convenient to the art museums, colleges, and Fenway Park. And there is absolutely no "hospital atmosphere" whatsoever!

The facilities are surprisingly abundant, with a modern museum-style cafeteria restaurant, The Jolly Poisson, opening off the inner courtyard. There's a cocktail lounge, beauty salon, bookstore, and other shops, plus free underground parking. Each of the 83 guest rooms is air-conditioned, pleasantly roomy, with a sitting area and TV. And the tariff is reasonable: $31 for singles, $33 for doubles, and $35 for twin doubles. Children under 12 are free with parents. Cribs are free, and guests may use the outdoor pool, open 8 a.m. to 8 p.m. Room service is available, 7 a.m. to 11 p.m.

IN BRIGHTON: If you'd like the peace and quiet of the suburbs combined with a location not more than 15 minutes away from the heart of the city, the **Terrace Motel,** a member of Superior Motels, Inc., 1650 Commonwealth Avenue (tel. 566-6260), is a good bet. Near Boston University, it's a complex of motel units just off one of Boston's major boulevards (and trolley-bus lines), and most of the rooms (some with ceiling-to-floor picture windows) face a pleasant residential street. Most popular are the rooms in the newer rear crescent.

This is a nice place for families, since there are two-room suites available, from $37 and up, and you can have the use of a kitchenette with a charge of $1 for equipment. Children under 16 can stay in their parents' room free, but an extra cot or crib costs $2. As for the other rooms, singles go from $20 to $23—doubles, from $24 to $27; twins, from $25 to $29.

A complimentary continental breakfast is served in the modest reception lounge.

Hotels in Cambridge and Somerville

Nicknamed "the pyramid on the Charles," the **Hyatt Regency,** 575 Memorial Drive, Cambridge (tel. 492-1234), is an exciting addition to the Greater Boston hotel scene. Terraced like a tower in ancient Babylon on the outside, and with a 14-story atrium accented with diamond-shaped glass elevators, fountains, and balconies on the inside, the Hyatt is an area showplace attracting locals and tourists to its two restaurants and revolving Spinnaker Lounge on the glass-enclosed rooftop.

Underneath all the glamor is some sound practicality. Of its 500 rooms, 15 on the third floor are designed to accommodate the handicapped—wide doors, special bathroom facilities. And the seventh floor is reserved for nonsmokers, with not a match or ashtray in sight! A soft color scheme of beige, brown, and rust is used throughout the hotel. Bedrooms have wicker headboards, desks, makeup tables, large mirrors, and graphics on the walls, plus a radio/TV/in-house-movie combination, air conditioning, and blackout drapes. The Concierge Department helps guests with arrangements for dining, theater, and travel. Prices ascend with the floor and the view you choose, or with luxury touches such as terraces overlooking the Charles, or balconies facing the atrium. Singles range from $43 to $71, and doubles, from $56 to $84. Terrace parlors are $43 to $56, and suites are $100 to $300 for glamor deals with bar. There is a $10 charge for an extra person, but children under 12 are free on the family plan. Good deals are the weekend plans that include dining privileges.

Try breakfast, lunch, dinner, or Sunday brunch at Jonah's on the Terrace, a bright, airy, and crowded restaurant, open to the atrium on one side and with a view of the river on the other. Hours are 7 a.m. to 11 p.m. and prices range from $5 to $8 at lunch and $5 to $12 at dinner. (Have a bowl of Russian cabbage borscht—almost a meal in itself—for $1.50.) The Empress Room, the hotel's gourmet restaurant, serves "Chinese cuisine in the continental manner." Peking duckling, enough for two (or more), is $22, and other delicacies range from $7.50 up. Open Monday through Thursday 6 p.m. to 11 p.m.; until 11:30 on Friday and Saturday; and Sunday until 10:30. An especially nice service is the ritual of choosing a tea ($1) and having it brewed to order. On the rooftop, the revolving Spinnaker Lounge serves

Statue of Paul Revere and Old North Church

A Budget Discovery

When we heard that there was a hotel in Boston offering "luxury accommodation" at ridiculous rates like $14.70 for one, and $18.70 for up to four, we were sure somebody was joking. But off we went to the **Suisse Chalet Motor Lodge**, 800 Morrissey Boulevard (off the Southeastern Expressway; tel. 287-9100), in Boston's Dorchester section, to see for ourselves, and we're here to tell you that it's all absolutely true. The attractive brown-and-orange chalet with balconies is the newest outpost of a chain of highly successful, economy-minded, and family-oriented New England skiing lodges. This one, however, is far enough away from the slopes to make it a convenient base for Boston living. A short bus or cab ride takes you to the subway station and a quick trip to downtown Boston, and by car, it's only ten minutes to the center of the city.

The rooms are more than adequate, they're delightful. All are large, nicely furnished, and carpeted wall to wall, with TV, FM stereo radio, direct-dial phones, electric heat and air conditioning, sliding picture windows, vanity-type washbasins, combination bath-showers, even infrared lamps in the bathroom to help you dry off a little faster! The single-bedded room is the same size as the double and is a favorite with salesmen who use the free space as a work area. There's a swimming pool in the inner court, a coin-operated washer and dryer, and a "vending area" with ice and snacks.

For all this largesse, the fee is, again, incredible: $14.70 for a room with one double bed, $18.70 for a room with two double-beds. The rates hold year round.

Where to eat will be no problem. The Swiss House Restaurant, just across the parking lot, is open from 7 a.m. to 11 p.m., featuring a pancake breakfast, among other selections, and a varied lunch and dinner menu with special children's prices. Incidentally, if you'll be driving from Boston to Cape Cod, staying here already puts you on the road.

lunch (\$4.50 to \$5.50) from 11:45 a.m. to 2:30 p.m., Monday through Saturday. Brunch from 11 p.m. to 3 p.m. Sunday. And drinks till 1 a.m. weekdays, 2 a.m. Friday and Saturday.

Parking for guests is $2 a day, with no "in and out" charge. Nonguests pay 50¢ an hour. The Hyatt Regency is convenient for college visiting, since it's halfway between Harvard and M.I.T., and across the bridge from Boston University. There's no public transportation nearby, but you can always join the

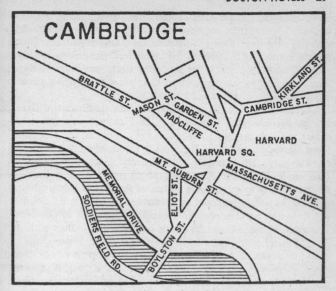

CAMBRIDGE

BRATTLE ST.

MASON ST.

GARDEN ST.

RADCLIFFE

KIRKLAND ST.

CAMBRIDGE ST.

HARVARD

HARVARD SQ.

MT. AUBURN ST.

MASSACHUSETTS AVE.

ELIOT ST.

BOYLSTON ST.

MEMORIAL DRIVE

SOLDIERS FIELD RD.

joggers along the Charles and head for Harvard Square or Massachusetts Avenue.

Although it's technically in Cambridge, **Sonesta Hotel,** 5 Cambridge Parkway (tel. 491-3600), is still very close to Boston; it's near Longfellow Bridge, M.I.T., and the Museum of Science. Its flavor is Boston at its most dramatic, with each room designed to provide an unforgettably lovely view of the Charles River and the city—no "back street" accommodations here. Everything is custom designed, with decorator furnishings, living-bedroom combinations, luxurious bathrooms, color TV, desks, space for social get-togethers. One wall of your room may have natural red brick; another, warm walnut paneling.

Singles are in the $39 to $48 range; doubles, from $46 to $56. Suites go up to $105 a day, but a great idea, for singles, is to rent only the living room of one of the suites. The sofa converts to a bed at night, and the big plus is the dramatic living room, with a picture window nearly 25 feet wide overlooking the twinkling lights of the Charles. Children under 14 are free in the same room with parents. There's an outdoor pool and free parking.

On the second floor, facing the river, is the Rib Room, one of Boston's leading restaurants. The Greenhouse Coffeeshop in the main lobby is fun for snacks and breakfasts. Public facilities include a babysitting service, ice machines, same-day laundry and dry cleaning, plus an outdoor pool where you can swim almost in reach of the yachts tied up at the docks along the river.

Incidental intelligence for shoppers: Lechmere Sales, a huge bargain center for cameras, stereos, appliances, camping goods, what-have-you, is right nearby.

Located in the most interesting and historic district of Cambridge, the **Sheraton-Commander,** 16 Garden Street (tel. 547-4800), is a substantial, 110-room hotel just across the Common from Harvard University. It claims to stand only a few feet from the elm where, on July 3, 1775, General George Washington took command of the American troops (in the front courtyard of the hotel is an impressive statue of the first U.S. president).

Traditionally patronized by parents of Harvard and Radcliffe students, the hotel successfully captures the spirit of Old New England. The neo-Colonial decor begins in the lounge with its Boston Hitchcock chairs and grandfather clock, and extends to the guest rooms, furnished with tall, slim four-poster beds, pine desks, Boston rockers, oil lamps. TV, of course. Singles go from $29 to $33; doubles and twins, from $36 to $40. Suites range from $50 to $100.

There are two dining rooms—the Colonial, for breakfast, lunch and dinner; and Dertads, highly rated for its gourmet continental French cuisine. A la carte dinners in this elegant room, with its arched wooden-beamed ceiling and stained-glass panels, start at $9.50.

Well-situated near the major Boston campuses—with Harvard to the right, M.I.T. to the left, and Boston University across the bridge—**Howard Johnson's Motor Hotel,** 777 Memorial Drive (tel. 492-7777), on the banks of the Charles River, is just ten minutes by car to the heart of Boston and less to Harvard Square in Cambridge. It's an attractive, modern motel, with plenty of peace and quiet, a swimming pool, and a court for paddle tennis.

Each of the bedrooms is equipped with a picture window (the better to enjoy the splendid views of the Boston skyline). Some have a private balcony. Rooms are large, nicely furnished, and the rates go from $31.50 to $36.50 in a single, and from $37.50 to $44.50 for doubles, the prices varying with the size of the room, the floor, and the view. It's $4 for each extra person, no charge for cribs; children under 18 free with their parents. Senior citizen discounts are available with AARP card.

Rooms are contemporary in style and have color TVs and air conditioning. The coffeeshop serves breakfast, lunch, and dinner, and the popular Red Coach Grill with a river view features a lavish salad bar and roast beef dinners.

Holiday Inn, 1651 Massachusetts Avenue (tel. 491-1000), is more modest than its larger sister located in downtown Boston. Nevertheless, it's a winning choice for many, designed in what it calls "Harvard red brick and enameled steel," and situated on the historic Cambridge Heritage Trail. A small, 135-room, air-conditioned structure, it is wide and spread out, on a busy boulevard, yet set back with enough parking space for cars in front. Parking is free.

Rates start at $28 for a single and $34 for a double, with $4 charged for each additional person sharing the same room. Children under 19 are free with parents. Families of students and faculty at Harvard, Radcliffe, Tufts, and M.I.T. stay here for comfort at moderate prices. There is an outdoor pool open 9 a.m. to 9 p.m. and room service from 7 a.m. to 11 p.m. Discount with AARP or NRTA card for senior citizens.

Still another **Holiday Inn** is the one at 30 Washington Street, Somerville (tel. 628-1000). It's a new high-rise of 184 rooms practically on the Cambridge and Charlestown lines, near Harvard, Tufts, and M.I.T., as well as Bunker Hill and the U.S.S. *Constitution.* Although the motel is about two and a half miles from the central area of Boston, it's near the Sullivan Square subway station and just four miles from Logan Airport.

The facilities include an indoor swimming pool, whirlpool, saunas, game room, and a sun lamp in each bathroom in case you prefer not to use the sundeck above the pool. The rooms are colorful and "busy" with blue-and-red rugs, modern blue-and-white furnishings, flowered spreads, air conditioning, and TV. Single rates start at $30, and doubles, $36. There's a charge of $4 for each extra person, but children under 18 are free with their parents. An attractive parlor suite with sofa bed, walnut furnishings, stand-up bar, and refrigerator is $40 single, and $45 double.

Practically in Harvard Square and convenient to everything, **Harvard Motor House,** 110 Mt. Auburn Street (tel. 864-5200), is a modern brick, six-floor motel, not in the least traditional, but a good base for Cambridge living. The rooms all have wide picture windows, and the furnishings are compact, comfortably Danish-inspired modern, with TV, radio, air conditioning, and combination tub-showers. Especially nice is the free continental breakfast—orange juice, assorted doughnuts, coffee or tea—included in the price of your room. Singles go from $26 to $28, doubles, from $32 to $34. An additional adult rollaway bed costs $5, but cribs are free (and so are children under 16). The top-floor suites rent from $55 to $65. No restaurants or cocktail lounges downstairs, but they're hardly necessary with the wealth of eating and drinking facilities in Harvard Square. Free parking is available for hotel guests. Senior citizens get a 10% discount with AARP card except during July and August.

Statue of Captain John Parker (Commander of the Minutemen)

Chapter IV

DINING OUT IN BOSTON

TO READ SOME travel writers, one would assume that Bostonians lived on a steady diet of seafood, cod, and baked beans, with perhaps a New England boiled dinner or two thrown in for good measure. It's just not that way, at least not anymore.

True, Boston is "the seafood capital of the world," and no seafood lover in his right mind would dispute the excellence of the Ipswich clams, Atlantic lobsters, quahog clams, cod, haddock, flounder, and mussels that have won the city this acclaim. The waters off the Massachusetts coast have abounded in these for centuries (at the Old State House, in fact, a wooden codfish commemorates the importance of the fish to the people of the Commonwealth), and the natives have responded by creating and maintaining a superb culinary tradition. And the old, cherished recipes—for oyster stew, for clam chowder, for steamed clams in drawn butter, for finnan haddie (smoked haddock,) and for that famed Boston scrod (the name for a small haddock or cod)—are still yours to enjoy when you visit the city. The baked beans, however, are seen now and then, and more likely to turn up in cans on supermarket shelves than in most Boston restaurants. And the New England boiled dinner is no longer as prevalent as it used to be, since the reason for its original existence has faded (in olden days, every ingredient—corned beef, carrots, potato, cabbage, whatever—was cooked in one pot, since that was all that would conveniently hang on a crane over the open fire).

What is prevalent, however, is a vast number of restaurants offering everything from regional New England to American to European and Oriental cuisines. And you'll find the Bostonian has as sophisticated a palate as the native of, say, New York or

San Francisco. Boston has its share of fine French and continental restaurants (this is, after all, the home base of Julia Child); the hallowed seafood temples, of course; the shrines to beef and hearty eating; and, since it has absorbed such a large immigrant population into its fabric, an outstanding selection of Italian and Chinese restaurants, plus an array of Jewish delicatessens where the pastrami and lox and seeded ryes are every bit as good as they are in the famed delis of New York. Add to that an ever-growing foreign colony of Middle Eastern, Mexican, Spanish, and Indian restaurants, plus macrobiotic and natural-food choices, and a bevy of spots for sumptuous brunches and relaxed outdoor dining. And if you run out of interesting places to dine in Boston, you're just not trying.

FACTS AND FIGURES: To simplify your dining selections, we've placed the restaurants into categories based on their price range and the nature of their cuisine. "Haute Cuisine" includes those restaurants charging upward of $16 per meal; "Upper Bracket," from $12 and up; "Moderate," from $8. Remember that if you choose lobster, currently in a state of scarcity everywhere in the world, prices will probably go above these figures. As for the "Budget" category, meals around $5, Boston has a good share of restaurants, especially in nearby Cambridge, with its vast population of money-conscious students.

Now for some general rules. It's always wise to phone ahead and make reservations, particularly for dinner and at the better restaurants. When you call, check, too on whether or not they accept the credit cards you're carrying; some of the finer places accept only their own house cards or cash. Also check on dress requirements; although Boston is not a "dressy" city, most of the better restaurants do require jacket (but not necessarily a tie) for men. For the ladies, pants, we are happy to report (but pants, *not* jeans), are acceptable everywhere, even in such once-haughty shrines as the dining room of the Ritz-Carlton.

As for tipping, it's a standard 15% everywhere, more if you're especially pleased, or if there's a captain. There's a 5% meal tax, added to all bills. And even in expensive restaurants, it's perfectly okay to ask for a bag to take home for the doggie.

If you have a car, it's wise to call ahead to see if there are any facilities for validated parking.

So then, let's begin.

Haute Cuisine
(Meals from $16)

CONNOISSEUR'S CHOICES: Rarely is there agreement among gourmets in choosing the finest restaurant in town, especially in Boston where there are so many superb dining rooms. But there are three that make everyone's list (arranged here in alphabetical order since each is tops in its own fashion): Cafe Budapest, Maison Robert, and The Ritz-Carlton Restaurant.

Cafe Budapest, 90 Exeter Street (tel. 734-3388), is in the lower level of the Copley Square Hotel, with its own mirrored entrance on Exeter Street. Edith Ban, the hearty empress of this Hungarian restaurant, runs a tight ship, supervising every detail personally and tolerating no errors on the part of her staff. Result: consistently excellent food and service. Mrs. Ban herself, in her traditional white gown, may greet you at one of the three dining rooms—the elegant Pink Room, with pale-pink cloths and napkins and green brocade chairs; the peasant-style Blue Room, with garlands painted on the ceilings to match the flowered dinner plates; or the wood-paneled main dining room, accented with stained glass, ruby goblets and napkins, and red leather chairs. If you're splurging, you can order a superb dinner for two for $30; it consists of a mixed grill of filet mignon, wiener schnitzel, pork chops, and other delights, topped off by a rich pastry and coffee. Well recommended on the à la carte menu are beef stroganoff, $11.50, turkey-stuffed mushroom caps, $9.95; and veal goulache, $10.50. A special favorite is veal cutlet supreme at $11.95—pan-fried veal cutlets layered with Swiss cheese and Virginia ham, and served with potatoes au gratin and asparagus with a remoulade sauce, plus a fresh salad. Entrees start at about $8. And whatever else you have, be sure to start with soup (around $2). We've heard that the cream of cauliflower and the chicken broth with chicken-liver dumplings are excellent, but we've never been able to pass up the iced, tart cherry soup with French Médoc wine. For dessert you must have the Hungarian strudel, $1.90, with Viennese coffee (ground fresh every hour), or tea brewed at your table. Dinner is served from 5 p.m. to 10:30 p.m., Monday through Thursday; 5 p.m. to midnight on Fridays and Saturdays; and from 1 p.m. to 10:30 p.m. on Sundays. A complete luncheon including entree, soup, salad, roll, coffee or tea, and pastry is served daily from noon to 3 p.m. À la carte entrees are also available.

The **Budapest Lounge** is open evenings for drinks, coffee, and pastries or special crêpes, served to romantic strains of Hungarian violinists.

Maybe it's the Julia Child influence (her program originates here) or just the fact that Boston appreciates fine cuisine, but Boston's French restaurants rank with the best. One of the people responsible for this is Lucien Robert, a man of uncompromising standards, the kind of restaurateur who has had turbot flown in from France to make a bouillabaisse! His **Maison Robert,** 45 School Street (tel. 227-3370), is considered one of the finest French restaurants anywhere. Centrally located, just off Tremont Street in the building that was Boston's Old City Hall, Maison Robert offers diners a choice of two restaurants—the elegant **Bonhomme Richard** on the first floor and **Ben's Cafe** on the ground floor.

Decorated in French Second Empire style, the Bonhomme Richard is a gracious dining room with ornate moldings and butternut window panelings, crystal chandeliers, potted palms, and fresh flowers. Lunch and dinner are served in the classical French tradition, with entrees starting at $9 and going up and up. You'll feast on the likes of mignon de veau, l'homard au whiskey (lobster with whiskey sauce), and le poulet Bonhomme Richard (roast chicken with Calvados and cream). The service is as superb as the food, and there is a wine list of vintage bordeaux and burgundies.

What were vaulted storage rooms are now the charming dining rooms of Ben's Cafe. The fresh flowers and white linen contrast with the oak woodwork, textured brick walls, and handsome vaulted brick ceilings. Try the roulade maison, the chef's specialty; it is a seafood crêpe stuffed with lobster, shrimp, and crab. We can also vouch for the properly done roast rack of lamb and the light Dover sole. The onion soup is thick and cheesy, and escargots or oysters make great appetizers. Desserts are French classics. Prices on the à la carte menu run from $5.75 to $12.50.

Although both rooms serve lunch, our personal choice would be Ben's Cafe, where you can get a complete meal, including soup, vegetable, salad, and beverage, from $5.50 to $8, and the entrees include a light and crusty quiche Lorraine and that famous roulade maison.

If you're here in summer, get a table in the outdoor terrace next to the statue of Benjamin Franklin which marks the site of his childhood home. (He's the Ben of the Cafe, in case you were wondering.) Ben's Cafe is open daily from 11:30 a.m. to

9:30 p.m.; Bonhomme Richard is open for lunch from 12 to 2:30 p.m. and for dinner from 6 to 10 p.m. Closed Sunday.

The **Ritz-Carlton Restaurant,** 15 Arlington Street (tel. 536-5700). A unique fame attends the elegant second-floor restaurant of this hotel, overlooking the Boston Public Garden. Whether it's Sunday brunch by the blue-and-white-draped windows, or an evening dinner under the soft lights of the crystal chandeliers, all with soft piano music, French menu, and attentive waiters, a meal here is a memorable experience. The menu is extensive, sophisticated, and expensive. Your least costly dinner might tally up about $12, the average around $16, and with hors d'oeuvres, soup, and dessert, you could spend $22, not including wines.

Nearly 20 in all, the appetizers range from baked clams casino at $4.75 to the pâté maison at $9.25 or Beluga caviar at $18. Chilled vichyssoise is $1.50 and the Ritz green turtle soup with a pastry turtle floating on top and sherry stirring within is $3. Entrees include the chef's pride, Maine lobster "au whiskey," with rice pilaf and an artichoke clamart, $16. Other substantial offerings feature roast leg of spring lamb in the Breton style, with vegetables, $12.50; and broiled prime sirloin steak, Cafe Paris, $13.25. For that extra-special dessert, order soufflé Grand Marnier, $8 for two, or the fluffy, delicate chocolate soufflé. Soufflé Suchard, at the same price.

Jacket and tie are required for men, and reservations are accepted. Dinner is served from 6 p.m. to 9 p.m., Sunday; 6 p.m. to 10 p.m., Monday through Thursday; and until 11 p.m., Friday and Saturday.

Breakfast, lunch, dinner, and supper (9 p.m. to 12:30 a.m.) are served in the **Ritz Cafe.** Prices are more moderate than the dining room, but the food is still excellent. Afternoon tea is served in **The Lounge,** and cocktails in the Lounge and the cozy **Ritz Bar.**

BOSTON CLASSICS: **Locke-Ober,** 3 Winter Place (tel. 542-1340). Those who lament the passing of the grand old traditional restaurants of America are usually heartened by a trip to Boston and to this legendary cafe. Locke-Ober's mahogany-paneled serenity is treasured. On the second floor is the "new" dining room. Downstairs, it's a world of carved paneling, of plate-glass mirrors, and a long bar with eight mammoth Germanic silver dishes. Women have finally been welcomed in both dining rooms.

And what would an 1880s bar be without a peach-complexioned nude? Red leather and brass-studded chairs, art nouveau light fixtures with exposed bulbs (after all, electricity was a novelty then)—all this forms the setting for what Lucius Beebe called "a temple of gastronomy." A pair of brass poles are used as a kind of dumbwaiter to send a tray of drinks up to the second-floor dining room, incidentally.

There are at least a dozen dishes that win accolades. The best way, in our view, to launch your meal is with a dazzling selection of hors d'oeuvres, $5.25, although many prefer the baked oysters, prepared in several different ways and ranging in price from $3.50 to $4.50. If you'd like to have perhaps the greatest dish on the menu—preferred by gastronomes from around the world whenever they descend on Boston—then make it baked lobster Savannah at $22—a lot of money, but well worth the once-in-a-lifetime splurge. Other popular dishes include filet mignon of beef mirabeau, $13.50; chicken Richmond, $7.25; sweetbreads Eugene (under glass), $9.50.

For dessert, try the sultana roll in a claret sauce, $2.10; or the Indian pudding with vanilla ice cream, also $1.25; baked Alaska for two is $6 and crêpes suzette are flamed for $4.50. There is also an excellent luncheon menu, 11:30 a.m. to 3 p.m., with prices from $4 to $17.50. Dinner is served from 3 p.m. to 10 p.m. Closed Sundays.

The **Cafe Plaza** is probably what you have in mind when you think of *The* Plaza. This gourmet restaurant in the Copley Plaza Hotel (tel. 267-5300) has a decor to match its elegant menu— Waterford crystal chandeliers, ornately sculptured vaulted ceilings, banquettes upholstered in red, fresh flowers, and soft background music. Chef Lydia Shire wields her talents on the fine à la carte continental menu, performing wonders with the grilled swordfish, topped with a cold cucumber sauce, $9.95; and the roast duckling à l'orange, $10.50. For a splurge you might try the chateaubriand with jardinière of vegetables, $26 for two; or the roast rack of lamb, $25 for two. And if you've just won the lottery, have Lobster Anita, 1½ pounds of lobster sauteed in white wine sauce and heavy cream, and served on a silver platter, $17.95. We advise saving some room for the desserts, especially the flaming specialties, like cherries jubilee, $3, or crêpes suzette for two, $8. Dinner is served daily from 5:30 to 10:30 and lunch from 12 to 2:30 with luncheon entrees (quiche Lorraine, shrimp in ale batter, and filet mignon) in the $4.25 to $7.95 range. The Cafe Plaza has one of Boston's finest wine cellars with many vintage treasures.

Back in the time of Emerson and Longfellow, the Parker House, 60 School Street (tel. 227-8600), was *the* place in town—home to Boston's literati and an elegant dining spot. Now, after many years of faded glory, the main dining room has been re-opened as **Parker's**, a bastion of haute cuisine for "Proper Bostonians." From the moment the manager hands each lady a yellow rose and each man a cigar, the touches are all elegant. Tables are set with Rosenthal china and sterling-silver flatware, and the menus are covered in leather. The decor is beige and brown, set against walnut-paneled walls.

The menu is divided into two categories—fish and crustaceans, and meat and fowl—and all entrees include vegetable, potato, Parker House rolls, and Boston baked beans. Prices range from $8.95 for boiled Parker House tripe with mustard sauce (based on a 120-year-old recipe), to $13.25 for steak Diane and escalope de veau Raphael (veal with a port wine sauce and white asparagus and avocado). An excellent poached Dover sole is $12.50, and a roast rack of spring lamb for two, $29 (there's a 45-minute preparation wait for this—a good time to sample the offerings of the wine cellar). The dessert specialty is Parker's Sparkling Strawberries, fresh strawberries laced with strawberry liqueur and served in a large snifter with a half bottle of Charbaut brut champagne, $7.95 for two.

The luncheon menu features Boston favorites and American and continental offerings, with choices of Boston scrod, $6.50; New York–cut sirloin steak, $8.95; and shirred eggs Pontalba, $4.50, among the entrees. Dinner hours are 5:30 to 9 p.m., Monday to Friday, until 10:30 p.m. Saturday. On Sunday, brunch is served at 11:30 a.m. and 1:30 p.m., and dinner from 5:30 to 10 p.m. Lunch, Monday through Friday, 11:30 a.m. to 2:30 p.m. Jackets are required, and reservations are suggested.

THE NEW ELEGANTES: Devotees of **Lechner's**, 21 Broad Street (tel. 523-1016), consider this gourmet restaurant superior to the venerable Locke-Ober. While that's a matter of taste, we recommend it highly for excellent food, gracious service, and old-world charm. Continental in style, with German accents, Lechner's is located in an oasis-like courtyard slipped in between the stone and steel of the financial district. A narrow stairway leads from the first-floor lounge to the small dining rooms on the second and third floors, with their crystal chandeliers and oil paintings.

You can spend from $25 to $50 and more for a dinner for two, depending on your menu choices and wines. For example, your appetizer can be plain tomato juice or Strasbourg pâté de foie gras. Herring in sour-cream sauce with onion and apple bits is $2.50; baked oysters, $4.25; and an hors d'oeuvres platter with shellfish, Westphalian ham, and cheese is around $10. Entrees include veal Cordon Bleu—veal cutlet stuffed with ham and cheese—at $9; a seafood mornay baked in lobster sauce and sherry, about $12; and a weiner roastbraten—a tender sirloin steak. Flaming foods are presented with theatrical flair. Try the duck Bigarade, a tender duckling sprinkled with Grand Marnier, flambeed with cognac, and served with an orange brandy sauce. Our choice of a flaming dessert is fresh strawberries marinated in liqueur, flamed with white rum, and served in layers of whipped cream. And we could easily become addicted to the Black Forest cherry cake, with its chocolate whipped cream and sweet black cherries.

Lunch is served in the same fine style, Monday through Friday from 11:45 a.m. to 2 p.m. Dinner hours are 5:30 p.m. to 10 p.m., Monday through Saturday. There is on-street parking only, but Lechner's is near the State Street "T" station.

Rosenthal china, champagne used as a marinade, snails flamed in chablis—these are some of the touches of elegance that beckon gourmets to **Zachary's,** the continental restaurant at the Colonnade Hotel, 120 Huntington Avenue (tel. 261-2800). The à la carte menu is expensive; dinner for two, without drinks, can run $40 or more.

If you're adventurous, sample the frog legs, which are sauteed to perfection and served, for $11.50. Our tastes run more to steak au poivre, in which the sirloin is combined with crushed peppercorn, dry wine, cognac, sweet butter, and heavy cream, wrapped in a thin crêpe, and prepared and flamed at your table, $14. Rouennais duck with champagne and cognac is served in two sequences: the leg is served roasted and very crisp, and the breast is fileted at the table and cooked and flambeed in champagne and cognac, $13.50. The service is excellent and the food is brought to your table on a rolling cart, while still being warmed on a special heating section.

For dessert, try the trifle—sponge cake, peaches, and strawberries laced with sherry and topped with whipped cream, or the pièce de résistance, home-baked Black Forest torte. We liked the Spanish coffee, $3.25; but you could also choose Irish coffee, or espresso. The restaurant is open for dinner, Monday through Saturday, 5 p.m. to 11 p.m.; and for lunch, Monday through Friday, 11:30 a.m. to 2:30 p.m. Parking is $1 at the Colonnade garage.

Borscht in the Museum of Contemporary Art? Well, how about caviar or chicken Kiev? All quite possible, since there's an Imperial Russian restaurant on the first-floor and basement levels of the museum. The **Hermitage,** 955 Boylston Street (tel. 267-3652), takes its name from Leningrad's magnificent museum, but its decor comes from its contemporary setting. Tan-and-chocolate backgrounds, candles, yellow roses, and pottery on the tables, and paintings on the white walls create a relaxed mood for dining.

The menu changes frequently, but you'll probably find beef stroganoff, $9.95; chicken Kiev, $7.95; and shashlik (marinated skewered lamb served with a dip of Oriental plum sauce) among the entrees. And as for that borscht, $2.25—you'll never find anything like it on your supermarket shelves. And chestnut mousse makes a lovely dessert. The pot au crème is excellent, especially when accompanied by a creamy cappucino Hermitage, blended with liquors and liqueurs ($2.50).

Dinner hours are 6 p.m. to 9 p.m., Sunday and Monday; until 10, Tuesday to Thursday; and until 11, Friday and Saturday. Lunch is served, Tuesday through Saturday, from noon to 2:30 p.m., and there is a Sunday brunch from 12 to 3 p.m. Closed Sundays during the summer.

Upper-Bracket Restaurants
(Meals from $12)

FOR SEAFOOD: One of the most outstanding restaurants in New England, winner of the Business Executive's Dining Award as America's most popular restaurant for five straight years, is **Anthony's Pier 4,** 140 Northern Avenue (tel. 423-6363). Over 30 years of devotion by Anthony Athanas has produced this extraordinary restaurant, spacious enough to serve a thousand people a day some of the best seafood in America. Dramatically situated at the end of a pier, its waterfront walls are made of glass, allowing clear views of incoming liners, fishing boats, tugs, and yachts (especially interesting ships are announced over the

For That Special Dinner
A Cookbook Author's Own Place

Madeline Kamman, chef and gourmet author, must be doing something right. In fact, she does everything right! That's why her new restaurant **Modern Gourmet**, Piccadilly Square, 93 Union Street, Newton (tel. 969-1320), is booked two months in advance for a Saturday night dinner. Connoisseurs rate the superb French and Italian food the best in Massachusetts. One sitting an evening, by reservation. Prix-fixe, Tuesday through Thursday, $13.50 plus wine. À la carte, Friday and Saturday: entrees, $18; appetizers, $3.50 to $6.00; and desserts, $3.50 to $4.00.

Elegant Dining in a Town House

Nine Knox, 9 Knox Street (tel. 482-3494), is a charming little 1850 town house in Boston's Bay Village section where, in a sophisticated Edwardian setting on the parlor floor, you can have a complete gourmet's repast from $12 to $18.

You'll be served an excellent full-course meal, beginning with either watercress, French onion soup, or vichyssoise; continuing with an onion-and-cheese quiche, coquille Knox Street, or escargots; going on to salad and a choice of entrees that includes, among others, beef Wellington ($18), filet mignon ($18), chicken Kiev ($14), shrimp Knox Street ($16). Dessert—a rich cream-and-fruit pie—and very good coffee. On Saturday, beef Wellington is the only entree, with set seatings at 6 p.m. and 9:30 p.m. Open Monday through Friday from 7 p.m. to 9 p.m. Closed Sunday. Reservations are imperative.

loudspeaker). The walls are lined with photos of Athanas with the famous in the world of arts, sports and government; and the restaurateur is usually there in person receiving the compliments of the diners and keeping an eagle eye on all phases of the operation.

There is often a long wait for a table, but once seated you're served hot popovers, marinated mushrooms, corn on the cob, and relishes. You drink from Sandwich stemware, and can choose either imported or domestic wines. There are dinner specials every night starting at $6.95 for baked stuffed filet of sole; and you can order swordfish en brochette for $7.95 or swordfish steak, $8.95. Dover sole from the English Channel (flown over especially for Athanas) is $11.95, and elegant baked lobster Savannah (with mushrooms, peppers, spices, wines, and mornay sauce) can be enjoyed for about $25. The Pier 4 Clambake Special features whole boiled lobster, Gulf shrimp, steamed clams, baked potato, and salad, $13.95. For an unusual appetizer, try smoked rainbow trout, $4.50; bouillabaisse, $3.50; or one ounce of Malossal caviar, $18. And Pier 4 is not all seafood, either. The roast beef ($8.95) and steaks ($10.95) are excellent. (Leave a little room for ice-cream pie or baked Alaska.)

Pier 4 is open every day but Christmas, serving lunch Monday to Saturday from 11:30 a.m. to 3:45 p.m., and dinner from 3:45 to 11 p.m. On Sunday, dinner is 12:30 to 10:30 p.m. And there's a Sunday morning brunch, too, for which reservations may be made. Jackets are required in all the Athanas' restaurants except his original **Anthony's Hawthorne** in Lynn on the North Shore. (You can get many of the specialties here at moderate prices since it is in the center of the city, rather than on the waterfront.)

Jimmy's Harbor Side Restaurant, 242 Northern Avenue (tel. 423-1000), is the domain of Jimmy Doulos, "Chowder King of the Nation." It was his chowder that settled the Senate "debate" over the merits of New England clam chowder vs. that of Manhattan. Emigrating from Greece almost 60 years ago, Jimmy started his restaurant career as a vegetable worker in a Greek cafe. He built his first restaurant in 1923 and it grew over the years to accommodate those seeking top-notch shore dinners.

There's a fine view of the harbor and Logan Airport in both the large main downstairs dining room with its nautical decor, and the smaller Pilot House upstairs, which has a more intimate touch. The overall feeling in both rooms is warm and friendly. As for the food, we wish you could try everything. But if you

Fishing boats in Boston Harbor

only come once, take one of the shore dinners, perhaps broiled scallops à la Jimmy at $7.50, or colossal Alaskan king crab legs at $11.25. Dinners include appetizer (order the creamy fish chowder with generous chunks of white fish), salad, potato, dessert, and beverage. (A bowl of fish à la carte at $3 makes a fine lunch.) Occasionally there are specialties not listed on the menu that only the regular diners ask for, such as gray sole. Check to see if it's available—excellent and not too expensive. There are many à la carte entrees, plus creations from Jimmy's Private Galley, including famous finnan haddie at $7.75; shish-kebab Athenian style, $7.75; and roast beef, $8.75. Special dinners are available for children, and there is a special menu for lunch. Lunch from 11:30 to 3:00, dinner from 3 to 9:30, Monday to Saturday. Closed Sunday. Reservations are accepted on weekdays.

While you're waiting to be seated, you can enjoy delicious hors d'oeuvres in the lounge—and you don't necessarily have to have a drink!

MOSTLY FOR BEEF: The 57, 200 Stuart Street at Park Square (tel. 423-5700). This is the famous old 57 Carver Street restaurant, now in an elegant rust-and-beige dining room next to the Howard Johnson Hotel. Happily, it still features the roast beef that made it famous, a thick, succulent 20-ounce rib for $9.50. The steaks, too, are outstanding. You can choose a New York cut for $10.50, or Boston cut sirloin for $11.50, or a peppercorn sirloin for $10.75. The menu is large, but one of our favorites is the unusual shrimp Athenian-shore style. It's a Greek-inspired classic—large Gulf shrimps sauteed with whole tomatoes and feta cheese, $7.75. All entrees are served with potato, vegetable, and salad. The excellent onion soup, $1.25, is served every day, but try the lobster bisque if it's available. Desserts are worth resigning from Weight Watchers for, especially the grasshopper pie, a crème de menthe chiffon concoction, $1.25. The shortcakes and tarts made with fresh fruit are also good. Lunch is a good buy; you can get an omelet and soup for $3.25, or a hot roast-beef sandwich au jus, served with soup and french fries, for $4.25. It is served Monday to Saturday from 11:30 to 3. Dinner is from 3 to 12.

Before or after your dinner, have a drink in the adjacent lounge, attractive and cozy, with couches and small tables, where a pianist and guitarist provide background music every night except Sunday.

There's more than scotch and sirloin at the **Scotch 'n Sirloin,** 77 North Washington Street (tel. 723-3677). There's an excellent steak-house menu with 17 entrees, unusual decor, and an all-points view of Boston from huge window walls.

Occupying the eighth floor of a former trade building near the Boston Garden sports area, the restaurant uses the old industrial fittings as focal points. Fire doors have been sprayed bright colors and are now backdrops for the three well-stocked salad bars, structural pipes are exposed, and a drill press and a printing press are reminders of the building's former occupants. Early 1900s photographs and plants and hanging baskets of greenery accent the red brick walls.

Menus are stenciled on black lunch boxes with prices ranging from $5.95 to $12.45. Portions are large and well prepared. The teriyaki sirloin at $8.95 is excellent, as is the prime rib at $9.95. Ale-battered shrimp (shrimp dipped in a batter of flour and ale, and deep fried), broiled scrod, and king crab are other good choices. Mushroom caps sauteed in butter ($1.95) are just about the best we've had, and the cheesecake is a bargain at $1.25.

Dinner hours are 5:30 to 10:30, Sunday to Thursday, and till 11:30, Friday and Saturday. Reservations are accepted, and there is valet parking.

The waterfront isn't exclusively for seafood—there's a broad range of dining places to choose from including steak houses in recycled harborfront buildings. **The Chart House,** 60 Long Wharf (tel. 227-1576), is one of a chain of 31 restaurants extending from the East Coast to Hawaii. Housed in a building which was built in 1760 (tea was stored there at the time of the Boston Tea Party), the interior has been stripped to mellow red brick walls and decorated with hanging greenery, old ferry boat schedules, nautical paintings, and purple-cushioned window benches. An open staircase extends from the lobby to the third floor where a huge brass tub fulled with ferns hangs from a pulley anchored to an exposed beam. (Both were used in the original warehouse.) The view through the large windows is delightful.

Basically a steak house, The Chart House is several cuts above the ordinary steak house in style, quality, and service. The "salad bar," in the form of a wooden salad bowl with thermal lining, is brought to each table, along with a chilled salad plate and three salad dressings. Top sirloin, prime ribs, and some teriyaki marinated meats are featured, as well as fresh fish, shrimp, and

lobster. Prices range from $5.95 for teriyaki chicken breast to
$13.95 for lobster. Dinner is served from 5 p.m. to 11 p.m. on
weekdays; 5 p.m. to midnight, Friday and Saturday; and 4 p.m.
to 10 p.m., Sunday.

MOSTLY FOR THE VIEW: Top of the Hub, Prudential Tower
(tel. 536-1775). The meals here, like the Tower, are high. But
you're paying for the view from this 52nd-floor Stouffer's restaurant which crowns Boston's major modern landmark, and it's
worth it. On a clear day you can see Boston below you and Cape
Cod or New Hampshire off in the distance. At night, the twinkling panorama of lights and music from the lounge create a
special magic. We suggest coming before sunset, and lingering
over your meal till dark. This way you get the best of both
worlds.

While the food isn't as exciting as the view, there are some
interesting selections on the menu. From the "flaming" group,
try steak brochette at $10.95, or roast duck à l'orange for $13.95.
The lowest priced entree is scrod, at $7.95. For a spectacular
dessert, order crêpes suzette or cherries jubilee, $3.95 for two.
Dinner is served from 5:30 to 10 p.m. daily. Lunch, from 11 to
3, is less expensive, with sandwiches starting at about $3. There
is also a Sunday brunch, from 11 to 2, $5.25 for adults, $2.95 for
children.

Now, if you can plan your visit so that you're here the night
of the full moon, you're in for a special treat. Have drinks at the
Thai Bar, adjoining the restaurant, as you watch the spectacular
sight of the moon rising high over Boston Harbor. By the way,
there's dancing in the Thai Bar, and dinner guests are invited to
join in.

THE FRENCH CONNECTION: Some of the best food in Boston
can be found in little unobtrusive cafes and continental dining
rooms specializing in the French touch. A case in point is **Cafe
L'Ananas,** at 281 Newbury Street (tel. 353-0176), near the Prudential Center. It's down a few steps from the street, easy to find
in the summer when tables with yellow umbrellas form a sidewalk cafe, but hard to spot otherwise. The small room is cozy
with banquettes along the wall, hanging greenery, and paintings.
The menu changes frequently; consequently, the prices vary. But
you can expect to find à la carte entrees in the $9.95 to $13.95
range, with broiled scallops in vermouth and garlic sauce at

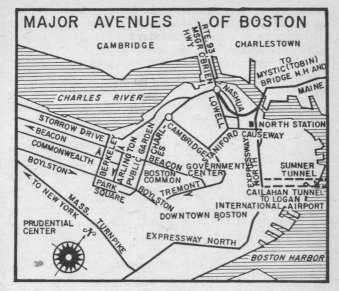

$11.95; pork tenderloin in port sauce with white raisins and currants, $11.95; and roast leg of lamb with fresh pineapple and mint sauce, $12.95. The creamed vegetable soups are superb—almost as good as the desserts. À la carte lunch prices range from $3.25 to $5.95; add soup, dessert, and coffee for $2 extra. Hours are noon to 12:30 for lunch and 6 to 10 p.m. for dinner.

Another little Boston hideaway that's a great favorite is **Another Season,** 97 Mt. Vernon Street (tel. 367-0880), near Charles Street. The menu is limited to about six entrees with two or three soups and appetizers, but each selection is created with an expertise usually found only in the top dining spots. Nothing run-of-the-kitchen here, but offerings such as bluefish en paupiette, $7.50; poached sole with dill mousseline, $8; veal à la crème, $9.50; and chicken Marcel (chicken with shrimp and sausage, simmered in a tomato, pepper, and onion sauce), $8.50. Soups are $1.50, and the choice could be egg lemon soup, cream of broccoli, or a combination of fish, tomato, and saffron.

The dessert choices ($1.50) depend on the inspiration of chef Odette Berry, but usually include a mousse (could be chocolate or lemon sherry), a gâteau with a liqueur-flavored whipped cream topping, or perhaps strawberries Romanoff served in a wine glass. Open for dinner only from 5:30 to 10:30 p.m., Monday through Thursday; and until 11 p.m., Friday and Saturday. Closed Sunday.

In mythology **Cybele** means "woman of the caves." Perhaps that is why Rebecca Caras and Bob Sweet choose that name for their excellent restaurant tucked away among the boutiques in the basement of the South Market Building in Quincy Market. Two small rooms with off-white walls, dark-brown carpeting, exposed brick and beams seat 36 diners; but the large paneled mirror on one end enlarges the room visually. Green plants, white tablecloths, fresh flowers, red glasses, and photographs of Mediterranean scenes obliterate any cave-like feeling. The menu has French, Greek, and Italian entrees, with the kitchen giving the French attention to detail that creates a fine meal. Baked stuffed sole ($8.25) features a stuffing of minced clams, scallops, shrimp, and shallots, and is cooked in lemon and white wine; veal Marsala ($8.95) has a thick, creamy Marsala and mushroom sauce with a subtle taste of herbs; and the coquille St. Jacques ($7.95) is also expertly flavored with wine and herbs. The top-priced item is tournedos with bearnaise sauce ($10.95), with a classic French bearnaise of butter, egg, and tarragon. Desserts include the Viennese sachertorte, $1.50; homemade fruit pie, $1.25 (said to be baked by Rebecca's mom); and a tray of fruits and cheeses, $2.50. And since you're down in the wine cellar, check the wine list.

In the adjoining cafe area under the open stairway, you can have dessert and espresso, cappucino, or cafe Viennoise. Or one of the appetizers from the regular menu. We recommend the spinach turnovers—three puffs of filo pastry filled with pureed spinach and Gruyere cheese and baked with sesame seed, $2.50. Open daily for lunch (slightly different menu including sandwiches) and dinner, 11:30 a.m. till 10 p.m., Monday through Wednesday; and till 11 p.m., Thursday through Saturday. Sunday, noon to 8 p.m.

We first discovered the **Houndstooth Restaurant** tucked away in a brick courtyard in one of Boston's back streets. It was a small, charming place with French provincial specialties. However, its fame spread so rapidly that the owners have moved it to larger quarters in the heart of the theater district at 150 Boylston Street (tel. 482-0722). The menu has been enlarged, too, and now has many continental offerings priced from $7.75 to $13, including vegetable and salad. They still have beef Toulouse (cooked in red wine with roquefort cheese), $9.50; and onion soup gratinée, a rich stock with lots of good Gruyere cheese on thick bread floating on top, $1.50. Desserts include a homemade linzer torte and rum cake, delightful to have with coffee-liquor combinations, as you look down on the Boston Common from the second-floor dining rooms. There is also a Pub in the basement where a lighter menu is featured. Open for lunch, Monday through Friday, 11:30 a.m. to 2:30 p.m.; and for dinner, 5:30 to 11 p.m. During the height of the theater season, special seatings are arranged before and after curtain time.

St. Botolph Restaurant, 99 St. Botolph Street (tel. 266-3030), is located in a remodeled town house with a picturesque turret, a setting just right for superb French dining. The upstairs dining room has large windows overlooking the street and a bright, cheerful decor. All foods are prepared to order and they're worth waiting for, especially the roast duckling with Bigarade sauce, $10.50; the prime French-cut lamb chops, $11.90; and the fresh filet of sole Caprice, $8.50. A chateaubriand bouquetière for two with bearnaise sauce is $29. If you prefer something less expensive, try one of the "Petits Entrees" such as chilled beef vinaigrette, $5.90; or "Le Plat Bleu," a daily special served with soup, $4.50 to $7.50. Indulge, perhaps, in one of the appetizers such as shrimp remoulade, $6.50; or escargots de Bourgogne, $4.25; and top off the meal with key lime pie or pecan pie, $2.75. Dinner is served 5:30 p.m. to midnight; lunch, 11:45 a.m. to 2:30 p.m. Valet parking is available or you can use the nearby Prudential or Hotel Colonnade garages.

TURNING BACK THE CLOCK: Last Hurrah, 60 School Street, in the Parker House (tel. 227-8600), is one of Boston's more successful attempts to recreate a turn-of-the-century eating and drinking place. The style is captured with Tiffany shades, a mahogany bar, bentwood chairs, red banquettes, and photographs of the politicians, sports figures, and other celebrities dear to the heart of Bostonians, lining the walls.

While the prices haven't been "turned back" along with the decor, some good values are offered: Boston scrod, $5.95; baked stuffed shrimp, $7.95; and roast beef, $7.50 and $8.95, depending on size. And with the beef you can choose from seven sauces, including sauce bearnaise, sauteed fresh mushrooms in wine, and brandied cheese. Soups and chowders also come in sevens, one for each day of the week. Daily specials are listed on the blackboard; and cold seafood on the half-shell, at 50¢ for oysters or

You Can Bank on These

You've probably heard of breakfast at Tiffany's, but dinner in the vaults of the Shawmut Bank? Not impossible, since Boston has two new restaurants serving elegant dinners where bank officers once arranged loans. (You don't need one to pay your tab.) **Gallagher,** 55 Congress Street (tel. 523-6080), has put blue carpeting and Wedgewood trim in the bank where *The Thomas Crown Affair* was filmed, stored the wines in the former vault, and turned out a continental menu with "French sauces." Entrees are in the $7 to $12 range, with a six-course fixed-price dinner at about $15. Less expensive meals are served in **Truffles,** next to the formal dining room, where pizzas, burgers, crêpes, and pasta share the menu with "Real Meals." Price range is from $3 to $9, and there's live jazz piano in the evening. Gallagher is closed on Sunday, but is open for lunch and dinner from noon till about 10 p.m. other days. Truffles keeps going from midafternoon to midnight.

Schroeder's, 8 High Street (tel. 426-1234), near South Station, caters to the same clientele that came there when it was the State Street Bank. But now the financial executives dine on hearty meals in the impressive hemispherical room with its brass chandeliers, beige-and-brown arched walls, and tables set with white linen and silverplate. Waiters in brown dinner jackets serve guests (also in jacket and tie, even at lunch) from a basic meat-fish-poultry menu that is highlighted with specialties with a German accent: wiener schnitzel, $7.95; braised sauerbraten with red wine, cabbage, and potato pancakes, $6.50; and kassler rippchen (smoked loin of pork with Canadian bacon) with sauerkraut and pancakes, $7. Other entrees go from $5.95 to $12, with an excellent roast duck at $7.95. Desserts include strawberry shortcake on biscuit with real whipped cream, $1.50; and cheeses, including liederkranz, 90¢. Open for lunch and dinner daily, but on Monday only lunch is served, and on Saturday, only dinner. Hours are usually 11:30 a.m. to 9:30 p.m. (10 p.m. on Saturday).

clams, is also offered.

The enormous do-it-yourself salad bar is outstanding, and even includes pineapple chunks and candied apples with the usual salad fare. Unfortunately, there's an extra charge—95¢ with an entree, but only $3.50 as a meal. Luncheon choices run from $3.95 to $7.95 and include scallops, finnan haddie, and crêpes. Last Hurrah is open from 11:30 a.m. to 1 a.m., Monday through Thursday; till 2 a.m., Friday and Saturday; and from 2:30 p.m. to 12:30 a.m. on Sunday. Dancing to the big-band beat is featured Monday through Saturday evenings.

Copley's Bar & Restaurant at the Copley Plaza Hotel, Copley Square (tel. 267-5300), is a restaurant with one name but several faces. There's the barroom with a raised oak-and-leather bar and mirrored walls decorated with oil portraits of local personalities; the lounge with stained-glass fixtures and plants, for cocktails and light sandwiches; and three small dining rooms where Proper Bostonians and others dine in style. These rooms remind us of private English clubs with their Edwardian decor, books, paintings, and other memorabilia. The menu is English-continental eclectic, and we found the carpetbagger steak, a prime filet stuffed with mushrooms, peppers, and onions, and wrapped in bacon, tip-top at $11.95. Hot pecan pie topped with fresh ice cream, $1.75, is an impressive dessert, and so are the homemade ice creams: try the cranberry brandy sherbet!

We've found that lunches are great fun here. They're served in the same elegant atmosphere, and four menus are rotated on a daily basis featuring such "delicacies" as toad in the hole (meat pie with fried onions), $4.25; and Indian curry pie, $4.25. The soups are $1.50: order steaming hot French onion or a smooth lobster bisque. Each menu has meat, fish, soup, salad, sandwiches, and egg dish, quiche, and littleneck clams, as well as the same delicious desserts that are served at dinner. Open for dinner 5:30 to 11:30 p.m. daily; and for lunch from 11:30 a.m. to 3 p.m., Monday through Saturday, and noon to 4 p.m. on Sunday.

INTERNATIONAL FAVORITES: Boston has many international restaurants in all price brackets. We'll cover the dollar-wise choices later, but herewith is a sampling of foreign restaurants in the expense-account category:

Casa Romero, 30 Gloucester Street, Back Bay (tel. 261-2146). The atmosphere is handsome Colonial Mexico (high-backed leather chairs, charming pottery, art works everywhere, inlaid tiles), and the cuisine is authentic Mexicana, on the hotly spiced side and great for those with cast-iron stomachs. If you're not a true aficionado, ask the waiter to go easy on the spices. The specialties include a very good mole poblano (chicken in a chocolate sauce), $7.95; camarones Veracruz (giant shrimps sauteed in a spicy tomato sauce, in the style of Veracruz), $8.95; and puerco adobado (pork tenderloin marinated in oranges, tamarind, and smoked peppers), $8.95.

After the heat of the meal, we suggest a change of pace with something sweet and cooling, perhaps the cold mango soufflé, $2.50.

Casa Romero is open from 6 p.m. to 10 p.m., Sunday through Thursday, and till 11 p.m., Friday and Saturday for dinner; and from 12 to 2:30 p.m. Tuesday through Friday for lunch.

Stella, 74 East India Row (tel. 227-3559), on the waterfront facing the Aquarium, is all Italian Renaissance with plush carpets, soft chairs, and background music. The menu is extensive —and expensive. One of Stella's best dishes is the braciolettine di pollo al Ferri (broiled chicken and ham), $7.50; but piccata di vitello al limone (sliced veal with lemon sauce), $7.75, is also nicely done. Fish lovers should try the baked haddock alla partenopea, $6.75. You have your choice of about 40 entrees, plus pastas, soups, salads, and appetizers in the price range of $3.75 to $15.50. Desserts are quite special, and we find it the height of luxury to savor the zabaglione al Marsala, $1.75; followed by a flaming cup of caffee diablo, $2.75. Stella is open from 11:30 a.m. to 11:30 p.m., with lunch served until 3 p.m. There's free parking in the adjacent Harbor Towers Garage.

Dom's, 236 Commercial Street at the corner of Atlantic Avenue (tel. 523-8838), is a chic Italian restaurant whose staff is devoted to the preparation and serving of good food. Everything is prepared from scratch, which guarantees top quality; even the pasta is homemade, a mere three pounds in one hour. The excellent entrees include osso bucco (a special veal dish including the marrow), $12; lobster Savannah, $20; caciucco (an unusual Italian fish chowder), $11; and pesto, that marvelous basil-flavored pasta dish, for $7.75. If you have the strength for it, you can have a complete meal, including antipasti, soup, a pasta sampler, main course, salad, cheese, fruit, dessert, and espresso for $20. A standout for dessert is the zuppa inglese, $3, made right in Dom's kitchen.

Dom's has a few special wrinkles up its sleeve. Children under ten are guests of the management for spaghetti, meatballs, and beverage; a 5% discount is offered for cash payment; and, in lieu of tipping, a 15% surcharge is added to the bill. Open daily from noon to midnight for complete meals, even later for snacks. Sunday brunch. Valet parking.

Dining Disco-Style

There are dining rooms with music and nightclubs with food, but Jason's, 131 Clarendon Street (tel. 262-9000), is in a class by itself. And Jason's is a classy discotheque, with terraces carpeted wall to wall in rich brown, art-deco styling, little corners for dancing, and huge tanks of expensive tropical fish to divide the rooms. The main dining room is set back from the disco area so the music doesn't intrude too much while you're eating. (You can be served early enough to finish before the dancing starts, but it's fun to stay and dance, or watch, or take a disco lesson.)

But the surprise is the food. If disco ever goes the way of the Lindy, Jason's can still pack in the crowds on the merits of the dining room alone. Baked fish en papillote (filet rolled with shrimp, scallops, crabmeat, herbs, and wine, and baked in parchment), $11; veal Oscar, with crabmeat, asparagus, and hollandaïse, $11.50; and chicken Cordon Bleu, $7.50; are among the impressive entrees. Appetizers include escargot bourguignon, $4; and lobster bisque, $1.25 and $2. If you've come mostly for dancing, there are salads and sandwiches, too. Lunches, without disco, are in the $3.50 (for quiche) to $5.25 (baked, stuffed shrimp) range. Jason's is open for lunch, Monday through Friday from 11:30 p.m. to 3 p.m.; for dinner, every evening, 5 p.m. to midnight; and for Sunday champagne brunch, from 11:30 a.m. to 4 p.m.

Moderate Restaurants
(Meals from $8)

OLD BOSTON: One of the unwritten laws of Boston seems to be that you must not leave town without visiting **Durgin-Park**, 30 North Market Street (tel. 227-2038), and judging from the mobs of people (several thousand a day) always waiting in line to get into this restaurant in the Quincy Market, it's a law that's pretty well obeyed. Although Durgin-Park has been here forever, it's now part of the chic new market area (which was built around it), but there's still nothing chic about Durgin-Park: the place *is* noisy, uncomfortably crowded, and you must share a long table with about 19 other patrons. But if you don't expect gracious service, don't mind clutter, are in a convivial mood, and think that exposed heating pipes and large fans (in summer) are period pieces, then join the long line of kings and commoners (you'll brush elbows with politicians and businessmen and market butchers and Back Bay society matrons here) and wait your turn (no reservations) for good, old-fashioned New England food. The food is still of the highest quality, the portions are very large—and after all, food is what you do go to a restaurant for.

If you can, go for dinner (quaint Boston-ese for the noontime meal), when hearty meals begin at $2 for Poor Man's roast beef or Yankee pot roast. Other entrees are priced from $3.25 to $6.50. At supper (served 4 to 9), prices range from $4 to $9 à la carte. A tremendous slab of prime rib of beef with vegetable is $9. All steaks and chops are broiled on an open fireplace over real wood charcoal. Seafood is received twice daily and fish dinners are broiled to order. Be sure to try the Boston baked beans, which must have been invented here. They're homemade, done the old-fashioned way, in stone crocks. And cornbread, also homemade, comes with every meal. For dessert, we staunchly recommend that venerable New England specialty, baked Indian pudding, a molasses and cornmeal concoction, slow baked for hours and hours, luscious with ice cream, 75¢; or the strawberry shortcake with fresh berries, $1.25.

If you're going for "dinner," beat the crowd by getting there before 11:30 a.m. Otherwise, the long line may drive you to drink; happily, a stop at the Gaslight Pub downstairs permits you to wait in a shorter line before being seated in quarters upstairs.

Durgin-Park is open every day, serving dinner from 11:30 to 2:30; supper, from 4 to 9 p.m.

Union Oyster House, 41 Union Street, between Faneuil Hall and City Hall (tel. 227-2750), started serving oysters in 1826—it's the oldest restaurant in Boston—and has continued ever since with the stalls and oyster bar "in their original positions." At the crescent-shaped bar on the lower level, you can enjoy half a dozen oysters on the half-shell at $2.95, perhaps sitting "where Daniel Webster drank many a toddy in his day." On the second floor of this building lived the exiled Louis Philippe, who gave French lessons to 19th-century Bostonians until he returned to France to become "Citizen King."

From the windows of the upstairs dining room you can look down on City Hall Plaza. Furnished like a simple New England inn, the Oyster House has traditional New England food, too. An oyster stew doused in fresh milk and country butter makes a good beginning. Count the oysters! A complete shore dinner with a chilled fruit cup with sherbet, steamed clams, a broiled live lobster, fried oysters, clams and scallops, dessert, and coffee is priced at $16.25. Ye Olde Seafood Platter is $8.25; fried Ipswich clams, $6.50; filet of scrod, $6.95. For dessert, try traditional Boston gingerbread at 85¢. Daily luncheon specials run as low as $1.60. Open every day from 11 a.m. to 3 p.m. for lunch; and from 3 to 9 p.m. for dinner (until 10 on Saturday).

Note: Daniel Webster also quaffed a pint or two in the building that is now the **Warren Tavern,** 2 Pleasant Street, Charlestown (tel. 241-8500), near the Bunker Hill Monument. The front section is a restored 1780 tavern and the main restaurant was added in 1972. The menu is continental gourmet, not the Early American you might expect, and the food is very good. You can call after 3 p.m. to find out what the evening's menu will be. Prices start at about $7.

FROM THE GASLIGHT ERA: We don't know if there really is a J.C. Hillary, but we do know that his "English Father's Irish Beef Stew," featured at the restaurant **J.C. Hillary's,** 793 Boylston Street (tel. 536-6300), is one of the best in Boston at 85¢ a cup and $1.50 a bowl. It has the usual meat, potatoes, carrots, and celery, but the seasonings give it a special zing. Add a dessert and beverage and you have a filling lunch. The menu features beef, fish, sandwiches, onion soup, and chowder, as well as the stew. Dinner choices include bone-in 1¼-pound sirloin steak, $7.95; shish-kebab, $5.95; and broiled chopped sirloin, $3.95. Broiled scrod and sole and fried Ipswich clams are $5.95. Salad, potato, and rolls are included in the dinner price, and a glass of wine or a mug of beer is only 25¢ with an entree! Sandwiches include hamburger, roast beef, and hot corned beef, $2.25 to $2.95. And a thick, chewy brownie with ice cream and chocolate sauce is $1.35. Lunches are priced from $2.95 to $4.50.

The decor is turn of the century, with a splendid mirrored entrance. Tables are set into an alcove or placed under arches of dark mahogany. Stained-glass panels, hanging plants, and prints in the early-1900s style adorn the walls. Hillary's is open Monday to Thursday from 11:30 a.m. to midnight; Friday and Saturday, 11:30 a.m. to 12:30 a.m.; and Sunday, noon to 11 p.m. Brunch is served on Sunday, noon to 3:30 p.m., includes a Bloody Mary or champagne for only 26¢, along with omelettes, soups, eggs, and steak.

Hillary's also has a "Lighter Side," an adjoining restaurant featuring "Mrs. Hillary's" choices which include crêpes, ome-

lettes, salads, sandwiches, and entrees like chicken breast Floren-
tine, $5.50; and seafood Newburg, $6.50. Prices start at $2.85 for
omelettes; $2.95 for sandwiches; and $2.95 for salads. The decor
is also "light," with mirrored walls, a beamed ceiling, plants, and
yellow-and-orange touches on chairs and tables. An old-fashioned traveling fan system moves up and down the room—far
more interesting than air conditioning! And if you choose the
right table, you can watch the espresso machine in action.

In case you've wondered what happened to the five-cent mug
of beer, it's right here in Boston, at the very popular **Charley's
Eating & Drinking Saloon,** 344 Newbury Street (tel. 266-3000).
That's the price of beer when you have dinner at this Victorian
restaurant-saloon with its 65-foot-long brass-rail bar, authentic
Tiffany-era lamps, old-time barber's chair, and bartenders and
waiters in period costumes. There are several beef and fish favorites including prime rib, $8.25; London broil, $5.95; barbecued
spareribs, $5.95; and baked stuffed shrimps, stuffed with Alaskan
king crabmeat, tiny shrimp, and bay scallops, $7.50. (It's listed
on the menu as "Charley's Mistress' Favorite.") The sandwiches
are tremendous in both size and quality, and are priced from
$2.40 to $3.50. The quality of the beef is excellent and Charley's
has a regular following to attest to that.

It's also a fun place to stop after the theater or concert for
late-night specials like sirloin steak and egg or sirloin steak and
cheese, each $5.95, with french fries and onion roll. Bartenders
"free pour" all drinks. It's just around the corner from the
Prudential Center and is open from 11:30 to 3:30 p.m. for lunch,
Monday to Saturday, and from 3:30 p.m. to 1 a.m. for dinner.
Open from noon to 1 a.m., Sunday. The bar is open until 2 a.m.
(1 a.m. on Saturday).

There is also a Charley's Eating & Drinking Saloon at The
Mall at Chestnut Hill, and at the South Shore Plaza, Braintree,
same hours, same menu, and no parking hassle.

SEAFOOD: The Half Shell, 743 Boylston Street (tel. 423-5555),
across from the Prudential Tower, is virtually impossible to
ignore, what with the vast array of sails, masts, chains, and ship's
rigging hanging over the sidewalk. A popular seafood spot in the
midtown area, it offers a wide variety of dishes in a theatricalized
setting; there are many nautical antiques from London's Por-
tobello Road, for instance. The menu offers a very good bouillabaisse (that saffron-flavored stew of lobster, scallops, shrimps,

crabmeat, and clams) at $6.95, broiled scrod at $3.95, and halibut at $5.95. Oyster stew is $2.95. Luncheon specialties run to hot dishes like creamed finnan haddie, $3.95. The clam chowder is excellent. Choose a cup at 75¢, a bowl at $1.45.

The Half Shell is open daily, serving lunch from 11:30 a.m. to 4 p.m., and dinner from 5 p.m. to 1 a.m. The Oyster Bar opens at noon, and does not close down until 1 a.m.

Quite the opposite in style from the Half Shell is **The Salty Dog,** in the Quincy Marketplace (tel. 742-2094). It's crowded, noisy, all the utensils are plastic, and the salt and pepper are in boxes on the counter—but it's mobbed. Everyone comes for the fresh, excellently prepared fish, served up in generous portions. Top of the line is the salmon, $5.50; and the halibut, $4.95. The fried clams are excellent at $3.50 and $3.95; and the fish stew, a thick brew of fish stock and four or five kinds of fish, is filling enough to serve as a lunch, $1.50. There are also salads, fish rolls, and appetizers—raw oysters, cherrystones, and shrimp cocktail, and cooked shrimp in the rough, 25¢ a shrimp. Open daily from 11 a.m. till 10 p.m., 11 p.m., or even later in the summer. The Salty Dog is in a corner in the west end of the market, (the side nearest Faneuil Hall) down a steep flight of stairs. And if you can't find a seat, just take your plate to one of the outdoor benches.

Budget Restaurants
(Meals around $5)

The English Room, 29 Newbury Street (tel. 262-5566), noted for its good home cooking, is a modest and economical place just off the Boston Public Garden. It is a tiny, very-Boston establishment with even tinier tables, but good-sized portions of food. The full meals are highly recommended: they include an appetizer, a salad, vegetable (one for lunch, two for dinner), dessert, and beverage. And the price range is from $2.06 to $3.32 at lunch, from $3.66 to $4.81 at dinner. The least expensive is hamburger with onions, bacon, or mushroom sauce; and the top-priced entree is fried jumbo shrimp with tartar sauce. Other listings include veal cutlet, stuffed chicken, grilled liver, and broiled halibut. There are also omelettes and sandwiches (salad is extra with these) and several imaginative desserts, all prepared on the premises. Try the lime Bavarian pie with whipped cream, 60¢; pecan pie with ice cream, 75¢; or old-fashioned peach or strawberry shortcake, 75¢. The menu changes twice daily! Hours are

Meet the Ladies

Forget the old image of the Beacon Hill matron and meet Bette and Lulu. Bette, Boston's own incarnation of Texas Guinan, presides over her old-time saloon **Bette's Rolls Royce**, 1 Union Street (tel. 277-0675). Since it's located opposite the rear of the new city hall at Government Center, the local "pols" and visiting celebrities are often there for the hearty food and sing-alongs at the upright piano. Steaks in various forms range from $2.95 to $6.95; and you can get a bowl of chili for $1.25 or knockwurst and hot sauerkraut for $1.95. Home fries are a specialty here, and so is the soused shrimp—marinated in beer. There's a good wine list, cheese platters going along with the booze, and dancing, too. On Saturday and Sunday, Dixieland jazz bands hold forth. Bette's Rolls Royce (named for her cherished auto) is open every day from 11:30 a.m. to 2 a.m. No cover, no minimum.

Lulu White, 3 Appleton Street (tel. 423-3652), with its red-flocked wallpaper, glass chandeliers, and black wrought-iron railings around the dance floor, is a copy of a New Orleans "jazz, dining and pleasure emporium." It's Boston's only Creole restaurant, so of course there's jambalaya, gumbo, red snapper en papillote, shrimp creole, and pecan pie. A Creole buffet ($6.50) gives you a taste of barbecued chicken and ribs, pickled eggs, salad, beans, and rice. What draws the crowd, however, is the good jazz, the live music that is featured every evening except Monday until 2 a.m. Dinner is served from 5 p.m. till midnight; lunch, from noon until 2 p.m., Monday through Friday; Sunday brunch, 11 a.m. to 2 p.m. Free valet parking.

11 a.m. to 4 p.m. for lunch, and 4 to 9 p.m. for dinner. They usually close a few weeks for summer vacation, so check first if you're here in July or August.

The Magic Pan, with two locations, 47 Newbury Street (tel. 267-9315), and the Quincy Market at Faneuil Hall (tel. 523-6103), is a very popular crêperie, with 27 varieties filled with chicken, beef, fish, ice cream, or sweets available. Salads and excellent soups are also offered (but there isn't a roll or slice of bread in the place). Try a crêpes-and-salad luncheon $3.20 to $4.25. A French bistro dinner with beef bourguignon, ratatouille crêpe, and salad is $5.95. Desserts range from $1.60 to $2.25 and include concoctions such as cherries royal crêpe. And as a reminder of its San Francisco origin, Magic Pan serves eggs

Sausalito on its Saturday and Sunday brunch menu, $4.25, from 11 a.m. to 4 p.m.

The atmosphere in both restaurants is charming, with cascades of greenery, flowers on the tables, and candlelight. Hours are 11 a.m. to midnight, Monday through Saturday, and until 10 p.m. on Sunday.

Note: Even though this is listed as a budget restaurant, the tab can go high unless you order carefully.

The Proud Popover, Quincy Market at Faneuil Hall Marketplace (tel. 523-6982), glorifies the popover the way Magic Pan enhances the crêpe. (Both are subsidiaries of the Quaker Oats Co., and share the top floor of the marketplace.) But the atmosphere is Colonial, rather than French. You can have your popovers stuffed with chicken or beef, or soaking up roast-beef juices; holding a pudding at dessert time; or in your breadbasket waiting to be layered with butter and honey. Prices at lunch are under $5 but can go up to $9 for the roast-beef entree at dinner. Soups (clam chowder and English beef and vegetable) go for $1.25, and three versions of quiche for $3.50. Real whipped cream is layered on the desserts—old-fashioned popover pudding with apples, raisins, pecans, and honey, $1.35; and a lemon soufflé cake with fresh strawberries (when they are in season), $1.50. Hours are Monday through Thursday, 11 a.m. to 11 p.m.; until midnight, Friday and Saturday; Sunday, until 9 p.m. Brunch is served Sunday, 11 a.m. to 3 p.m., and costs $3.95.

Charles Street Steak House, 21 Charles Street (tel. 227-6111), is a self-service restaurant on a street running along the side of Beacon Hill. The decor consists of an original old brick Beacon Hill facade, beamed ceiling, an open charcoal grill in the window, and warm wood paneling. A proper but inexpensive steak costs only $3.65, and with it you get a salad with a choice of dressing, a crusty baked potato, and warm garlic bread. For a little less, you can have chopped steak, but for big spenders, there's a giant one-pound sirloin at $4.55. Fish dinners start at $2.99 and include salad bar, baked potato, and garlic bread. You can choose from a variety of desserts and beverages as well. Open daily from 11:30 a.m. to 10 p.m.

You might not expect a budget restaurant in the financial district, but bankers know how to make every penny count. **Brandy Pete's,** at 82 Broad Street, serves everything in large portions: huge sandwiches, big bowls of soup, and martinis in water glasses (no water, just martini). Also, generous portions of fish, chops, chicken, and steak; a sirloin with french fries is $6.95.

You can get lunch for under $3 from 11:30 to 2:30, and dinner from 3 to 9 p.m. And those huge bar drinks are only 85¢ from 4:30 to 6:30 p.m.!

Dini's Sea Grill, 94 Tremont Street (tel. 227-0380), specializes in that mysterious-sounding Boston scrod, which is nothing more than a small cod prepared in a distinctive New England style. You'll find it listed on the extensive menu with the array of seafood cocktails, soups, chowders, sandwiches, salads, omelettes, steaks, chops, and lobster. Complete meals at lunch start as low as $4.25, and full dinners are $5 to $8.50. Dini's also serves "Bruncheon" from 10 a.m. to 11 a.m., Monday through Saturday. This includes a choice of several entrees, perhaps scallops, chicken, or Spanish omelettes, plus dessert and coffee for $3.25. Open every day, serving lunch from 11 a.m. to 4 p.m., Monday through Saturday, and dinner from 4 to 10 p.m. Open Sunday from 11 a.m. to 10 p.m.

A Fish Tale

No Name Restaurant, 15½ Fish Pier (tel. 338-7539), started out almost 60 years ago as a little place on the pier where fishermen could come and eat the pick of their catch. They told their friends about the excellent food and the word spread. And suddenly No Name was the "in" place to go. Everyone wanted the clams and scrod and chowder. So owner Nick Contos added more tables and then another room. And more and more people came, so many that now it's just another busy fish house on the wharf—noisy, crowded, and very rushed. But the bright spot to this story is that the food is still good, and if you're not expecting a little hideaway, you'll enjoy it. A large plate of broiled scallops with a butter sauce is $4.45. Same price for salmon. The seafood plate is $3.95, and the broiled scrod, $3.15. Chowder is 50¢ a cup.

The restaurant is hard to find, but don't give up—or drive off the pier looking for it. From Northern Avenue turn onto the Commonwealth Fish Pier near the guard's booth where the sign says, "Do Not Enter." Open daily for lunch and dinner.

VEGETARIAN—MACROBIOTIC: Sanae, 272-A Newbury Street (tel. 247-8434), the first macrobiotic restaurant in Boston, is run by a staff dedicated to "cooking for health." Following the precepts of Michio Kushi, the macrobiotic "guru," the restaurant concentrates on grains, beans, and vegetables in season. Everything is made fresh from scratch, including breads and desserts, and in season Sanae buys local organic produce. The fish, of course, is fresh, bought daily at the Boston Fish Pier. The most popular dish is "A Square Meal," a combo plate with soup, grain, two vegetables, beans, and tea, $3.50; and they do very well by a vegetable tempura, $3. Also featured are traditional Japanese foods: tofu, $1.90; miso soup, 80¢; and brown rice. Herb teas, grain coffee and real coffee (fresh ground), and spring water, 10¢, are also served. Sanae—comfortable, informal, and just recently remodeled—is open every day but Tuesday from noon to 9 p.m.

Seventh Inn, 288 Boylston Street (tel. 261-3965), also concentrates on cooking macrobiotically. From the outside it looks like just another Oriental eating place, but inside it's all natural foods, organically grown fruits and vegetables, and not a trace of meat. Broiled bluefish is $4.50; and shrimp tempura with vegetable tempura, around $6. Miso soup shares honors with fish chowder, and salads vary from fruit with soybean curd to watercress with alfalfa sprouts and green vegetables. Desserts feature carob in preference to chocolate, ice cream, fruit pies, and sauces sweetened with honey. There's a small wine list and a selection of unpasteurized beers. Lunch is served Tuesday through Saturday from noon to 2:30 p.m.; dinner is from 5 to 9 p.m., Tuesday through Sunday.

Note: Boston is a national headquarters for the macrobiotic movement. Michio Kushi lives here, and there are numerous "macrobiotic" houses throughout the city. Erewhon, one of the leading purveyors of macrobiotic staples, is at 342 Newbury Street and also in Cambridge and Brookline.

Conscious Cookery, 30 Massachusetts Avenue, between Marlboro and Beacon streets (tel. 247-7947), is a small, immaculate restaurant run by a local group of spiritual seekers who prove that there is more to vegetarian cooking than brown rice and beans. There is an excellent variety of very good Mexican, Indian, and other international dishes. No meat, of course, but lots of cheese and dairy products. Try the Adi Shakto enchiladas, a specialty made with corn tortillas, sour cream, tomato sauce, and two kinds of cheese, served with Mexican black beans and Guru's Garden salad, all for $4.50. Or your taste might tend more to the Samurai sandwich, a Japanese spread of tofu, walnuts, mushrooms, and miso topped with tomato and sprouts and served on hearty seven-grain bread ($2.50) with soup. There are delicious fruit drinks that vary with the season, herb teas, ice cream, and cakes made with whole-wheat flour. Pineapple upside-down cake ($1.20) is delicious. Conscious Cookery is open from noon to 9 p.m. Monday through Thursday, and until 10 p.m., Friday and Saturday. (Closed on Sunday as this is written, but their enthusiastic patrons may change that.)

Soul Food, Boston-Style

Chef's Restaurant, 604 Columbus Avenue, is Boston's "home of soul food" in Roxbury. Here's a warm link between the cuisine of the South, Harlem, and New England. You get wonderfully cooked food, in generous portions, at low-budget prices. Just a block from Massachusetts Avenue, Chef's is immaculately kept. Here you'll find friendly service, family style.

The price of the chef's special dinners—$3.75 for two smoked meaty hamhocks; $4.25 for large sirloin steak; $4.75 for soul chitterlings; and $4.50 for barbecued spareribs. Luncheons go for $2.50 and up, and include a choice of vegetable (everything from blackeye peas to mashed turnips to "smothered" fresh cabbage). Homemade desserts are 60¢ extra. You'll be tempted by a "glorified" fried chicken or perhaps the tasty meat loaf. From the kitchen, the wafting aroma of sweet-potato pies and hot, homemade "soul bread" drifts in. Hours here are until 9 p.m. daily, except Sundays and Mondays when Chef's is closed.

SOUP AND SALAD: We had always associated "soup and salad" with lunch-counter quickies until we discovered **Stockpot**, down a flight of stairs at 119 Newbury Street (tel. 267-5711). The soups change daily—you could eat there for a month and have a different soup each time. We've relished a thick vegetable soup, a hearty cream of broccoli, and a thick baked onion gratinée. Cold fruit soups are on the menu in the summer. A small, ten-ounce soup is $1, and a 16-ounce soup is $1.50. Quiche is also offered. You can have a combination of soup and salad for $2 or $2.50. Open daily noon to 8:30 p.m.

There is another Stockpot in Cambridge, 57 Boylston Street, in the Crimson Galeria. Hours are 11:30 a.m. to 10:30 p.m.

Our special favorite is **Salad Days**, 41 Charles Street (tel. 723-7537). We love the atmosphere, the plants, and, of course, the food. In addition to the soup ($1, small; $1.50, large) and the salad bar ($2.25), there's tasty lasagna and eggplant parmigiana ($3.25) and chicken ($3.50), plus quiche and chile. Desserts are very special at $1.25. The carrot cake sounds "healthy," which it probably is, but it's also delicious with cream-cheese frosting and chunks of pineapple. Open 11:30 a.m. till 11 p.m., Monday through Friday; and from noon till 11 p.m., Saturday and Sunday. Another branch with the same high standards is at Harvard Square in **The Garage** (tel. 661-8979).

FOR DELI AND BURGERS: Delicatessens and hamburger places can get pretty fancy around town. Try **Ken's** at 549 Boylston Street at Copley Square (tel. 266-6106), and **The Fatted Calf Saloon and Eatery,** 4 Beacon Street (tel. 523-2425), for proof. At Ken's you can have a dinner for under $7 that includes such appetizers as gefilte fish and knishes, beverage, and dessert, and a good selection of entrees. Orange-baked chicken is $4.85, and London broil, $6.50. At lunch, indulge in potato pancakes or cheese blintzes, $1.65. Come early—from 7 a.m.—for breakfasts of kippers and eggs or lox and cream cheese, or late—anytime up to 3 a.m.—for some scrumptious desserts. Our favorite: the ice-cream fritters, banana fritters topped with ice cream, fresh strawberries, and whipped cream, a lovely way to end the evening at $1.95.

The Fatted Calf takes the hamburger and turns it into a production. You won't find the lawyers and judges from the nearby court and State House arguing the merits of this case. They agree that the burgers are good, starting with the basic calfburger, served with fries, lettuce, and tomato, $2.25; and moving on to a more complex burger with mushrooms, cheddar or blue cheese, or even bacon and melted Swiss. There is a Victorian setting with wood paneling, smoked-glass windows, and old-style photographs. In addition to the bar that serves up the Bloody Marys, a "raw bar" is open weekdays from 4 p.m. to 8 p.m. with clams and oysters on the half-shell, 25¢ apiece. Open Monday through Friday, 11:30 a.m. to 10 p.m.

There's another Fatted Calf at 581 Boylston Street which is cafeteria style and strictly for burgers—no bar.

At the other end of the spectrum, and at the other end of town, is **Premier I** in Boston's South End, at East Berkeley and Washington streets. It's an old-fashioned deli with a loyal following who come for food rather than atmosphere. For there aren't many places serving kashe varnishkas (dumplings made of buckwheat groats), knishes, boiled flanken, and chopped herring along with the usual delicatessen sandwiches. And matzo-ball soup, too! Open from 5 a.m. to 9 p.m., daily except Sunday.

Neither deli nor salad bar, but a nice place to go if you're in the Newbury Street–Boylston Street area and want to eat quickly is **Romano's Bakery and Sandwich Shop,** 33 Newbury Street (tel. 247-8988). The minestrone is always excellent, and the soup du jour is also well made, both at 95¢. Try antipasto, $2.50; knockwurst, $1.25; or a salad bowl, $1. And buy some of the pastries and cookies to take along with you, especially the blueberry muffins.

For kosher foods, nary a restaurant in all Boston. If, however, you take a Commonwealth Avenue or Beacon Street trolley out to Harvard Street in neighboring Brookline, you can find two. **Rubin's,** 500 Harvard Street, is open from 9 a.m. to 8 p.m. except Saturday; Friday, from 8 a.m. till before sundown. **Cafe Shalom,** 14-A Pleasant Street, Brookline, is also kosher, but leans more to Israeli style: falafel, chick peas, and hummus, and of all things, pizza!

For more budget restaurants, see the sections that follow.

The Foreign Colony

There are so many "foreign" restaurants in Boston that at times we think Chinese, Italian, and Greek foods are more native to the town than the bean and the cod. Here is a sampling of some our favorite ethnic restaurants in the Moderate and Budget price categories. (Check the Upper Bracket and Cambridge listings for others.)

ITALIAN RESTAURANTS: Italian men might still be boss at home but it's mama who rules the kitchen in Boston's "Little Italy." Just look at the names of the Italian restaurants in the North End—Felicia's, Ida's, Mother Anna's, Regina's, Francesca's, Lucia, Florence's. Each one is a favorite in someone's list, some for quantity, some for quality, and some for value. But the most famous of the lot is Felicia's.

Felicia's, 145-A Richmond Street (tel. 523-9885), takes its name from its owner, chef, inspiration, and motivating force, Felicia Solimine. Her informal, personalized restaurant has made her somewhat a celebrity in Boston. And she has many celebrity friends, from the Kennedys to Arthur Fiedler to Bob

Hope, whom she visits yearly to prepare the meals for some of his Palm Springs parties.

Felicia's food is excellent. One of the specialties is chicken Verdicchio, boneless breast of chicken cooked with lemon, mushrooms, artichoke hearts, sauteed in Verdicchio white wine and served with spaghetti or salad, for $6.50. There's a complete dinner that includes the chicken or a veal scallopine, plus shrimp marinara, fetuccine, salad, dessert, and coffee, $10.45. Homemade cannelloni is another favorite, especially when filled with scallops and crabmeat and served with a sauce of melted cheese, $7. The dining room has dark wooden booths, tables with red cloths, and candles that drip into colored patterns over a bottle. Open daily, 5 to 10 p.m.

The Pushcart, 61 Endicott Street (tel. 523-9616), is right where you'd expect it to be—in the heart of the Haymarket pushcart district in Boston's North End. It's a family enterprise with papa and mama in the kitchen, daughters waitressing, and uncles and cousins helping all around. The restaurant is quite small so you may have to wait a while to be seated. However, you don't need lots of money. There are a number of dishes including eggplant parmigiana, and an antipasto full of meats, cheeses, and vegetables, chicken cacciatore, and occasional specials including tripe (which the waitress will let you sample before you order). Price range is $2.50 and up; and if you are going up, try the chicken Vilanese with linguine, shrimp, clams, and mushrooms at $6.75. Pushcart is open for lunch on Tuesday through Saturday, 11:30 a.m. to 3 p.m.; and for dinner from 5 p.m. to 11 p.m. Closed Sunday and Monday.

There are new little places cropping up constantly and many other old standbys each with its own devotees. Francesca's, 147 Richmond Street (tel. 523-8826), gets plus marks in every category—soup, salad, fettucine, vegetables, veal, seafood, and homemade desserts, including cannoli, filled at the table. Price range is between $5 and $10. The European, 218 Hanover Street (tel. 523-5695), has complete dinners for $6 to $7, a vast menu (you can concentrate on pizzas, too, $2.50 to $4.50), and fast service. It claims to be Boston's oldest Italian restaurant (since 1917). Much newer is Ristorante Lucia, 415 Hanover Street (since 1978), but it already has a devoted following. The chef is a master from Abruzzo and has a very full menu with soups, veal, chicken, pasta, and exceptional house salads and Italian bread. The espresso and cappuccino are excellent. Pasta dinners are as low as $2.95, chicken and veal go up to $7. For reservations, phone 523-9148. Now, if we can add a man to the list, try **Joe Tecci's,** 53 North Washington Street (tel. 742-6880), near Haymarket Square. It's unmarked on the outside, but look for the blue ceramic tile with family crests. The entrees are hearty and on the expensive side, and Joe expects you to fill up on them since there are no soups or desserts. The atmosphere is "Sorrento." Open Monday through Saturday, 5 p.m. to 11 p.m.; Saturday, until midnight.

You don't have to stay in the North End for good Italian food. There's **Marliave,** 11 Bosworth Street, a small street between Tremont and Washington streets (tel. 423-6340). Located at "Ye Olde Province Steps" since 1875, Marliave still features the old-world atmosphere that attracted guests a century ago. The food is not the commercial overspiced Italian found in so many restaurants, but a milder version accompanied by homemade soups and vegetables that even kids like to eat. There are close to 50 offerings on the menu with about 16 Italian specialties, over a dozen steak and chop entrees, six chicken dishes, ten seafood, and over ten veal. Many of them are quite excellent, including the veal cutlet Antonio (a house specialty), $7.80, which combines veal, anchovies, melted cheese, green pepper, and pimiento. Linguine with clam sauce features fresh chopped littleneck clams, and if you wish, you can get a big bowl of spaghetti or fettucine Alfredo. Prices range from $3.90 to $5.75 for complete luncheons; $6.25 to $8.85 for dinner à la carte.

Marliave is open every day except Sunday and holidays, serving lunch from 11 a.m. to 4 p.m. and dinner from 4 p.m. to 10 p.m. There is a parking garage next door.

CHINESE RESTAURANTS: Chinese restaurants in Boston are quite specialized now. You can go for Cantonese-style cooking (eggrolls, spare ribs, butterfly shrimp, and chow mein), Szechuan (hot and spicy moo shi and yu hsiang), and Peking (Peking ravioli and the more subtle flavors of northern Chinese cooking). Most of Chinatown's menus are geared to American palates, but sometimes there's a second menu for Chinese patrons. Ask for it, or tell your waiter you want your meal Chinese style. Most Chinese restaurants are open every day, begin serving around lunchtime, and stay open until 3 a.m., which makes them fine for a bite or a meal after many other places have closed down. Chinatown is perfectly safe during the daytime, but since you must pass through the "Combat Zone" (Boston's new red-light district that replaced Scollay Square) to reach it, it's not particularly recommended for women alone at night. The area is just a few blocks around Beach Street, near the expressway, on the south side of town. You can also approach from the expressway and park in Chinatown's garage, avoiding the Combat Zone. Herewith, some of our favorite places in and out of Chinatown.

China Pearl, 9 Tyler Street (tel. 426-4338), features Cantonese specialties, the familiar chop suey, pork strips, and eggrolls served in generous portions at moderate prices. Some of our favorites are the sweet-and-sour shrimp, and goldfingers, pieces of sliced chicken fried to crisp perfection. Among their specials are a seafood plate, Imperial eggroll, $3; spare ribs, $3.45; and flaming lobster Hawaii, $8.50. Opens at 11 a.m. and closes at 2 a.m., except on Fridays when it closes at 3 a.m., and Sundays, when the hours are noon to 1 a.m.

Fung Won, 8 Tyler Street (tel. 542-1175), isn't especially known for its atmosphere (Formica and linoleum), but it excels where it counts: the food. Ask for the Cantonese menu, over 100 items priced from $3.50 to $8, and noodle dishes for under $3. Cantonese fried clams in black-bean sauce are $4.25 (actually, the clams are steamed); delicious steamed bass is $6; and fung won steak, $5. Open from 11 a.m. to 3 a.m. Dinner is served until midnight.

Carl's Pagoda, 23 Tyler Street (tel. 357-9837), is an easy place to order in. Just tell Carl Seeto that you want seafood, or chicken, or whatever, and he takes it from there, creating a delicately flavored Cantonese treat. Carl sets the price for all dishes, so if you're budgeting, let him know your limit. You can get a full-course meal for under $10 American.

Shanghai, 21 Hudson Street (tel. 482-4797), is known for Mandarin cuisine, so if you're one of those North Chinese nuts, this is your palce. It's a very casual atmosphere, with many local Chinese families sitting around and enjoying the good food at reasonable prices. Lunches start at 99¢; dinners average $3.95. There's a delicious dim sum or dumpling menu, Saturday and Sunday, 11:30 a.m. to 2 p.m. Try Peking ravioli at $2.40. If this kind of food is a new adventure for you, ask the waiter for guidance. You can usually rely on dishes like moo shoo pork and shrimp with black-bean sauce in all northern Chinese restaurants. Open Monday through Friday, 11 a.m. to 10 p.m., and Saturday and Sunday, 11:30 a.m. to 10 p.m.

Dim sum could be called the Chinese hors d'oeuvres meal, but it's really much more than that. The offerings include dumplings filled with meats and vegetables, steamed breads, ravioli, and items like thousand-layer cake, which is only a stack of steamed crêpes with a dab of fruit. Many of the Chinese restaurants feature it at lunchtime and often it's a substitute for Sunday brunch. **The 70 Restaurant, Moon Villa,** and **King Wah** (all in Chinatown) feature dim sum from 9 a.m. until 3 p.m. You order—and pay—by the piece, usually from 25¢ to 75¢.

The chefs at **Mandarin Yen,** 671 Boylston Street (tel. 266-9367), bring spicy Szechuan cooking to Copley Square, just across the street from the Boston Public Library, and they don't even use MSG! The menu is quite extensive, and the "hottest" dishes are starred. One of the house specialties is ta-chien chicken with Chinese celery, red and green peppers, scallions, and hot, dried red pepper, $4.65. Sweet-and-sour fish at $5.35 is dipped in a batter of egg white, wine, and cornstarch, deep-fried, and served with a sweet-and-sour sauce typical of Szechuan. There are some strictly vegetarian dishes and mildly flavored seafood, meat, and chicken entrees in a price range from $2.25 to $5.50. A cafeteria-style lunch with specials from $2.10 is served weekdays. Dim sum, the Chinese "pastry" menu, is offered Saturdays and holidays from 11 a.m. to 4 p.m., and on Sundays from noon to 4 p.m. Prices from 40¢ to $3.30. Open seven days: from 11 a.m. to 10 p.m., Monday through Thursday; and until 11 p.m. on Friday and Saturday. Sunday hours are noon to 10 p.m. A sidewalk cafe is open summer afternoons.

No discussion of Boston's Chinese restaurants would be complete without mention of Joyce Chen, the Julia Child of Chinese cooking, a celebrated TV cook and cookbook author. **Joyce Chen Restaurant,** in a new building at 390 Rindge Avenue, Cambridge (tel. 492-7373), dishes up authentic Mandarin and Szechuan delights. (Szechuan and Hunan cooking is hot and spicy; Mandarin, or Peking, is spicy in a more subtle manner; and the Cantonese style is usually bland.) We've enjoyed such exotic dishes as Shanghai duck ($5.95 for a half, $11.50 for a whole duck) cooked in soy sauce and star anise; and Mandarin sweet-and-sour shrimp, $6.25. The wonton soup, $2.95 for a bowl large enough for four servings, is delicious; and the pork and Szechuan pickles soup, $3.25, is, well, let's say unusual. So is the octopus, Hunan-style (cold), at $2.75.

Buffets are served Monday, Tuesday, and Wednesday evenings from 6 to 7 p.m. The Monday buffet is all vegetarian. Joyce Chen's is open Sunday to Thursday from noon to 10:30 p.m., and Friday and Saturday until 11:30 p.m.

Joyce Chen's Small Eating Place, 302 Massachusetts Avenue (tel. 492-7272), is across the street from M.I.T., but it hasn't become computerized yet. The food is still carefully prepared, consistently good.

Also worth trying in Cambridge is Hunan, 700 Massachusetts Avenue at Central Square (tel. 547-1130), with excellent Mandarin and Szechuan food, and Yenching Restaurant, 1326 Massachusetts Avenue at Harvard Square (tel. 547-1150), where the Szechuan cooking follows the precise recipes of that region.

And if you're near a China Sails in Salem, Brookline, Peabody, or Danvers, try the jumbo fried shrimp—the best anywhere.

POLYNESIAN RESTAURANTS: Kon Tiki Ports, Sheraton Boston Hotel, Prudential Center (tel. 262-3063). A lush tropical setting for luscious tropical food. We especially like to come here for the fabulous Sunday Polynesian luau brunch at $5.75, which includes all the Mai Tais and Bloody Marys you can drink, and for the daily luncheon buffet served Monday to Saturday from 11:30 to 3:00 and certainly one of the best deals in town at $4.75 (you can forget supper after that). The fans claim that Kon Tiki Ports serves the best Mai Tais, and we won't dispute them. At dinner, entrees begin at about $6, and average about $9.75 for a complete dinner. Open every day for dinner from 5 p.m. to 11:30 p.m.

And if you're driving to the North Shore along Route 1, the Kowloon in Saugus is a very pleasant, very large restaurant, elaborately decked out with a waterfall, a volcano, and other South Seas hoopla. And there's dancing, too!

JAPANESE RESTAURANTS: There are two kinds of Japanese restaurant currently popular in Boston—the slice-dice-grill type, where the knife-wielding chef cooks the meal with lavish showmanship before your eyes; and there is the traditional restaurant style of ancient Japan, where the meal is a thing of beauty to see as well as taste.

Restaurant Genji, 327 Newbury Street (tel. 267-5656), serves in both styles. The teppan, or steak house, where you watch the chef perform at your own table grill, is on the street level. The traditional room is downstairs. There, diners take off their shoes and climb into cubicles consisting of a table and benches, and are served by kimono-clad waitresses. Table settings and even the arrangement of food on the plate is planned with the Japanese skill for detail in color and texture. The "variety dinners," including tempura and teriyaki chicken, are served in black Bento lacquerware—a seven-compartment bowl (used for picnics) with a place for appetizers, vegetables, entree, salad, rice, and dessert. Tempura includes deep-fried shrimp, fish cutlets, sesame and rice balls, eggplant, carrot, zucchini, hard-boiled egg, horseradish, salad, grapes, and orange slices (around $9). Teriyaki chicken (about $7) is served with rice, shrimp, mushrooms, tomato, and lettuce. The "Nabe" dishes are those brought to your table in large pots for do-it-yourself cooking. Included are Genji Nabe, $6.75 to $8.95, and the ever-popular sukiyaki. And for dessert, ginger ice cream with azuki sauce is perfect. Open Monday through Saturday for lunch and dinner, and Sunday for dinner.

Hai Hai (Yes Yes), 429 Boylston Street near Bonwit Teller's (tel. 536-8474), started life as a two-level cafeteria with birch tables and an orange-and-brown decor, and has metamorphosed into a pleasant, moderately priced restaurant. The authentic Japanese dishes are slightly Bostonized, and there is a "pedantic menu" which explains all about domburi, katsu, yaki, teriyaki, tempura, and soba, the different styles of Japanese food preparation, so that you can order knowledgeably. All lunches are accompanied by a bowl of soup, except the sobas, which are soups filled with meat, chicken, shrimp, or vegetables, added to a base of buckwheat noodles, $1.95 to $2.25. Dinner prices range from $2.85 for tamago domburi, an all-vegetable omelette, to $5.95 for beef teriyaki tenderloin. Desserts include a rice pudding and a sweet "domino-shaped jelly bean," each at 45¢, and mitsumamé, a fruit cocktail, 75¢. Lunch is served from noon to 2:30 p.m., and dinner from 5 to 9 p.m., daily.

GREEK CHOICES: There aren't any wealthy Greek shipping magnates in Boston, but there's a wealth of excellent Greek food at moderate prices. Two favorites are Aegean Fare, with restaurants in the marketplace area, at Kenmore Square, and Cleveland Circle, Brookline; and Athens Olympia, 51 Stuart Street.

Aegean Fare, 16 North Street (tel. 723-4850), specializes in Greek dishes, even though it is just across the street from the hallowed Faneuil Hall. But the old Yankee merchants of the area probably would have appreciated the baked lamb in casserole, tender and nicely flavored, served in a tomato sauce, and thrifty, too, at $3.50. We enjoyed the very good vakalaos gemistos, baked stuffed filet of haddock with scallops, $4.50. Entrees are in the $1.50 to $4.50 range for lunch, and are $2.50 to $6.50 for dinner. They are served with a Greek salad and french fries or rice pilaf, so you can dine here quite inexpensively. The place opens at 11 a.m., and meals are served until 2 a.m. And if you want a quick snack, try their "stall" in the Quincy Marketplace, open 9 a.m. to 10 p.m.

Aegean Fare, at Kenmore Square (tel. 267-2203), is a good choice for breakfast (feta cheese omelettes, and bagels and lox are among the choices). The same Greek specialties are offered, as well as American food and Jewish delicatessen. Open from 7 a.m. to 4 a.m. Aegean Fare at Cleveland Circle (tel. 232-7900) is open from 11 a.m. to 2 a.m.

In the block between Tufts Medical Center and the theater district is Boston's oldest Greek restaurant, Athens Olympia (tel. 426-6236). A Grecian facade marks the entrance and stairway that leads to this excellent second-floor dining room with its murals of Greece. Souvlaka à la Oriental, $6.35; moussaka, broiled scup, taramasalata, and authentic Greek yogurt are featured, along with an excellent sirloin with fried onion rings. À la carte dinners, $3.15 to $8.95, are served all day. Lunches are offered from 11 a.m. to 3 p.m. and range from $2.05 to $4.95. Open Monday through Saturday from 11 a.m. to midnight, and on Sunday until 10 p.m. Closed Sunday during the summer.

Discounting Calories

If you're counting calories, relax. Boston has a restaurant for you, too. **The Thin Place,** 154 State Street (tel. 723-9380), has all the calorie calculations listed on its menu. For example, a raw vegetable salad is 95 calories and $1.40; a tomato stuffed with egg salad is 125 calories and $1.65. Ingredients for homemade soups and the daily specials are chosen to keep the pounds off. The management doesn't encourage seconds or lingering over desserts, and has lined the walls with pictures depicting the consequences of overeating. And to help you stick to your diet, they have frozen low-calorie dinners to take home. The Thin Place is open for breakfast, too. Hours are 7 a.m. to 3 p.m., Monday through Friday. Weekends, you're on your own.

Boston Cafes

OUTDOORS: If, like us, you love sidewalk cafes—the bright umbrellas, the continental feeling, the people-watching—check this list of where to dine outdoors in Boston.

Ben's Cafe at Maison Robert, 45 School Street, Old City Hall. Dine at the statue of Ben Franklin with a tree-shaded view (actually the Old Granary Burying Ground) next door. Complete French meals. Expensive.

Cafe Marliave, a courtyard over "Ye Old Province Steps," 10-11 Bosworth Street, near Bromfield Street. This Italian rooftop cafe features complete meals at moderate prices.

DuBarry, 159 Newbury Street, a courtyard surrounded by a high wall. French food, complete meals. Moderate to expensive.

Magic Pan, 47 Newbury Street, one of the most attractive sidewalk cafes, with striped umbrellas and potted shrubs. Serves soup, salads, and desserts from lunchtime till early evening.

The **Stockpot,** 119 Newbury Street, brings its soups, salads, quiches, and desserts to little sidewalk tables daily except Sunday.

Cafe Florian, 85 Newbury Street, the oldest and most authentic sidewalk cafe in Boston, is perfect for leisurely sipping European coffees and exotic teas, wine or beer, and for dining on light lunches and full-course continental dinners.

Travis Restaurant, 135 Newbury Street. A "takeout" place. You can take out your hamburgers and sandwiches to the tables and breezy deck chairs out front. Informal, inexpensive.

Dante's on Beacon Hill, 21 Joy Street. Open evenings and for lunch on weekdays, this fascinating courtyard garden with its lovely fountain is great for medium-priced Italian meals.

Cafe L'Ananas, 279 Newbury Street. A real sidewalk spot with umbrellaed tables, pretty flowers, and plants. Features à la carte French cuisine.

The waterfront is a perfect spot for outdoor dining and **Lewis Wharf,** off Atlantic Avenue, has two dockside cafes. The **Winery** is the lovelier. There is a view of the ocean from its brick terrace, and musicians to serenade you in the evening. **Taisei of Japan** has outdoor tables at lunch where you can sip plum wine and look at the flower garden that has been added to the wharf.

Also on the waterfront, **Stella,** 74 East India Row, has a charming terrace facing the Aquarium. Dolphin-watching, anyone?

The **Cafe at Lily's** in the Quincy Marketplace is one of the best people-watching spots in Boston with its view of the stalls in the shopping areas and of the busy plaza with the flower market and outdoor displays. In the manner of a Parisian cafe, Lily's serves light meals from early morning until late at night, including soup, quiche, salad, seafood, and beef. Try some of the dessert coffees and pastries, too. The **Bar at Lily's,** facing Durgin-Park, is also an enclosed-type cafe where you can sip cocktails, listen to music, and watch the shoppers stroll by. A very popular singles spot in the evening.

Cricket's, under the same management as Lily's, is in the South Market building, and has a streetside cafe with an over-hanging balcony; beamed ceilings and a profusion of hanging plants suggest the feeling of being in a greenhouse. **Cityside** in the Central Market is another noisy, bustling sidewalk cafe that's put under glass when the weather turns cold.

. . . AND IN: Deserving a special word here are three indoor cafes. The **Promenade Cafe** at the Colonnade Hotel, 120 Huntington Avenue (tel. 261-2800), has a quiet elegance and a view of the Prudential Center, weekly buffets and fashion shows. You can have a Monte Carlo or Reuben sandwich, $4.50; an avocado stuffed with shrimp, $4.50; a "petit" filet mignon, $7; or an omelette prepared at your table, $3.25. The Promenade is open for all meals, 7 a.m. to 11:30 p.m.

If you've always wanted to try English set tea, you can find it served from 3 p.m. at **Copley's Court** in the Copley Plaza Hotel (tel. 267-5300), among the palms in the lobby. For $3.75 it includes thinly sliced salmon, chicken, and watercress sand-wiches, scones with whipped cream and strawberry preserve, and tea. And for afternoon tea at the marble-topped tables you may also choose hot buttered crumpets, $1.75, or an English trifle, also $1.75.

In the North End, **Joe Tecci's,** 53 North Washington Street (tel. 742-6210), has an indoor cafe with a real street scene from the '30s, including lamps, street signs, curbs, hydrants, and mu-rals. Open seven days a week, 11 a.m. to 1 a.m., serving light meals, coffees, liqueurs, and fruit frappes.

The Breakfast Menu

Breakfast in Boston need not be dull. Some of the more inter-esting possibilities include:

The Steaming Kettle, 65 Court, opening onto a plaza fronting the new City Hall, is marked by an overscale copper kettle over the entrance, constantly steaming. A Boston symbol since 1872, the kettle holds 227 gallons of water. Upstairs, the policy is self-service, and offerings include the makings for a slightly expanded continental breakfast: pure orange juice for 30¢; hot coffee, 30¢; tasty Danish pastries. Many Bostonians also come here for a quick luncheon, enjoying a large bowl of New England fish chowder for $1.45, or a cup for 90¢; a hot pastrami on rye, $1.30; warm apple pie with cheddar cheese, 70¢. There are other Steaming Kettles at 235 Washington Street and at 100 Summer Street. Open 7 a.m. to 4:45 p.m.

Zeke's. Three locations—899 Boylston Street, 170 Tremont Street, and 1379 Beacon Street (Brookline). A good breakfast here is only $1.17 for two eggs, toast or muffin, and a "bottomless" cup of coffee. Have the pancakes or hot apple pie if you want something special. If you're too late for breakfast, try the regular menu; the food is good. Open 7 a.m. to midnight, every day.

For a breakfast to really make you feel pampered, the **Cafe Plaza** in the Copley Plaza Hotel has delicacies such as fresh raspberries (in season), broiled scrod, fresh-squeezed orange juice, and homemade muffins, served in style with flowers on the tables. You can also have breakfast done up quite elegantly at the **Ritz Cafe** in the Ritz-Carlton Hotel.

And you can always have a good breakfast at **Brigham's,** with several locations around town (and excellent ice-cream and hot-fudge sundaes for later in the day); or **Pewter Pot Muffin House,** which has many branches in the area and features 24 different kinds of warm, luscious muffins.

If you're planning on spending the morning in Cambridge, start with breakfast at the **Coffee Connection** in **The Garage** with homemade granola, 95¢, and freshly squeezed citrus juices. **Piroshka,** 24 Dunster Street, has excellent breakfast specials, and almond, chocolate, and plain croissants from 40¢. (We saw Caroline Kennedy having breakfast there one morning.) Try **Patisserie Française,** 54 Boylston Street, for French coffee and apple pastry. **Golden Temple,** 95 Winthrop Street, has an unadulterated natural-foods breakfast with whole-wheat pancakes and real maple syrup.

The Boston Brunch

Breakfast, lunch, afternoon tea, with a Bloody Mary thrown in for kicks—that's Boston's Sunday-brunch picture. It's a great value, too, for that one meal can last you through supper. We're listing some of the most popular for you.

Tops on most everyone's list is the lavish brunch served from 10 to 3 at **The Falstaff Room** in the Sheraton Boston Hotel (tel. 236-2000). It's like a Bar Mitzvah in an Elizabethan setting. Before 11:30 you are offered eggs, croissants, brioches, kippered herring, and corned-beef hash. After 11:30, there's beef stew, chicken, and shrimp Newburg. And all through the brunch you can have fruit salad, cold cuts, cheeses, scrambled eggs, ham, salads, vegetables, lox, bagels, and cream cheese. There are Jell-O molds, 15 types of pastry for dessert, and coffee. You can fill your plates as many times as you want, all for $6.95 for adults and $3.95 for children. Don't forget to admire the wall decorations—coats of arms and pictures of Shakespearean heroes.

Break your diet 52 stories over Boston with Sunday brunch at the **Top of the Hub,** Prudential Tower (tel. 536-1775). Ask for a table near the window so you can enjoy an unsurpassed view of the city between trips to the bountiful tables. You don't have to choose, take a little of everything—eggs, sliced roast beef, chicken Newburg, Swedish meatballs, cheese soufflés, pastries, fruits, desserts, and coffee. Served between 11 a.m. and 3 p.m.; $5.25 for adults, $2.95 for children.

The brunch at **Anthony's Pier 4** is reminiscent of one of the gala buffets aboard a cruise ship, for you have an ocean view along with the eggs Benedict, chicken livers, finnan haddie, ham, blintzes, fresh fruit, bagels, and lox. You can have your crêpes filled to order, or pile whipped cream on your chocolate mousse as you forget about the calories. It's all yours for $7.95 (children, $4.95), paid in advance at the door. Reservations accepted. Pier 4 brunch is served from 10 a.m. to 12:30 p.m.

An elegant brunch is served at **Parker's,** at the Parker House, at 11:30 a.m. and 1:30 p.m. for $9.50. It's a lavish meal, with finnan haddie, quiche, bacon, eggs, melons, cheeses, and delicious mousses for dessert. The tables are set beautifully, and there's soft background music.

If you prefer your music a bit louder, there's the Swing Brunch in **Last Hurrah,** also in the Parker House. Music and edibles from 11:30 a.m. to 3:30 p.m. Price is $6.50 for adults, $3.95 for kids, and you can fill your plates as often as you wish with the varied egg dishes and desserts from the sweets table.

The lines are long for the buffet brunch at **Jonah's on the Terrace,** in the Cambridge Hyatt-Regency (tel. 492-1234), so come early if you want to heap your plates with eggs, sausages, roast beef, salads, cheeses, desserts, pastries, as well as a choice of hot dishes. The serving tables are decorated with flowers and an ice sculpture, and your own table overlooks either the river or the terrace. Price is $8.95 for adults, $6.95 for children under ten. Served from 10 a.m. to 3 p.m. (but be in line by 1 p.m.).

Many Boston restaurants offer late Sunday breakfasts with eggs Benedict, quiche, omelettes, and other choices. They include the **Hampshire House,** 84 Beacon Street (Sunday newspapers available); **Delmonico's** in the Hotel Lenox, 710 Boylston Street; **Cafe Vendôme,** at the corner of Dartmouth and Commonwealth Avenue (Sunday newspaper included); the **Hermitage,** 955 Boylston Street; and the **Ritz-Carlton. St. Botolph,** 99 St. Botolph Street, offers brunch for $5.90 including a pitcher of Bloody Marys; and **Jason's,** at 131 Clarendon Street, includes a glass of champagne and fresh fruit with its brunch—$3.75 to $5.95, from 11:30 a.m. to 4 p.m.

Dining Around the Clock

Should the 3 a.m. munchies strike and the urge become irresistible for, say, pickles or tacos or chocolate matzo balls or baklava, take heart; Boston has a number of eating places that never—or almost never—call it quits. All of the following are open after 12, some until the wee hours of the morning, and some never close.

Aegean Fare at Kenmore Square and 16 North Street in the market area are open until 2 a.m. on Friday, Saturday, and Sunday and until midnight the rest of the week. **Lily's Cafe** in the Quincy Market is open till 2 a.m., and many of the other clubs around there and on the waterfront are also open till 2 a.m. **Ken's,** the huge deli at 549 Boylston Street, is open until 3 a.m. nightly; and **Rainbow Ribs,** 97 Massachusetts Avenue, barbecues the ribs, chicken, and seafood until 2:30 on weekends, other nights till 12. Most of the restaurants in Chinatown keep late—or rather, early—hours. **Moon Villa,** 23 Edinboro Street, serves till 4 a.m.; **The 70 Restaurant,** 70 Beach Street, is also open till 4 a.m. And **Kim Toy Lunch,** 2 Tyler Street, threw away the keys—it's open 24 hours. **Brigham's** in the Prudential Center and at Harvard Square are also open 24 hours, as are the branches of **International House of Pancakes** in Brighton and

Brookline. **Yellow Submarine** on Cambridge Street near the Massachusetts General Hospital, fixes some of the best subs in Boston until 3 a.m. And **Caffee Pompeii** brews espresso, cappuccino, and caffe latte until 5 a.m. every morning.

Note: **Store 24,** with branches in Boston, Cambridge, and several other cities is open 24 hours a day selling everything from snacks and toothbrushes to furniture and teddy bears.

Dining in Cambridge

Even if you're not staying in Cambridge, you'll certainly be visiting there, and it's pleasant to combine a meal with your sightseeing excursions. And Cambridge is so close to Boston—most of the restaurants listed here can be reached on foot from the Harvard Square subway stop, just across the Charles River from the center of Boston—that it's no more difficult to dine here than any other place in Boston. Many of your fellow diners will include Harvard, Radcliffe, and M.I.T. students and faculty, members of the huge academic community that makes Cambridge one of the most exciting cultural centers in the country. Venture on to Inman Square, a polyglot community, to sample the fares of a varied ethnic population.

THE UPPER BRACKET: High-style dining with each element orchestrated beautifully, from the preparation to the service, is pretty much a lost art these days, so we were delighted to find it again at **Dertads** in the Sheraton-Commander Hotel, 16 Garden Street, near Harvard Square (tel. 354-1234). Oak-paneled walls, vaulted ceilings with stained-glass inserts, and smoked mirrors provide a handsome backdrop for the tables set with white linens and accented with single red roses. There is always a waiter or busboy standing by unobtrusively to serve, carve, or pour the wine. The continental-French cuisine is expensive: à la carte dinners start at $9.50, and dinner for two reaches $40 quickly. (Taxes and tips, 15%, are included.) Your perfect meal could include boula-boula (turtle and pea soup braced with sherry and topped with cream), $2.50, crab Edward, California dungeness crab stuffed into its own shell along with minced shrimp, tarragon, and cream sauce accented with wine, $12.50; or escallope de veau clamart, veal scallops sauteed with slivers of bacon, peas, and onions, and coated with a thin glaze, $10.50. You might also have a hot vegetable platter framed with a border of rippled duchesse potatoes, $1.50; salade à la Dertads, tossed at the table, $1.25; and, for a grand dessert, cherries jubilee, $4.50. Open Tuesday through Sunday from 6 p.m. to 11 p.m. Reservations are necessary.

Ferdinands, 124 Mt. Auburn Street (tel. 491-4915), is a popular French restaurant near Harvard Square. From the parchment menu—handprinted in old script—you might order onion soup parmesan, 95¢; or gratinée with Swiss cheese and brandy, $2.25. Main courses include fresh lemon sole meunière, $7.50; softshell crabs, $11.50; roast duck with orange sauce, $9.50; and veal Dijonnaise, $9.75. Individual rack of lamb is $11.75. Luncheon prices, which include entree, salad, bread and butter, and beverage, range from $3.25 to $5.75. Those in the know claim it's one of the best French restaurants and advise a midweek visit to avoid the weekend crowds. Open for lunch, Monday through Friday, 11:30 a.m. to 2:30 p.m.; and for dinner from 5 to 10 p.m., until 11 on weekends. Sunday brunch from noon till 3 p.m., and dinner from noon to 10 p.m. Free evening parking in the Nutting Road lot.

THE MIDDLE BRACKET: The **Peacock,** 5 Craigie Circle (tel. 661-4073), is a study in simplicity. But it's a simplicity that is akin to elegance. The portions are modest and only lightly seasoned. The vegetables are arranged carefully on the plate—a single stalk of broccoli and a small russet potato, for example, arranged as if for a still life. The menu changes to take advantage of the best offerings in the market and might include a bouillabaisse, $5.50; roast lamb, $7.95; or duckling, $5.95. Soups at $1.25 have included zucchini and tomato soup and fish chowder. The flourishes of the peacock come across only in showy desserts like chocolate cake filled with fresh strawberries and bordered with rosettes of whipped cream, vacherin (meringue with apricots and hazelnuts), and mocha meringue, each $1.50. Located in the basement of an apartment building near Harvard Square, The Peacock has two small white-and-yellow dining rooms. Open for dinner Tuesday through Saturday, 5:30 to 10:30 p.m.

The theme is music and the music is jazz at the **Sunflower Cafe,** 22 Boylston Street (tel. 864-8450), in Harvard Square. Poster-size stills of local jazz artists, inverted instruments brimming with dried flowers, and columns plastered with old sheet-music set the mood in this popular hangout for the local student crowd. The food is good, too, with dinner specialties mostly in the $3.75 to $6.95 range, offering such intriguing possibilities as

Moroccan chicken, roast duckling with almond sauce, and scallops sauteed with mint. Sandwiches, burgers, and salads are available for lunch and dinner, or you can create your own omelette, choosing from something like 28 different fillings—any two can be yours for $2.50.

Contemporary jazz artists are featured at the Sunday jazz brunch, 11 a.m. to 4 p.m., where the $4.95 tab includes a cocktail. Live jazz at Sunday lunch, too, 11 a.m. to 4 p.m. Sunflower is open from 11 a.m. until 1 a.m. daily, with dinner available from 5 to 10 or 11 p.m. The downstairs bar presents live jazz nightly, from 9 p.m. to 1 a.m., with no cover.

Athenian Taverna, 567 Massachusetts Avenue (tel. 547-6300), is a Greek restaurant with high-quality food, good service, and low prices: a perfect combination. On the second floor of George and Nick's steak house (also good) in Central Square, Athenian Taverna creates its Greek atmosphere with murals, background music, and specialties like baked lamb, $4.50; and stuffed grape leaves, $3.95. Also on the menu: fried squid, $4.25; and moussaka, $4.25. Be sure to have one of the appetizers—tzatziki (cucumber yogurt and garlic), or the taramosalata pâté, 95¢. Top it all off with baklava or rice pudding. Open daily from 11:30 a.m. to 11 p.m.

Peasant Stock, 421 Washington Street, Somerville (tel. 354-9528). A popular hangout for the Cambridge-Somerville student and gourmet population, Peasant Stock is a very simple restaurant that puts all its emphasis on the food: very good French provincial cooking at very reasonable prices. The menu changes every day depending on the inspiration of the cooks, but they always have good soups and stews (it started out as a soup-only place), quiches and omelettes, and such specialties as boeuf bourguignon, $5.40; ternera al jerez (boneless veal roasted in sherry and vegetables), $5.95; or halibut marguery (stuffed with fresh mussels and served in a sauce made with bay scallops), $5.40. Add an extra $1.50 for a full dinner and get a good Canadian split-pea soup (75¢), a chocolate pecan pie, and beverage.

Don't expect to find the ersatz peasant atmosphere of pretty costumes on the servers and Tyrolean designs on the walls. This is real peasant—wood floors that creak and drab walls—but it's the food that's the attraction. Open Tuesday through Friday for lunch and dinner, and on Saturday for dinner only. Sunday, it's brunch from noon till 3 p.m., $2 to $3.

Note: Live classical chamber music is featured some evenings in the back room. These concerts are by reservation only, so call ahead.

THE BUDGET RANGE: Legal Sea Food, 237 Hampshire Street, at Inman Square (tel. 547-1410), has nothing to do with the courts, although judges and law school students do eat there. (At one time, it seems, they gave out "legal" trading stamps.) But it is the favorite of families and food editors and just about everyone from miles around Cambridge who wants good, fresh fish at good, low prices. The menu consists of whatever comes in fresh in the market, and prices range from $3 to about $6. It's a hustle-bustle kind of place; you order your lemon sole, fried fish (or broiled or baked), clams, shrimp, or lobster from the waitress, and then help yourself to tea, coffee, and "go-withs." There are two dining rooms and an oyster bar upstairs, where you can drink, eat oysters, shrimp cocktails, or Japanese appetizers while you wait for a table. Among the most enthusiastic patrons here are the Japanese residents and visitors who have discovered that sashimi is available, served with french fries!

Legal Sea Food is sometimes also known as "that fishy place," since there's an equally famous fish market next door which boasts that all the fish sold are fresh the same day. Open daily, from 11 a.m. to 9 p.m.

If you crave a dessert after your fish meal (although you probably won't need it), stop in next door at **Legal Sweet Shop,** a tiny bakery-ice-cream bar, with just a few tables, serving cake, pastries, 22 flavors of natural ice cream, and other assorted snacks.

There's another Legal Sea Food on Route 9 in the shopping center at Chestnut Hill. *Note:* You have to pay in advance at both locations.

The famous **Wursthaus,** directly on Harvard Square (tel. 491-7110), is very German and very crowded. It's open from 8 a.m. till midnight, and the bar with an attached eating counter is always jammed with a mixed bag of students, politicians, passersby, and the occasional businessman. The Wursthaus claims to feature the world's largest selection of foreign beers, and specializes in such items as bratwurst, knockwurst, sauerbraten, and imported wieners. Most main courses are in the $2.95 to $6 range, and over 30 varieties of sandwiches ($1.15 to $3) are also available. Luncheon specials start at $1.85 and are served from 11 a.m. to 3 p.m. Monday through Friday. Dinner is served till midnight Sunday through Thursday, and until 1 a.m. Friday and Saturday.

Colorful paintings and posters decorate the underground walls of the **Patisserie,** 54 Boylston Street, Cambridge (tel. 354-9850), a charming little coffeehouse with a French flavor and authentic croissants. The best in town! With your delicious espresso or regular coffee, you can have a sandwich or choose one of the French specialties: pâté, quiche Lorraine, meat pies, or omelettes at à la carte prices of $1.35 to $2.65. Special French lunches are priced from $2.95 to $3.50. Open Tuesday through Saturday from 8 a.m. to 6 p.m.; Sunday, from 10 a.m. to 5 p.m.

INTERNATIONAL FARE: You can get some of the best food bargains in the area in the little Portuguese restaurants in Cambridge and Somerville. Sometimes we suspect they keep their dreary storefront appearances to keep tourists away. A case in point is **Terra Foods,** 1193 Cambridge Street, Cambridge (tel. 864-1730). We passed it by several times until a friend with sophisticated food tastes insisted we try it. We found Portuguese pot roast done the Azorean way (with burgundy wine and tomato) for $3.50; pepper steak with wine, $1.95; and kale soup, 50¢. The fried fish is even more of an attraction than the Iberian selections, $2 with chips. Complete meals come with soup, chowder or fruit cup, potato, salad, and a good hunk of bread at $2.50 to $4.25. Terra Foods, a few blocks from Inman Square, is open Monday through Friday from 7 a.m. to 9 p.m. Saturday, they close early—at 6 p.m.

Just across the street is **Casa Portugal,** 1200 Cambridge Street (tel. 491-8800). It's classier than Terra Foods, with murals and candles and displays of pottery. Meals are a good buy here, too, with dinners in the $3.95 to $6.95 range and lunches as low as $2 for tortilhas. There are lots of fish and meat dishes and Portuguese wines.

If you visit **Savarin,** 156 Prospect Street, Cambridge (tel. 876-9475), try to go on Monday or Tuesday when soup or salad is free. But you get good value every day in this excellent Czechoslovakian restaurant. The price range is from $3.75 for chicken to $5.50 for shrimp Catalina. A different special is served each day, including a fine assortment of soups at 75¢. Salads are also 75¢. Open Monday through Thursday from 5 to 11 p.m., and Friday and Saturday until midnight.

India Restaurant, 1780 Massachusetts Avenue, Cambridge

(tel. 354-0949), has a reputation for authentic and inexpensive Indian cooking. The pride of the house is the chicken tandoori dinner at $3.95, à la carte, and $6.25, full-course. They also have a wide variety of curries, with the spices ranging from mild to hot and the ingredients ranging from spinach and mushrooms to meat, fish, and chicken. It's a popular place with the local vegetarians, too. Don't miss the desserts: there are not many places in the Boston-Cambridge area where you can sample the likes of ras malai (baked homemade cheese with cream) or laddoe (a sweet dish made of chickpea flour), both 75¢. Open daily for dinner from 5 p.m. to 10:30 p.m.

The Rendezvous, 24 Holyoke Street, Harvard Square, Cambridge (tel. 547-5005), is a small restaurant with the most surprising menu in the city—exceptional Vietnamese and French foods at exceptionally low prices! Don't be turned off by the entrance, which is a fast-food emporium on the street level. Rendezvous, with its exotic food, is downstairs. The offerings include shrimp paste on sugar cane, $3.85; barbecued beef with lemon grass (imported from Thailand), $3.95 (this is a sweet, gingery dish served with noodles, vegetables, and fish sauce—for dunking). Appetizers are around $1.50 (be sure to try the spring rolls); and desserts go from 70¢ to $1.25. The French entrees are also under $4. Dinner is served Tuesday through Sunday, from 5 p.m. to 10 p.m.

We've finally found a natural-foods restaurant in Cambridge with delicious food for under $3. **Conscious Cookery Restaurant,** 95 Winthrop Street (tel. 354-0365), serves no additives, no sugar, no chemical preservatives, but does offer homemade soups and sandwiches, enchiladas and tostadas. The Golden Temple sandwich of whole-wheat Syrian bread is crammed with mushrooms, tomatoes, sprouts, and hummus, and crowned with grilled cheddar cheese, $2.75. A feast for both the eyes and the palate is the Sat Nam salad—mounds of sprouts, mushrooms, carrot slices, and grated cheddar atop salad greens, $2.70. Desserts include honey-sweetened frozen yogurt with a carob sauce or maple syrup, 95¢. The white-turbaned Sikhs who run the restaurant also serve the only natural-foods breakfast in the Boston area with whole-wheat pancakes and waffles, real maple syrup, and fresh orange juice. The restaurant, which is below street level (but still open and airy), shares space with a natural-foods store, so if you're really impressed with your meal, you can buy the fixings to duplicate it at home. Open Monday through

Thursday, 7:30 a.m. to 10 p.m.; and till 11:30 p.m., Friday and Saturday. Special Sunday brunch and dinner, 9 a.m. to 9 p.m.

OTHER CAMBRIDGE SUGGESTIONS: The Blacksmith House
(formerly the Window Shop), 56 Brattle Street, has Viennese, Hungarian, German, and French tortes, cakes, and pastries to eat there, with coffee and tea, or to take out. Best linzer torte and dobos torte we could find! . . . **Restaurant Brasilia,** 58 Boylston Street, is the only Brazilian restaurant in New England. You can get a good meal here and excellent Brazilian coffee and desserts . . .**Swiss Alps,** 56 Boylston Street, is a cozy underground cafe with traditional red-and-white checkered tablecloths. Quiche ($2.75), raclette, onion tarts, and chocolate mousse are the typical fare.. . .**Natarj,** 419 Massachusetts Avenue, near M.I.T., caters to the local Indian crowd. . . . Mexican aficionados alternate between **Casa Mexico,** 75 Winthrop Street, Harvard Square, and **Boca Loca,** 1300 Cambridge Street, Inman Square

Harvest Restaurant, 44 Brattle Street, in the Design Research building, is the gourmet choice for Cambridge fashionables. . . . For outdoor dining, try the patio at **Harvest Passim's,** 47 Palmer Street, or **Cafe Pamplona,** 12 Bow Street. . . . Not only typical Mid-eastern foods, but unusual Moroccan dishes with a French flavor as well, can be found at **Ahmed's** on Winthrop Street in Harvard Square.

Faneuil Hall

Chapter V

SIGHTS OF BOSTON

BOSTON IS AN eminently pleasant town for leisurely sightseeing and strolling. You can see the city by sightseeing bus, guided walking tour, or even sightseeing boat (more about which later), but you can also walk around on your own, poking your way into odd little corners as you go; and since Boston is not a large city (geographically), this is, for us, the most rewarding way to see it. You can see most of the major sights in two or three days. Take the subway or a cab to the major areas you want to see, then explore in depth the best way of all: by walking. For an overall view of the city, start at one of its dazzling observation towers: the **Prudential** or **John Hancock**. See details in Chapter II, "Finding Your Way Around Boston."

And for a kaleidoscopic insight into the city—scenes and sounds of the diverse neighborhoods, museums, sports, nightlife —be sure to see *Where's Boston?*, the 55-minute sight-and-sound show at 60 State Street, just a few steps away from Faneuil Hall. Shown daily, on the hour, from 10 a.m. to 10 p.m., this multi-image, quadraphonic-sound show is a very pleasant orientation to the city. Admission: $2.25 for adults, $1.50 for children under 13, $1.25 for senior citizens. Information phone: 661-2425; theater phone: 367-6090. Special parking rates are available at the adjacent parking garage with validated tickets.

Visitor Information

Now, before you start your walk around town, stop by one of Boston's Visitor Information Centers for free maps, folders, weekly listings of special exhibits, and a list of visiting hours and fees at the historic shrines.

The National Park Service Visitor Center, at 15 State Street, right next to the Old State House and the State Street "T" station, is a good place to start your tour of historic Boston. The audio-visual show, *Walking the Freedom Trail,* gives you basic information on those 16 historic sites and the knowledgeable guides (with distinctive Park Service uniforms and hats) answer all questions politely. There are special ramps for the handicapped, comfortable chairs for relaxing, and rest rooms. Shuttle buses from the Boston Common Underground Garage take you directly to the center. Open daily from 9 a.m. to 6 p.m. (tel. 223-3764).

The City Hall Visitor Hospitality Center is open Monday to Friday, 9 a.m. to 5 p.m. Get brochures there, look at the exhibits, perhaps use the storage lockers, and if you have little children in tow, try the child-care center. (Bypass the steps at City Hall Plaza by walking up State Street toward Government Center, by the "Steaming Kettle" to the Plaza.)

The Freedom Trail Information Center is on the Tremont Street side of the Common, open daily from 9 a.m. to 5 p.m., and there you can get maps and brochures. To guide you, there's a red brick line in the sidewalks from the Common to the end of the trail.

In the Back Bay area of Boston, the visitor information center is in the **John Hancock Tower** (corner St. James Avenue and Trinity Place), open Monday to Saturday from 9 a.m. to 10:15 p.m.; and Sunday, from 10 a.m. to 10:15 p.m. during the months from May to October, and noon to 10:15 p.m. the rest of the year, with the exception of Thanksgiving and Christmas.

The Foreign Visitor Center, on the fourth floor at 15 State Street, offers interpreters, guides, and other help to tourists. Open Monday through Saturday from 9 a.m. to 5 p.m. (tel. 262-4830).

And the **Greater Boston Convention and Tourist Bureau,** at 900 Boylston Street, has a live number, 338-1976, from 8 a.m. to 5 p.m., Monday through Friday, to give the latest information on goings-on about town. It offers recorded information at all other times.

Maps

At one time you could always tell tourists from natives by the maps they carried, but there has been so much reconstruction in the "New Boston" that the locals find maps helpful, too. Free maps of downtown Boston and the rapid transit lines are available at the visitor information centers; and the Park Street Station of the MBTA has free wallet-size maps of all subway lines. Or write in advance to the MBTA at 150 High Street, Boston,

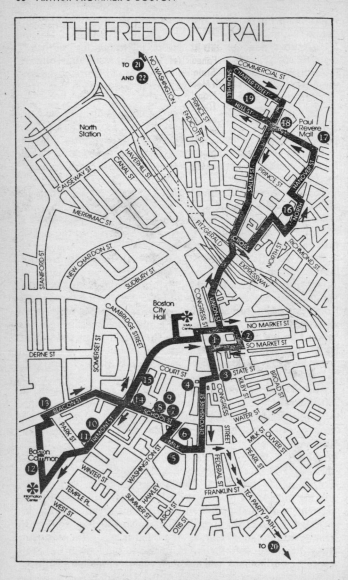

THE FREEDOM TRAIL

KEY TO THE NUMBERED REFERENCES ON OUR MAP OF THE
FREEDOM TRAIL: 1.—Faneuil Hall; 2—Quincy Market; 3—Boston
Massacre Site; 4—Old State House; 5—Site of Benjamin Franklin
Birthplace; 6—Old South Meetinghouse; 7—Old Corner Book Store;
8—Statue of Benjamin Franklin erected 1856; 9—Site of the First
Public School—1635; 10—Granary Burying Ground; 11—Park
Street Church; 12—Boston Common; 13—State House and Archives
Museum; 14—King's Chapel; 15—King's Chapel Burying Ground;
16—Paul Revere House; 17—Paul Revere Mall; 18—Old North
Church; 19—Copp's Hill Burying Ground; 20—Boston Tea Party Ship
and Museum; 21—Bunker Hill Monument; 22—U.S.S. Constitution
("Old Ironsides").

MA 02110. The Prudential Life Insurance Company has a
neighborhood map of Boston which it distributes at its Skywalk
viewing platform. Very helpful for your walking trips of Beacon
Hill, North End, Chinatown, South End, Charlestown, and Harvard Square.

Arts Boston, 73 Tremont Street (tel. 742-6600), has an excellent map-guide that shows which MBTA lines and stations to use
to reach museums, theaters, concert and dance sites. The listings
are color-coded to match the Red, Green, Blue, and Orange lines
of the "T" system. Very clear and easy to follow, it's also a good
street map to use around town. Free at visitor information centers, it's a red folder titled "Getting to the Art of Boston."

The Metropolitan District Commission (MDC) has an excellent map of the reservations, parks, and recreation areas in
Greater Boston. It tells where to find salt- and freshwater beaches, swimming and wading pools, picnic areas, foot trails and
bridge paths, playgrounds, tennis and golf courses, freshwater
and saltwater fishing, bicycle paths, and ice-skating rinks. Write
to the MDC, 20 Somerset Street, Boston, for a copy. Also check
the Department of Environmental Management, Division of
Forests and Parks, 100 Cambridge Street, for a free guide to
touring in the Bay State and for a vast range of booklets and
pamphlets on cultural and recreational activities.

Check also with the New England Innkeepers Association, 25
Huntington Avenue, Boston, MA 02116. The Essex County
Tourist Council, P.O. Box 1011, Peabody, MA 01960, will send
you a handy guide if you write to them. Three guides listing
historical houses and museums in New England are available

from the **Society for the Preservation of New England Antiquities,** 141 Cambridge Street, Boston, MA 02114. **The Massachusetts Association of Campground Owners (MACO)** has a free pamphlet listing private campgrounds in the state. Write to MACO, Sutton Falls Camping Area, Manchaug Road, West Sutton, MA 01527. Ski maps and campground maps as well as a Travel Tips map are available from the National Survey, Chester, Vermont.

The Freedom Trail

The one walking tour that everyone must make, of course, is the **Freedom Trail,** which consists of 16 numbered historical sights spread out over an area of three or four square miles in the downtown section and Charlestown. In two to three hours, depending on how long you spend at each site, you'll cover 2½ centuries of America's most important history. "A visit to Boston is a must for every American," say the historians, "for without Boston there would have been no free American life."

And to show how free Bostonians are, the Freedom Trail has been expanded and rerouted in the last few years. There are now two loops—one through downtown Boston and the other through the North End—making the trail easier to follow. Although the new "official" start is at the City Hall Hospitality Center, we like to stick to tradition and begin the tour at the **Boston Common.** Either way, there are trailblazer signs and a red sidewalk line to mark the trail.

To reach the Boston Common, take the subway to Park Street, or drive and park in the Common's 1,500-car underground garage (entrance on Arlington Street). From there a free bus takes you to the Information Booth on the Common. The Common is an integral part of Boston's past and present. It is the oldest public park in the country (1634), a place where cows once grazed, soldiers drilled, witches were hanged, and "common scolds" were dunked in the Frog Pond (now used for wading and ice skating). Today you'll find Hare Krishna dancers, band concerts, rock concerts, sidewalk musicians, soap-box orators, demonstrations for or against almost anything, a free playground for the young, park benches for the elderly, Bostonians brownbagging their lunch, annual flowers and ancient trees, and pigeons—and street people—begging for handouts.

Now that you've got your bearings, proceed to the "new" State House, with its great gold dome, one of the masterpieces of the career of Charles Bulfinch (to the original Bulfinch building have been added new wings, none as handsome). Although the building is called "new," it was actually built in 1795 to replace the smaller "old" State House (which you'll see later on your tour). Samuel Adams laid the cornerstone, and the original dome, now gold-leafed, was done in copper purchased from Paul Revere. The building is replete with flags, paintings, and such specialties as "the sacred codfish," a pine wood fish which hangs opposite the Speaker's desk. But you'll probably enjoy the Archives Museum in the basement most. Here you can view, among other things, old documents, maps, guns, witchcraft acts, and the original manuscript of William Bradford's *History of Plymouth Plantation*. The Doric Dames provide a volunteer daily guide service, on the hour from 10 a.m. to 4 p.m. through October 12, and Monday through Friday, thereafter. State House and Archives are open Monday through Friday, from 9 to 5.

Heading down one side of five-sided Boston Common, from which the British troops set off for Concord in 1775, the trail next pauses at the **Park Street Church** at the corner of Park and Tremont streets, built in 1809 and once described by Henry James as "the most interesting mass of bricks and mortar in America," with its white steeple and original exterior designed by Englishman Peter Banner. The church is rich in its associations: William Lloyd Garrison gave his first antislavery address here on July 4, 1829. Incidentally, the site on which the church stands has long been known as "Brimstone Corner," since gunpowder was stored in the church's basement during the War of 1812. During July and August, the church is open from 9:30 a.m. to 4 p.m., Monday through Saturday, and 9 a.m. to 1 p.m. and 4:30 p.m. to 9 p.m. on Sunday. At other times of the year, hours are geared to the availability of tour guides, or are by reservation.

Just to the left of the church on Tremont Street is the **Granary Burying Ground**, once part of the Common and later the site of a public granary. Pause for a moment and pay tribute to some illustrious Americans who are buried here: John Hancock, Samuel Adams, Paul Revere, Benjamin Franklin's parents, the victims of the Boston Massacre (five colonists shot in a fracas with British troops on March 5, 1770), and the wife of Isaac Goose, otherwise known as "Mother Goose," from the nursery rhymes of the same name. But don't try any gravestone rubbing. Once a popular pastime, it has been prohibited in Boston's historic cemeteries as the rubbing process was beginning to wear off the engraving on the tombstones. Open daily, 8 a.m. to 4 p.m.

King's Chapel is next on your tour: built in 1754 and worshiped in by the royal governors, it was the first Episcopal church in Boston. George III sent gifts, as did Queen Anne and William and Mary, who presented the communion table and chancel tablets still in use today before the church was constructed. The crown's religion was never too popular with the colonists and after the Revolution, it became the first Unitarian church in America. Unitarian-Universalist services are now conducted here. Open Tuesday through Sunday, 9:30 a.m. to 4:30 p.m. through October 12, and then Monday through Friday from 10 a.m. to 4 p.m.

Now follow the red brick line to School Street, where you'll find two stops on the trail: the Site of the First Public School, Boston Latin School, where Adams, Franklin, and Cotton Mather were students (Boston Latin is now in the Fenway Area); and the statue of Benjamin Franklin, the first portrait statue erected in Boston. If you look closely you'll see that one side of the statue is smiling, the other serious. (Old Ben is probably wondering how to react to the fact that the location of his old school is now a chic French restaurant. It was Boston City Hall until the new building was erected.) Next on the trail is the building that once housed the Old Corner Bookstore, and the publishing house of Ticknor and Fields. This was the literary center of America, where such Boston literati as Longfellow, Lowell, Thoreau, Emerson, Hawthorne, and Harriet Beecher Stowe used to meet and chat. It is now a business office for the Boston *Globe* and is somewhat restored to what it was in the old days.

The Old South Meeting House, at the corner of Washington and Milk streets, next on your walk, was used by the early colonists for both religious and political meetings, overflowing from nearby Faneuil Hall. It was here, in 1770, that an angry crowd met to wait for Governor Hutchinson's promise to withdraw British troops after the Boston Massacre. And it was also here, on December 16, 1773, that several thousand citizens sent messengers to the governor that the newly arrived tea be removed from the harbor and sent back to England. At last, they were informed by Samuel Adams of the governor's refusal; a whoop went up from the citizens disguised as Indians who then rushed to the docks to begin the famous Boston Tea Party. Today the Meeting House is a fascinating museum of revolutionary history, with its pews still on the ground floor; a centuries-old clock ticking away; exhibits of old books, plateware, engravings; a sign reading that "Boston Tea Party started here December 16,

1773," with a vial of the tea (washed up on the shore of Boston Harbor the morning after) to prove it. Open daily, 10 a.m. to 4 p.m. in the winter, and 10 a.m. to 6 p.m. in the summer. Admission 50¢, children free.

Now plan to spend a little time poring over the priceless collection of Colonial and Revolutionary memorabilia at **The Old State House,** Washington and State streets, which dates back to 1713. It was the seat of the Colonial government of Massachusetts before the Revolution, and the state's capitol afterward. It was from its balcony that the Declaration of Independence was first read to the citizens of Boston in 1776. In 1789, George Washington, as president, reviewed a parade from the building. The Old State House is an impressive building with a magnificent spiral staircase, and as you roam around, you'll see rooms filled with old furniture and paintings, and a varied collection of early Boston memorabilia: ship models, uniforms, guns, policemen's hats, and a few leaves that survived the Boston Tea Party. From November 1 to March 31 it is open from 10 a.m. to 4 p.m., Monday through Friday; from 9:30 a.m. to 5 p.m. on Saturday; and from 11 a.m. to 5 p.m. on Sunday. Hours from April 1 to October 31 are 9:30 a.m. to 5 p.m., Monday through Sunday. Admission, 75¢; senior citizens, 50¢; children under 12, 25¢.

Outside the Old State House, a ring of cobblestones marks the site of **The Boston Massacre,** March 5, 1770, an event which helped consolidate the spirit of rebellion in the colonies. Colonists, angered at the presence of British troops in Boston, stoned a group of Redcoats who panicked and fired into the crowd, killing five men.

Faneuil Hall, at Dock Square, is the next important stop on the Freedom Trail. Built in 1742 and given to the city of Boston by merchant Peter Faneuil, it became known as the "Cradle of Liberty" because of the frequent protest meetings that took place here, while orators such as Samuel Adams exhorted the crowd against the British. The upstairs is still a meeting hall for state and local civic and political groups and the new breed of political protesters, the downstairs still a produce market, all according to Faneuil's will. On the top floor, the military-minded can examine the weapons collection of the Ancient and Honorable Artillery Company of Massachusetts, open weekdays, 10 to 4. Faneuil Hall is open seven days a week, from 9 a.m. to 5 p.m. Hourly talks by the National Park Service. Free.

The North End Loop of the Freedom Trail starts at the Paul

Revere House, but before going on you might want to stop here and visit the Quincy Marketplace which is next to Faneuil Hall (we'll describe it fully later in this chapter). Or you may want to visit the City Hall Hospitality Center where there are a rest area, child-care center, storage lockers, and exhibits. (There are rest rooms also at the National Park Service Visitor Center, which is at 15 State Street, adjacent to the Old State House.)

To reach the Paul Revere House follow the red brick path that takes you under the expressway to the North End.

The **Paul Revere House** was already 94 years old when Revere bought it in 1770 (for some 213 pounds), and is still standing today, at North Square. The two-story wooden structure, the oldest in Boston, with its leaded windows and large fireplace, filled with many of the original furnishings and artifacts, is one of the major landmarks along the Freedom Trail. Revere, a brilliant silversmith as well as a patriot, had good training for his famous ride of April 18, 1775; he had occasionally been hired by the selectmen to carry news of their deliberations to other parts of the colonies. In 1774, for example, he bore dispatches to Philadelphia and New York calling for a congress; the year before, he had spread the news of (after taking part in) the Boston Tea Party to New York. You can gaze at Revere's saddlebags and a box of pistols—a silent reminder of what may well be the most famous horseback ride in history. The house is open daily. Hours are 10 a.m. to 4 p.m., November 1 to April 14; 10 a.m. to 6 p.m., April 15 to October 31. Closed Thanksgiving, Christmas, and New Year's Day. Admission is 50¢ for adults over 17; 25¢ for children 6 to 17; and 25¢ for senior citizens.

The area around Paul Revere's House is pleasantly unspoiled in some ways, although the architectural styles are mixed. You may want to note, too, at the beginning of the little cobbled street on which Revere's house stands, the **Moses-Pierce Hitchborn House**, another venerable one for Boston, built around 1680. A few blocks up, at James Rego Square, is a little park with a statue of Paul Revere on horseback. Here you'll also see **St. Stephen's Church**, a beautiful edifice created by Bulfinch in 1802. Walk into the park, pausing at the fountain in the square, and emerge at the **Old North Church**, Salem Street at Paul Revere Mall. It's a thoroughly beautiful structure which dates back to 1723, and is modeled in the style of Sir Christopher Wren's buildings, with its red brick facade and tall steeple. It was from this steeple, of course, that Revere had arranged for Robert Newman to hang two lanterns ("One if by land, two if by sea"), the signal that the

British were on their way to Lexington and Concord. The Revere family attended this church (you can still see their plaque on Pew 54), and other famous visitors who have attended services at Old North have included Presidents James Monroe, Theodore Roosevelt, and F.D.R. And more recently, Gerald R. Ford and Her Majesty Queen Elizabeth II. Have a look at the interior of the church, noting the pulpit shaped like a wine glass, the ancient chandeliers, and organ. Then stop at the museum-shop next door, also in an old building, where you can buy maps of Paul Revere's ride, pewter, and silver, as well as less historic-type items like maple sugar candy. Proceeds go to support the church. Old North Church is open daily from 9 a.m. to 5 p.m. And you can attend Sunday services at 9:30 and 11 a.m.

Also at the Old North Church, see the portraits in brass exhibited by the **London Brass Rubbing Centre,** and try your hand at brass rubbing. Materials and instructions provided for a small fee which is used to maintain historic churches in Boston and England. Open daily at 193 Salem Street, 9 a.m. to 5 p.m.

On your way to the last two stops on the Freedom Trail, pause for a while at the **Copps Hill Burial Ground,** just up the hill from Old North Church. Used by the colonists as early at 1659, this is where Cotton Mather and his brother are buried along with other early Bostonians. On this ground, once the site of a wind-mill, were planted the British batteries which destroyed the vil-lage of Charlestown during the Battle of Bunker Hill, June 17, 1775. Today, the deserted graveyard is mostly used by local people to walk their dogs in, but because of its height, you can see across the river to Charlestown, spotting the masts of the U.S.S. *Constitution.* The *Constitution*—*"Old Ironsides"* of War of 1812 fame—was built at a cost of $302,718 (that was back in 1797), and since she never lost a battle, this must have been one of the biggest naval bargains in history. First used to help drive the French privateers from West Indian waters, the *Constitution* won a succession of famous victories over the British fleet in the War of 1812. Participating in 42 engagements, she captured 20 vessels without ever being beaten. The ship is now preserved— "not only as a monument to its glorious past, but as a symbol of the spirit which established our nation." Open 9:30 a.m. to 3:50 p.m., daily. Kids love to climb up and down the ladders between decks!

There are two exhibits worth seeing right at Hoosac Pier No. 1 where "Old Ironsides" is docked: the **U.S.S. Constitution Museum** and the **Bunker Hill Pavilion.** The museum displays guns, powder buckets, and other artifacts and memorabilia of the ship. Open 9 a.m. to 5 p.m. daily except Thanksgiving, Christmas, and New Year's Day. Admission is $1 for adults; children under 16, 75¢; and includes a 15-minute color slide show depicting life aboard *Old Ironsides.*

The **Bunker Hill Pavilion** is a theater in the round With a 30-minute multimedia presentation of the Battle of Bunker Hill. Showings are continuous, seven days a week from 9:30 a.m. to 4:30 p.m. (till 6:30, June through August). Closed Thanksgiving, Christmas, and New Year's Day. Admission is $1.50 for adults, 75¢ for children. There is a special family rate of $4.

Reaching the *Constitution* is a bit confusing. If you'd like to take a chance on Boston's highway maze, try this. From Haymarket Square, follow the signs that direct you to Northeast Expressway and the Mystic River Bridge. Exit right before the ramp leading to the bridge. There is parking at the Charlestown Navy Yard near the *Constitution.* Best bet is to take a sightseeing bus or the MBTA. Try "T" Bus #93 from Haymarket Square. This takes you to City Square, Charlestown, a short walk to the U.S.S. *Constitution* and Bunker Hill. Or take the "T's" Orange line from Haymarket to Bunker Hill Community College, near the Bunker Hill Monument. If you're driving from the *Constitution* to the monument, get instructions from one of the guides at the naval shipyard, since there are narrow one-way streets to cope with.

The **Bunker Hill Monument,** a 220-foot landmark, was built to honor the men who died in the Battle of Bunker Hill, which took place on June 17, 1775. Although the colonists lost the battle, it speeded the events that eventually pushed the British out of America. Unless you're willing to climb 294 steps—there is no elevator—it's best to observe the tower from the distance. There are exhibits at the base. Open daily from 9 a.m. to 4 p.m. Adults, 75¢; children, 50¢. For a real sense of history, rent a hand-held tape recorder and listen to battle accounts on the spots where they happened in 1775.

The **Boston Tea Party Path** is marked with white discs and the logo "Blue Boston 200." It traces the patriot's route from the Old South Meeting House to Griffin's Wharf, where they threw the tea into the harbor. Moored at the wharf now is a replica of one of the ships they boarded, **The Boston Tea Party Ship and Museum.** Located at the Congress Street Bridge, it's a short distance from South Station and Faneuil Hill Marketplace. Parking is difficult on weekdays (we think if the patriots had had to park their cars in the area, the British would still be taxing tea in Boston), so weekends would be your best bet if driving. You can also take the MBTA Red line to South Station, or the Tea Party courtesy shuttle from the rear of the Old State House, corner of State and Devonshire streets, or the harborside entrance to Faneuil Hall Marketplace. The museum has three points of interest: the brig *Beaver II,* a full-size working replica of one of the ships involved in the Boston Tea Party; a museum with copies of historical documents, artifacts, and audio-visual presentations of the Tea Party period; and a gift shop with Tea Party replicas. And if you really want to get into the spirit of the rebellion, you can even throw tea chests from the deck into the water. (They're retrieved by their rope harnesses). The museum is open daily from 9 a.m. to dusk. Admission is $1.75 for adults, $1 for children (5 to 14), and no charge for those under 5. Complimentary tea is served.

The **Black Heritage Trail** covers 16 points of interest in the Beacon Hill section that relate to the history of 19th-century black Boston. A free brochure with a map of the trail is available at the Freedom Trail Information Booth, the National Park Visitor Center, or the Museum of Afro-American History, Smith Court, off Joy Street (tel. 723-8863 or 445-7400). Included in the tour is the African Meeting House, the oldest black church building in the United States. Guided tours of the trail are given Sunday afternoons at 2 p.m. by the staff of the Museum of Afro-American History. Fees are $3 for adults and $1.50 for children. Tours at other times may be arranged by calling the museum.

Shuttle Bus

If you're a bit foot-weary and still want to do the Freedom Trail, there is a shuttle bus leaving from the Boston Common Information Booth every 45 minutes from 8:45 a.m. to 3:00 p.m. You can get off and on at any of the 11 stops and stay as long as you want at each of them. These are narrated tours and the buses are air-conditioned. Rates are $3.50 for adults and $1.50 for children. Call Hub Sightseeing & Tours, 755 Boylston Street (tel. 267-5200).

Beacon Hill

Another historic area that's delightful to walk around is Beacon Hill on the northern side of the Boston Common, an architectural gem from the 19th century crowned by the gold-domed State House. The old brownstone and brick houses are virtually the same as they were when Louisa May Alcott lived at 10 Louisburg Square, Edwin Booth at 29A Chestnut Street, and Julia Ward Howe at 13 Chestnut Street. Happily, the area has now been designated as a National Historic Landmark and is safely beyond the reach of developers. One of the oldest black churches in the country, the African Meeting House, is on the Hill at 8 Smith Court.

The quaint narrow streets have red brick sidewalks (a second revolution almost occurred when the city dared to suggest repaving in concrete), gaslight lamps, and in spring and summer, flowering windowboxes on most of the town houses. Fashionable **Louisburg Square**, the famed turf of the Boston Brahmins with its cluster of 22 homes and a beautiful central park, is still home to the Old Money. (It was in these environs that the Cabots spoke only to the Lowells and so on.) And the iron-railed square is open only to residents with keys. Many of the homes on other parts of the Hill have been subdivided into rental apartments and young people—executives, secretaries, families, students, and nonconformists—have moved into the neighborhood, to the dismay of the old residents, who have been moving out. The change is most noticeable at the foot of Beacon Hill in the Charles Street neighborhood which counts itself, more or less, the Greenwich Village of Boston.

Charles Street, whatever you compare it to, is Boston in microcosm. There are expensive antique and florist shops, intimate, friendly coffeehouses, boutiques and head shops, neighborhood grocery and hardware stores, inexpensive restaurants, sub shops, ice-cream stores, launderettes, the Charles Street Meeting House, and Phillips Drugstore, which is open 24 hours. At one end of the street is the MBTA Charles Street station (Red line to Cambridge) and at the other, Boston Common and the Public Gardens. While you're exploring, take some time to browse in the stores. (See our chapter on shopping in Boston, ahead.)

When you explore this area, by the way, be ready for a good deal of walking and climbing. Charles Street is at the base of the Hill, but everything else goes up. Tourist buses don't make the rounds there—they probably never could turn the narrow corners—and a parking space is practically impossible to find unless you dare park under a towing sign. And the ever-efficient meter-maids do call the tow trucks.

If you're ever in Boston on a Christmas Eve, it's fun to take part in one of the city's nicest traditions: caroling on the Hill. A unique musical group called the "Bell Ringers" makes its appearance. And from your snowy vantage point up on the Hill, you can see the Boston Common below you, decked out in a blaze of holiday lights.

Incidental Intelligence: In Boston's early days, Beacon Hill was one of the three hills, and as the name implies was the site of a beacon. In the early 1800s, the ingenious Bostonians, who were becoming cramped for living space, solved their housing problem and unemployment problem with one bold stroke. For a period of 60 years, they removed earth from the top of the three peaks on Beacon Hill and built homes on the slopes. And they used that earth to fill in a pond to the north that is now the North Station terminal, and a bay to the west that is now Back Bay.

Visiting Boston's Old Houses

If you're still in the nostalgia mood, you'll enjoy a visit to some of the old houses of Boston which are still standing; here you can get a feeling of what life among the 19th-century aristocrats and upper middle class was like—from the inside. One of the most pleasant of these is the **Gibson House Museum,** 137 Beacon Street (admission $1, open 2 p.m. to 5 p.m., daily except Monday and holidays). It's full of the kind of curios that our great-grandparents found essential: petrified-tree hat racks, a sequinned pink velvet tent for the cat, a Victrola, gilt-framed photographs of every relative. What must be one of America's oldest telephones is mounted on a second-floor wall, supplementing the internal network of wired bells to summon servants from any part of the house. (Sounds like "Upstairs, Downstairs.")

Both the **Nichols House Museum** at 55 Mount Vernon Street (open 1 p.m. to 5 p.m., Monday, Wednesday, and Saturday; admission, $1.00), and **Harrison Gray Otis House** at 141 Cambridge Street (open all year, Monday to Friday, with tours at 10 a.m., 11 a.m., 1 p.m., 2 p.m. and 3 p.m.; admission, $1) were designed by the 18th-century architect Charles Bulfinch and are well worth seeing. (The Otis House is also headquarters for the Society for the Preservation of New England Antiquities.) So are the pair of period-furnished houses occupied by the **Women's City Club** at 39-40 Beacon Street, on view to the public from 10 a.m. to 4 p.m. Wednesdays; $1.50 admission for a guided tour. Lunch is available.

The oldest brick building now standing in Boston is **Hancock**

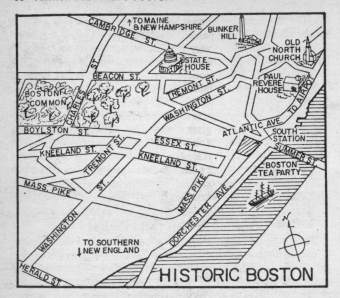

HISTORIC BOSTON

House, 10 Marshall Street, which dates from 1760. It was owned by John Hancock but occupied by his brother Ebenezer, paymaster of the Continental Army, who lived there from 1764 to 1785.

Note: Embedded in the side of the gift shop across from the Hancock House is the **Boston Stone,** the official centerpoint of the city. All distances to and from Boston are measured from this point.

City Hall, Government Center, and the New Boston

If you remember your history, you know that "Old Boston" was once considered very revolutionary. So, just consider "New Boston" as following tradition when you visit **Boston City Hall** (dubbed an "Aztec Tomb" by its critics), which overlooks the Quincy Market—Faneuil Hall section. The main approach is across an eight-acre red brick plaza, comparable—in size only—to St. Peter's Square in Rome. There are fountains at one end, good for foot-dunking in hot weather, and steps for sitting. But no trees or benches. The plaza comes alive at times with music and dance performances sponsored by the city; and with demonstrations and protest rallies not sponsored by the city. Food vendors hawk lunches and snacks from umbrellaed carts. City

Hall itself, whose design was chosen in national competition, was opened in 1969, accompanied by howls of protest from traditionalists who disliked the very unusual contemporary structure. It is dually regarded as "one of the great civic buildings of the 20th century" and as a cold, concrete-and-brick monstrosity, depending on whether you're talking to architects or plain Bostonians. Office workers and visitors say they get lost in the huge connecting passageways; designers extol the high lobby with its exhibition areas, the huge glass doors, the light shafts, and the imaginative use of space and irregular shapes and surfaces. And there seems to be general agreement that the balcony outside the mayor's office is a great place for visiting royalty—i.e., the victorious Bruins hockey team or the champion Red Sox or Boston Celtics—to greet the cheering throng below. Form your own opinion by taking one of the free guided tours given weekdays from 10 to 4. The building is open from 9 to 5, and at times there are very good art and photo exhibits in the lobby and fifth-floor galleries—even poetry readings. To reach Boston City Hall, follow Tremont Street from the Boston Common to Government Center or take the MBTA to Government Center.

Facing City Hall across the plaza are more new government buildings. The 26-story **John F. Kennedy Federal Office Building**, the **Center Plaza**, one of the country's longest office buildings, and the **State Service Center**, with a 30-story tower.

Another controversial building—or rather an addition to an old one—is the annex to the **Boston Public Library** at Copley Square. The style has no relation to the elegantly graceful Modern Baroque of the building, but is very simple and very functional. There are eight floors, a mezzanine, and an auditorium for educational programs. Both the new addition and the Central Library are worth visiting for their numerous art objects and architectural features as well as their books. And there's a tranquil courtyard in the Central Library where you can read, relax . . . or hold a secret rendezvous. Call 536-5400 for hours and special events.

Just beyond the B.P.L. in the few blocks between Boylston Street, Huntington Avenue, and Massachusetts Avenue, are Boston's other contemporary showpieces: the **Prudential Center** with its shops, restaurants, offices, the John B. Hynes Civic Auditorium, the Sheraton Boston Hotel, and the 52-story Prudential Tower; the new **John Hancock Tower**, rising higher than the Prudential Tower; and the soaring new **Christian Science**

Buildings which surround the Mother Church and its beautiful reflecting pool on Huntington Avenue.

Note: And there's fantasy in Boston's architecture, too. The back wall of the **Boston Architectural Center,** 320 Newbury Street, is resplendent with a mural of a five-story classical palace complete with balustrades, columns, arches, and a great central dome. The best place to see it is on Boylston Street, near the Institute of Contemporary Art.

Waterfront–Faneuil Hall Area

This is where the future takes on the shape of the past. Boston's history is tied to the sea—the early fortunes were made via the clipper ship route and colonial commercial life centered around the waterfront. Now, as Boston rebuilds, it turns to the source of its origins for inspiration. A small city within the city is taking shape as the old wharves are rebuilt and the ramshackle warehouses are recycled into chic restaurants, apartments, and offices. (You have "arrived" if you have a waterfront address.) The new Aquarium is there, plus several restaurants including seafood, steak house, Italian, and Japanese dining spots. On Lewis Wharf, a long-deserted warehouse has been transformed into a striking ground-level arcade with a florist shop, Greek and Polish import boutiques, clock shop, designer furniture shop, restaurants, and offices. On the upper levels are condominiums with views of the harbor. And it's all dramatized with cobblestone paths, a flower garden, and a boccie green. A similar type of rejuvenation is planned for the other piers and for the whole area along the harbor. The total effect will be similar to San Francisco's Ghirardelli Square, but with a historical background.

Part of the grand scheme is the new **Waterfront Park.** Use the Aquarium subway stop or take the Green line of the "T" to Government Center and walk down to the sea via City Hall Plaza, Faneuil Hall, and the Quincy Marketplace. Sit on the terraced steps facing the harbor and dream of the tall ships (perhaps with a picnic lunch and a bottle of wine purchased at Quincy Marketplace or the Haymarket for sustenance). This is one of Boston's most charming areas, with trees, flowers, and a 340-foot trellis which will blossom with roses and wisteria. The walks are paved in brick, cobblestone, and granite; the lights have a nautical design; the tot-lot comes with a crow's nest and a wading pool; and there's even a "restroom" for dogs—three brightly painted hydrants!

Quincy Marketplace, an exciting new addition to the Boston landscape, is a miniature city in itself, with stores, restaurants, exhibits, food markets, entertainment, and a swinging nightlife. The three-building complex, which is linked to Faneuil Hall by walkways and a plaza of brick, cobblestone, and granite is in the National Register of Historic Places, but it is very much alive with people—mingling, shopping, and eating in a bazaar-like atmosphere. The main structure, a three-level Greek-revival-style building, opened on August 26, 1976, 150 years after Mayor Josiah Quincy opened the original market. The South Market Building opened on that date in 1977, and the North Market Building on the same date in 1978.

Try to come early in the day to avoid the crush at the **Central Market Building.** The street level is where the action is, with the Bull Market and the colonnade and glass-canopied sidewalk aisles along either side. Here are the food stalls and market—crafts, craftsmen, and vendors—things to buy and eat. You could treat yourself to a pickup feast from the booths that line the marketplace: pizza at **Regina's II,** lamb in pita bread at **Aegean Fare,** chow mein at **Ming Tree,** shish-kebab at **Aris,** subs at **Jennettes,** kosher franks at the **Brown Derby Deli**—not to mention lobster salad roll at the **Great American Lobster,** shrimp roll at **Salty Dog,** and cherrystone clams at **The Walrus and the Carpenter.** You can even get fried dough at **Anna's Homemade Fried Dough Stand,** among other possibilities. But be warned: finding a place to sit down to eat is as hard as finding a seat on the subway at rush hour. There are benches outdoors and box-like tables and chairs in the rotunda, but sometimes there is no choice but to eat standing or sitting on the floor.

If juggling and balancing plates is not your dish, treat yourself to one of the restaurants. On the top floor, **The Magic Pan** (crêpes) and the **Proud Popover** (stuffed popovers, beef and fish); on the marketplace level, **Marion's** for hearty-type meals and **Cityside** or **Lily's** sidewalk cafe for a light lunch; and in the brick basement, **Lily's Restaurant** for gourmet dinners or **Salty Dog** for seafood. Also try the **Bar at Lily's** and the **Ames Plow Tavern,** a casual pub. Check out the unusual wares on the shopping wagons, too—baskets, prints, crafts, and even supplies for "lefties" such as scissors, notebooks, and tools. And don't forget to buy some flowers at the stalls or in the **Greenhouse.**

Now get your breath and try the **South Market Building** on the other side of the promenade—very elegant with expensive gift stores, high-fashion boutiques, and home-furnishing shops (see our Shopping section) adorning its three levels. There you'll find **Seaside Restaurant** (no view of the sea), the bustling **Cricket's Restaurant** with its glass-canopied "Palm Court," and **Cybele's,** a gourmet oasis of calm among the frenzied dining scene of the market. At night the promenade between the Central and South Buildings glitters with lights illuminating the shops, the planters of flowers, the trees, and the young entertainers who offer music, mime, and juggling.

The **North Market Building** has retail stores, offices, and the famous **Durgin-Park Restaurant,** which has been renovated along with the rest of the building.

Hours at the marketplace are 10 a.m. to 9 p.m., Monday through Saturday, and 1 p.m. to 6 p.m., Sunday, but some restaurants open early for Sunday brunch and remain open until 2 a.m. daily. There are three parking lots nearby, and a much-needed multilevel parking garage is planned for Dock Square. Until that's ready, your best bet is to use the garage near Haymarket Square or take the subway or bus to the State Street, Haymarket, or Government Center "T" station.

Two Walking Trips: To Little Italy and Chinatown

Boston's ethnic neighborhoods are distinct entities working hard to preserve their own cultural identities. Since Boston is such a walkable city, it's worth your while to take a few hours to stroll, browse, and taste (perhaps shop) your way through two of the most colorful enclaves: the North End (Little Italy) and Chinatown. Since the North End backs up to the waterfront, let's start there.

THE NORTH END—LITTLE ITALY: Pushcarts and festivals, old men playing boccie in the "prato," children playing hopscotch on the street, and Italian mamas calling from the windows. That's "Little Italy"—the North End. Here Boston's Italians, packed together in their historic old section, still maintain close family ties and try to keep the "newcomers" out. You see most of the North End when you tour the Freedom Trail (Paul Revere's house and the Old North Church), but there are two other times when you should go there—any weekend, when the pushcarts laden with fruit and vegetables clog the streets, and special weekends in July and August when feasts are held to honor the saints.

Take the subway to Government Center or Haymarket Square for the first stop on your way to the North End, and bring a camera and a shopping bag. This is the historic market area, Faneuil Hall and Quincy Market. On Fridays and Saturdays entire families, young business people, students, all wander along the narrow streets, squeezing vegetables, peering into boxes, comparing prices, haggling for bargains. It's a real multimedia experience—sight, sound, smell, and taste. Buy a sub sandwich or a pizza or hot chestnuts in the winter and, eating as you go, explore the tiny narrow streets that have been there for hundreds of years. Buy some cheese, salami, and Italian bread, and perhaps a bottle of wine, and save money on lunch that day.

Use the pedestrian walk under the expressway to get to the residential and restaurant area of the North End, where you'll also find the churches, the focal points of the feast days. When homage is paid to the Madonna or the saints, the streets are blocked off, and the garland-bedecked statues are paraded through the area. There are floats, flowers, and bands, and still more statues, followed by the pious as they wend their way to one of the churches. The local papers carry the listings of feast days.

Shopping in the North End means shopping for food, so browse through the groceries and little bakeries and buy a few thousand calories: cappuccino or an Italian fruit drink at the **Paradiso,** 296 Hanover Street; cannoli shells filled with ricotta cheese as you watch or marzipan sharks—Jaws I and Jaws II— at **Etnas's Pastry Shop,** 7 Prince Street. In the summer, buy some slush from the slush barrel on the stoop. Or try the **Prince Pastry Shop,** 2-A Prince Street for their macaroons and pastries. Indulge in the fried dough dripping with honey and walnuts at **Modern Pastry Shop,** 257 Hanover Street; or homemade ice cream at **Caffee Pompeii,** 280 Hanover Street. Buy salty French-style Italian bread at **Drago and Sons,** 275 North Street, and marvelous cheese to go with it at **Pace's,** a tiny place at 54 Salem Street. And don't forget the pizzas!

Follow Salem Street to Charter Street to **Copps Hill** from which you have a magnificent view of the harbor and the water-front, including *Old Ironsides* and Bunker Hill on one side; the Aquarium, the piers, and the new office towers on the other. You can walk to the waterfront by following **Commercial Street.** Remember this was once a busy fishing area and if you're lucky, you might get to see some fishing trawlers unloading the day's catch. Just follow the seagulls.

CHINATOWN: Home and shopping center for many of Greater Boston's Chinese families, Chinatown is a tiny, three-block long, 12-block-wide area, bounded by the expressway, the downtown shopping district, and the Tufts University medical complex. It's easy to reach by following Stuart Street to Harrison Avenue and Kneeland Street, through the Garment District, or by taking Boylston Street to Essex and Beach Streets. Or take the Orange line of the "T" to Essex Street. This way, you only briefly cross the "Combat Zone"—the cheap bars, girlie shows, and pickup areas. Perfectly safe in the daytime, but it's best not to go alone at night. (You can drive to Chinatown following this same route, or turning off the Mass. Pike extension and using the parking garages.) You can also use the parking garage at the Tufts–New England Medical Center on Harrison Avenue. When you see the red phone booths with pagoda tops and street signs in Chinese and English, you'll know you're there.

The best place for window shopping is along Beach, Tyler, and Hudson streets, and Harrison Avenue. On Beach Street, there's a poultry store with live chickens in coops, waiting to become dinner for some Chinese family. Go into one of the food stores, examine the exotic wares, perhaps choose some dried fish hanging from the racks or "thousand-year-old eggs" or packaged bird's-nest soup. You may see one of the basements where bean sprouts are grown (they don't always come in cans or packages). You can stop for a snack at **May Lee Ice Cream** on Oxford Street and indulge in an iced lichee or iced lotus-seed drink, some almond paste or grass jelly. They also serve chicken, fish bits, and rice dishes. Or have afternoon tea Chinese style at **Fung Won's,** 8 Tyler Street, daily till 3 p.m. It's called dim sum and consists of assorted Chinese hot hors d'oeuvres. Dim sum is also served at the **70 Restaurant** at 70 Beach Street daily, noon till 3 p.m., at **Bo-Shek,** 63 Beach Street, and **Moon Villa,** 23 Edinboro Street. Treat yourself to a winter melon dumpling with a delicious creamy filling, steamed sponge cake, moon cakes, or a bag of fortune cookies at **Ho Yuen Bakery,** 54 Beach Street, open 8 a.m. to 7:30 p.m. They'll even bake a birthday cake for you! You can check the schedule at the **China Cinema,** 84 Beach Street, for a movie with English subtitles, browse in the gift shops, or relax at one of the many good Chinese restaurants (see Chapter IV for details).

If you're in Boston at the time of the Chinese New Year (January or February, depending on the moon), join the crowds to watch the traditional festivities, as dragons weave up and down the streets to the accompaniment of Chinese music and very loud firecrackers. In August, try to see the Festival of the August Moon, a street fair sponsored by the **Summerthing** program. And don't forget those cameras. Call the Chinese Merchants Association, 20 Hudson Street (tel. 482-3972), for information on special events.

Chinatown Shopping: Chung Wah Hong Co., 55 Beach Street, has imported delicacies including ginger, lichee nuts, preserved plums, and Chinese teas. (How about chrysanthemum tea?) We like the assortment of gifts, toys, chimes, and soup bowls at **Asian Arts Association Importers,** 58 Kneeland Street.

Boston's Gardens

Boston's gardens rate a sightseeing trip of their own. They're not all within walking distance of each other, but with a combination of footwork and public transportation or auto, you can see them all in a long afternoon. (Give yourself time to relax and enjoy them.) The **Boston Public Garden,** adjacent to the Boston Common, is one of the prettiest public flower gardens anywhere, especially in the spring when thousands of tulips and pansies burst into delicate bloom. It's ideal for resting (but only on benches: the grass is becoming fragile), people-watching, or letting the kids (or yourself) have a ride in the famed Swan Boats that move gently along the pond, under the bridge, around the island, and back. Pay the captain 50¢ for yourself, 30¢ for the children.

Not noted for flowers, but for its trees, is the **Boston Common,** whose beautiful shade trees are identified with botanical labels. At the corner of Boylston and Tremont streets is a recently planted ten-foot oak tree, called the Liberty Tree. It is a replacement for the original one which was a rallying place for Revolutionary patriots, and was cut down by the British in 1775. The new one was planted as part of the Bicentennial celebration.

And not too far from Fenway Park, on Park Drive, are the beautiful **Fenway Rose Gardens.** Hundreds of rose varieties are grown in formal plantings in June and July. Take the subway to Kenmore Square to get there.

The most spectacular garden of all awaits you a short distance away: this is the **Arnold Arboretum** on the Jamaica Way, one of America's oldest parks. Opened in 1872 and often called America's greatest garden, it is open daily from sunrise to sunset. A National Historic Landmark, it is administered by Harvard University in cooperation with the Boston Department of Parks and Recreation. You can have a fine time wandering here through some 265 acres containing over 6,000 varieties of ornamental trees, flowers, shrubs, with plants hardy to the Boston area. Spring is heavenly, the air fragrant with dogwood, azaleas, rhododendrons, and hundreds of varieties of lilacs, for which the Arboretum is especially famous. You'll be sorry if you don't bring those cameras. There is no admission charge, and if you'd like information on what's in bloom, call 524-1717.

You can take the MBTA Forest Hills subway to the Forest Hills elevated station; the Forest Hills Gate of the Arboretum is just two blocks west.

And if you'd like to do a little mini-mountain climbing, there's the **Blue Hills Trailside Museum**, Route 138 off 128, Milton, just a short drive south from Boston. Public transportation is also available. There are exhibits of natural history and live native wildlife, plus trails to climb. Open Tuesday through Sunday, 10 to 5, year round. Closed Mondays, except holidays. Admission is 50¢ for adults, 25¢ for children.

Guided Tours

If you prefer guided walking tours to hoofing it on your own, you have your choice of several:

The Freedom Trail Walking Tours literally dresses up the tour with costumed guides playing the roles of characters from revolutionary Boston. You may even have "John Hancock" take you on the 2½-hour tour of the major sites! Sponsored by the Cobblestone Historical Association (tel. 482-2864), the tours leave the Boston Common Information Booth mornings, starting at 9:30, Monday through Saturday. Rates are $3.50, adults; $2.00, children 7 to 13; and free under 7.

Boston By Foot (tel. 367-2345) conducts architectural tours of Beacon Hill and the Government Center area. The guides, or *docents,* have taken a special educational program and are very knowledgeable about the architecture and history of the area. In addition to pointing out the distinguishing characteristics of Boston's architecture, they include history and anecdotes in the

1½-hour, $2 tours, conducted Tuesdays, Thursdays, and Saturdays at 10 a.m. and Sundays at 2 p.m., even in the rain. The Beacon Hill tour starts on the bottom steps of the State House on Beacon Street; and the "Heart of the Hub," which is the Government Center Tour, meets at the rear plaza of 60 State Street, near Faneuil Hall and the *Where's Boston?* exhibit. There are also "Tours of the Month" to Boston neighborhoods. Call for details.

Discovery Tours cover the North End and the financial and waterfront areas, Tuesdays and Thursdays at 10:30 a.m. from April through October. They are sponsored by the Historic Neighborhoods Foundation, 112 Water Street (tel. 523-1860), and cost $2. Tickets and details available at Paperback Booksmith, Quincy Market, or by mail from the Historic Neighborhoods Foundation.

Children have two very special tours of their own. **Make Way for Ducklings,** sponsored by the Historic Neighborhoods Foundation, and based, of course, on the children's classic of that name, goes through the Boston Common, the State House, and Louisburg Square, and ends with a ride on the Swan Boats in the Public Garden. Tours, $2.50, are given only on Wednesday and Friday at 10:30 a.m., reservations necessary; phone 262-1860. **Boston By Little Feet,** for children 6 to 12, is held Sundays at 2 p.m., and meets at 60 State Street near Faneuil Hall. Children are encouraged to see, touch, and talk about the buildings in the Government Center area. $1 per child; accompanying adults, free.

Sightseeing Cruises and Boating

Now, if you've done enough walking and you'd still like to do some more sightseeing, we suggest one of the harbor tours. There are several that you can choose from. If you'd like to muse on Boston's seafaring history aboard a sailing ship, then the thing to do is to take a two-hour cruise on the **Windjammer Spray,** flagship of the Bay State–Spray Cruise Line (tel. 723-7800), 20 Long Wharf (near the Aquarium subway station). The *Windjammer Spray* is a handsome, 55-foot sailboat that cruises through the inner harbor, right by *Old Ironsides,* the Old North Church, Bunker Hill, and the site of the Boston Tea Party. Then it goes on to the outer harbor, all of whose islands are steeped in history, legend—and hearsay. It sails daily at 2 p.m. during

July and August, and the charge is $5 for adults, $4 for children under 12.

Also on Long Wharf, you can take several sightseeing cruises via Bay State motor launch. These are 1½-hour trips with narration, and call at George's Island State Park, where you can stop over if you wish for a picnic (or hop a free water taxi to one of Boston Harbor's small islands for swimming). The weekend schedule is in effect from April through October with sailings at 10 a.m., 12 noon, 2 p.m., and 4:30 p.m. Weekday sailings, May through September, are at 10 a.m., 1 p.m., and 3 p.m. Tickets are $3 for adults, $2 for children. And you can combine lunch with ocean breezes on the 12:15 p.m. to 12:45 p.m. lunch cruise. Use the ship's galley or bring your own food. Tickets for all cruises are on sale at the red-and-white ticket office on Long Wharf opposite the Chart House.

BayState also runs **"Water Music"** cruises: The Dreamboat on Tuesdays at 7:30 p.m. and 9:30 p.m.; The Jazzboat, Wednesdays, 7:30 p.m. and 9:30 p.m.; and the Concert Cruise, Thursdays, 6 p.m. and 7:30 p.m. The Dreamboat and Jazzboat dance sailings are $5.50, and the Concert fee is $3.75 with a $1 discount for senior citizens and children under 12. Tickets are on sale at the wharf 45 minutes prior to the first sailing, at outlets in Boston and Cambridge, or through Concert Charge (tel. 426-8181) which adds a 50¢ service charge. Call Water Music, Inc. (tel. 876-8742), for programs.

Boston Harbor Cruises (tel. 227-4320), on Long Wharf, has 90-minute sightseeing trips hourly from 11 a.m. to 4 p.m., May 15 to September 15; and at 1 p.m. and 3 p.m., September 16 to October 30. In addition, there are sunset cruises every evening from June to Labor Day, 7 p.m. to 9 p.m., and a Disco Cruise every Wednesday and Thursday at 10 p.m. Fares are $3 for adults; $2, children; $2.50, senior citizens and students with IDs, except for the Disco Cruise, which is $5.

At Rowes Wharf, farther along Atlantic Avenue, the **Massachusetts Bay Lines** (tel. 542-8000) has daily sailings to George's Island, which go through to Nantasket Beach. Boats leave at 10 a.m., 1 p.m., 4 p.m., and 5:30 p.m. Round-trip fares (1½ hours each way) are $5.75 for adults and $3.75 for children (they'll love the Paragon Park amusement area). Tickets for George's Island only are $3 round trip for adults and $2 for children. Sailings are from June 24 through Labor Day, and on Monday (except for holidays) special family rates are in effect. The "Booze Crooze" with rock music and dancing sails Wednesday and Thursday from 8:30 p.m. to 11 p.m., $3.50, and twice on Friday—8:30 p.m. to 11 p.m. and 11:30 p.m. to 2 a.m., $4.50.

And at 5:30 on weekdays, try the Commuter Boat to Hingham, $3 round trip. You have the ship practically to yourself on the return trip.

You can cruise to Gloucester for the day from the Northern Avenue Pier, near Pier 4 restaurant. Leave Boston daily at 9:15 a.m.; leave Gloucester at 3 p.m. Round trip, $10 adults; under 12 and senior citizens, $4. Call 426-8419 for further details.

And for almost a full day at sea, there's the **M.V. Provincetown,** which sails from Long Wharf daily in late June, July, and August, and on weekends in early June and September. It's anchors aweigh at 9:30 a.m. for the three-hour trip to Cape Cod's picturesque Provincetown. The sail home starts at 3:15, giving you a few hours for shopping and sightseeing. It's $12 for the round trip for adults; $8, for children; $2, bikes. Special rates for senior citizens, Monday through Friday.

If you'd prefer a river cruise, **Charles River Cruises** (tel. 846-5577) has narrated one-hour rides from the Hatch Memorial Shell on the Esplanade and the Museum of Science. Boats leave from the Hatch Shell hourly from noon to 5 p.m. and from the museum hourly from 11:45 a.m. Tickets are $2 for adults and $1.50 for children and senior citizens.

On a Slow Barge

A horse-drawn boat? That's what we found on the Old Middlesex Canal in Woburn. On Sunday and holiday afternoons from June to Labor Day, you can cruise along the river in a replica of the 1803 packet boat *The Colonel Baldwin,* that ran from Boston to Lowell. You relax while horses on either side of the narrow canal slowly pull the boat up the river and back. *The Colonel Baldwin* runs from 1 p.m. to 4 p.m. Donations are requested. Call 935-2562 for directions on reaching the canal, near the junction of Routes 128 and 38.

And don't forget the most traditional ride of all in Boston, the **Swan Boats** in the Public Garden. A Boston institution for 101 years, the Swan Boats run daily through spring and summer (except for very windy or rainy days) from 10 a.m. to 6 p.m., and from noon to 4 p.m. after Labor Day. Season ends the last Sunday of September. Fare is 50¢ for adults and 30¢ for children under 12. Telephone 323-2700 for springtime opening date.

Time for a Swim

If you're ready now for a swim, you can take about an hour's drive south on Route 3 to **Nantasket Beach,** a large, well-equipped public beach in Hull. Paragon Park, an amusement park, will keep the kids happy. You can also take a boat to Nantasket (see Sightseeing Cruises). Or you can go farther south to Duxbury near Plymouth for a clean, quiet, nine-mile beach with dunes. The beach is located off Routes 3A and 139. Public parking is at the north end. Going north from Boston, try **Revere Beach,** once Boston's equivalent of Coney Island. But now many of the amusements are closed as plans are being made for apartment buildings on the waterfront. But there are still hot-dog and pizza and frozen custard stands, and an expanse of sandy beach with a gentle surf. Parking along the beach is free. Or take the MBTA to Revere Beach or Wonderland stations, 25¢ and 20 minutes from Boston. If you have a car, drive up to the end of the beach, near Point of Pines and the General Edwards Bridge, for less crowded swimming. Even more spacious, with clear, cold water for swimming is Nahant Beach, about three miles north. (We should warn you that the temperature of the water at North Shore beaches is apt to be quite low; they're not as cold as the beaches of Maine, but not as warm as those on the South Shore and Cape Cod.) If you're going to Nahant, get there early in the morning, especially on the weekends, since parking is just 50¢ and spaces fill up fast.

To the North Shore: If you're still in a summertime, beachy mood, you could continue driving north, on a one-day trip, to **Salem,** the original Witch City, where you can explore old houses and some outstanding museums, swim at **Salem Willows** and take a boat ride, or visit **Pioneer Village;** to historic **Marblehead,** home of the American navy and now host to the chic yachting set, a great place to walk around, with its quaint streets, vintage houses, and fun shops; on to **Gloucester,** home of the fishing fleet; and to the picturesque artists' colony at **Rockport.** But for the very best swimming on the North Shore, you should drive farther (a little over an hour from the city) to Ipswich, to beautiful **Crane's Beach,** with its picturesque dunes, miles of white sand, and crisp, cold water. Admission is $2.50 during the week, $4.50 on weekends, but it's worth it, since many of the other North Shore beaches are for residents only. The drive, incidentally, will take you through what we call "John P. Marquand country," those elegant little villages where the Boston Brahmins have long escaped the summer heat.

If the parking lot at Crane's is full, try some of the other North Shore beaches. There are two fine places in Gloucester. **Wingaersheek Beach,** which is off Route 128 (exit 13), has beautiful white sand, a fantastic view, and sand dunes for climbing or hiding behind to seek privacy. It's open through Labor Day and there's a charge of $4 weekends, $3 weekdays, for parking. **Stage Fort Park,** Route 128 (exit 13) is at Gloucester Harbor and has 100 acres of oceanfront with sheltered beaches, playgrounds, picnic and cookout areas, and an old fort site for the kids to explore. And if you'd like a stretch of several beach areas with magnificent dunes and a strong surf (surf fishing is allowed), follow Route 1A to Newburyport and **Plum Island,** which is part of the **Parker River Wildlife Refuge** with nature trails, observations towers, and wildlife. No admission or parking charge, but the small lots fill up early—sometimes cars are turned away at 9 a.m.

Just a word of warning: Wingaersheek, Plum Island, and Crane's beaches are hosts to Greenhead flies as well as swimmers for a few weeks in late July and early August. Bring insect repellent with you. The beaches have lifeguard services and bathhouses.

Other fine area beaches include **Salisbury Beach,** Route 1A, south of the New Hampshire border, which has spectacular surf; and **Good Harbor Beach,** Gloucester, also with a fine surf, on Thatcher Road off Route 127A.

Boston's Extraordinary Museums

The museums of Boston are among the finest in the country, and they offer a variety of choices for you to visit; museums devoted to art, science, transportation, plant, sea, and animal life, are all within easy access of each other. Here's a rundown of what they offer to help you arrange your sightseeing.

Whether or not you're a serious student of art, you should pay a visit to two of the loveliest museums in the country, which both happen to be in Boston: the Boston Museum of Fine Arts and the Isabella Stewart Gardner Museum.

MUSEUM OF FINE ARTS: Like the Metropolitan Museum of Art in New York (to which it ranks second among all the great museums of the country), the Museum of Fine Arts, 465 Huntington Avenue, is enormously popular among the local citizenry, usually drawing long-line crowds for its special exhibits. But even without anything special going on there is enough here, in the almost 200 galleries, to hold your attention for days—or at least many hours. The century-old museum is especially noted for its Egyptian and Asian, as well as European collections, but our particular favorites here are the Americans—Whistler, John Singer Sargent, Childe Hassam, with so many superb portraits and paintings that recall the young days of the colony and the country and the lovely days of Old Boston.

Pick up a floorplan at the **Information Desk** before you begin and decide what you want to see: perhaps the new and exciting Contemporary Gallery; the many splendid rooms of period furniture; the portraits of the founding fathers; the Zen garden of sand and rock leading to the Oriental collection, with its full-size Japanese temples and Chinese house compound dating back to early Sung Dynasty days; the world-renowned Egyptian tapestries, murals, tablets filled with hieroglyphics; the 9th-century Catalonian chapel, with organ music playing softly in the background. This only begins to suggest the wonders of the collection.

The museum is open Wednesday through Sunday from 10 a.m. to 5 p.m., and on Tuesday from 10 a.m. to 9 p.m. It is closed on Monday and holidays. Admission is $1.75, but there is a special Sunday rate of $1.25. Senior citizens go free on Fridays, Tuesday evenings from 5 p.m. to 9 p.m. are free for everyone, and children under 16 are free at all times. To reach the museum from downtown, take the Green line, Huntington Avenue trolley.

ISABELLA STEWART GARDNER MUSEUM: Stepping into the Isabella Stewart Gardner Museum, at 280 The Fenway, is akin to walking back into the past, into a Venetian *palazzo* of a century ago, right into the middle of a Henry James novel. Mrs. Gardner, the wife of a wealthy Bostonian, lived in this house for 22 years and had it constructed to fit her fondest dreams; much of the art collection within was chosen with the help of her friend, Bernard Berenson. Pièce de résistance of the place is a breathtaking courtyard filled year round with fresh flowers (lilies at Easter; chrysanthemums in the fall; poinsettias at Christmas) and covered by a skylight. Spotted all about, on every floor, are the treasures that Isabella Gardner chose to live with: Whistlers and Sargents, Matisses and Titians; Italian religious masterpieces (including Raphael's *Pieta*); stained-glass windows; exquisite antique furniture. Try to get here for one of the concerts given in the magnificent Tapestry Room, with its heavy-beamed ceiling, superbly tiled floor, and priceless tapestries. They're given at 4 p.m., Sundays and Thursdays, and at 8 p.m. on Tuesdays (except July and August). The Tuesday and Thursday concerts are free.

Hours are 1 to 9:30 p.m. on Tuesdays, and 1 to 5:30 p.m., Wednesday through Sunday. (Closed on Mondays and national holidays.) There is a voluntary admission fee of $1. For information on exhibits and programs, call 734-1359.

INSTITUTE OF CONTEMPORARY ART: We don't know if it was the fear of art thefts or another reason, but the Institute of Contemporary Art (tel. 266-5151) has moved into an abandoned police station at 955 Boylston Street, opposite the Prudential Center. The emphasis is on "art as contemporary as today." Gallery displays include exhibitions of local, national, and international contemporary art and photography. Admission is $1 for adults; 50¢, senior citizens, students, and children under 12. Hours are 10 a.m. to 5 p.m., Tuesday through Saturday, with an extension till 9 p.m. on Wednesday; noon to 5 p.m. on Sunday. Closed Monday. And while you're there, treat yourself to lunch or dinner at the **Hermitage Restaurant** on the lower level of the museum.

NEW ENGLAND AQUARIUM: One of the busiest museums in Boston is the New England Aquarium at Central Wharf (tel. 742-8870). Take the MBTA Blue line to the stop marked Aquarium, then the long escalator to the street, and you've arrived. And remember—aquariums aren't just for kids! This one will fascinate the whole family. Buy the guidebook, have a look at it, and at the ground-floor display, and then work your way up on the ramp alongside the glass four-story 200,000-gallon Giant Ocean Tank (the largest of its kind in the world) that holds the Aquarium's collection. At many times of the day you can see the scuba divers feeding the animals in the tank. You can see an electric eel, an octopus that changes color from white to bright red, a catfish, and even a variety of living sharks. The jackass penguins are fascinating, and so are the giant sea turtles. And a new 1,000-seat floating amphitheater, **Discovery,** has just been added with a dolphin and sea lion show. There are free movies in the Aquarium every morning, afternoon, and Friday evening. Just about the prettiest part of the Aquarium is the

Harbor Room, where you'll find yourself looking down on the water over the harbor—especially nice as the sun starts to set. Hours are 9 to 5, Monday through Thursday; 9 to 9 on Friday; and 9 to 6, Saturday, Sunday, and holidays. Admission is $3.50, adults; $2, children 5 through 15; under 5, free. Senior citizens, servicemen, students with ID cards, $2.50. If you're driving, find your way to Atlantic Avenue (under the expressway), and park in the large garage in the Harbor Towers near the Aquarium.

And if you've worked up an appetite climbing the ramps, some of the finest restaurants in Boston are nearby. *Note:* Construction is now under way for a public plaza with cascading waterfalls, reflecting pools, and a sculpture of eight bronze dolphins for the area fronting the Aquarium.

MUSEUM OF SCIENCE AND HAYDEN PLANETARIUM: The Museum of Science and Hayden Planetarium at Science Park (tel. 742-6088) have a little something for everyone. Little children, teenagers, adults—everyone seems to be fascinated by the exciting, look-and-touch place full of exhibits that engage the visitor personally. This is a look *and* touch museum. You can, for example, pat a reptile, confront a live owl or porcupine eyeball to eyeball, play tic-tac-toe with a computer (which usually wins), weigh yourself on a scale—in moon measurements—or climb into a space module. The West Wing exhibits run the gamut of the ages, from a life-size replica of Tyrannosaurus Rex to a full-scale model of the Apollo 11 lunar module, set on a simulated moon surface. And while your head is still above the clouds, visit the adjoining Hayden Planetarium for a lesson in astronomy. Shows are usually scheduled twice daily, but extra performances are sometimes added to accommodate visitors. The present hours are: Tuesday to Saturday, 11 a.m. and 3 p.m., with an extra performance at 8 p.m. on Friday; Monday, 11 a.m., except July and August when the showing is at 3 p.m.; and Sunday, noon and 3 p.m. Since the capacity of the Planetarium is limited, we suggest you buy your show tickets (50¢) when you enter the museum, even if it's quite some time before the performance. That way you'll be sure to get a seat.

The glass-enclosed skyline restaurant with its view of the Charles River and the Boston skyline is open for lunch from 11 a.m. to 2 p.m. and Friday night for dinner. You can also eat at Friendly's in the museum from 10 a.m. to 4:30 p.m. Museum hours are 9 a.m. to 4 p.m., Monday through Thursday; Friday, till 10 p.m.; Saturday, till 5 p.m. Sunday, 10 a.m. to 5 p.m.; and it is closed on Thanksgiving, Christmas, and New Year's Day. Admission is $3 for adults; $2 for senior citizens and children 5 to 16. Kids under 5 are free; and college students with ID cards, $2. Friday after 5 p.m. admission is $1 for all ages. You can walk to the Science Museum from North Station or the MBTA Science Park station if you go by subway; take the Green line from Park Street in the direction marked Lechmere. If you drive, the museum has its own parking garage. Hours and fees may change, so call before your visit.

MAPPARIUM: You can zoom out of the world at the Planetarium, but if you want a chance to walk right *inside* the world and view it from a new perspective, then take the family to the Mapparium (tel. 262-2300), inside the Christian Science Publishing Society at the corner of Massachusetts Avenue and Clearway Street. You'll find yourself in an enormous room the exact shape of a globe, illuminated from the outside and explored via a bridgeway, under, above, and around which are various parts of the globe. Esthetically, it's a delightful experience; the colors are done in the style of old European stained glass, and the acoustics have a distinct quality, since the hard surface of the room does not absorb sound and one's voice bounces off. Various characteristics of the world are pointed out; where the International Dateline falls, which are the deep-water parts of the ocean—and does one of them hide the lost continent of Atlantis? Meridians mark the time zones, so you can check the relative time in any section of the world.

Three tours are given: the Mapparium, the newsroom and printing plant, and the church. From April to October, the Mapparium tour (ten minutes) is given Monday through Friday, 8 a.m. to 4 p.m.; Saturday and holidays, 9 a.m. to 4 p.m.; and Sunday, noon to 4:45 p.m. From November through March, tours are 8 a.m. to 4:15 p.m., Monday through Friday; 9 a.m. to 4 p.m., Saturday and holidays; and noon to 3 p.m., Sunday. The Publishing Society tour (45 minutes) is at 9:30 a.m., 11 a.m., 1:30 p.m., and 3 p.m., Monday through Friday, throughout the year. Admission is free, and it's near the MBTA's Prudential and Symphony stations.

CHILDREN'S MUSEUM: The Children's Museum, Congress Street, near the Boston Tea Party Ship, isn't just for children.

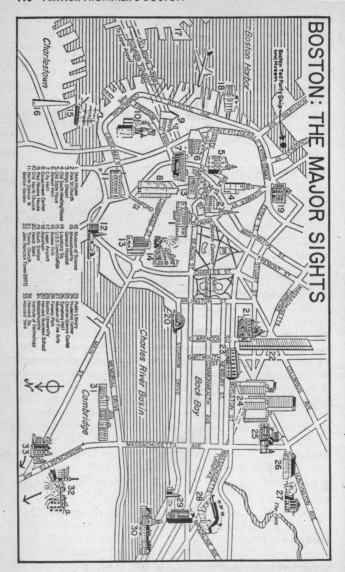

BOSTON: THE MAJOR SIGHTS

1. State House
2. Park Street Church
3. Kings Chapel
4. Old South Meeting House
5. Faneuil Hall
6. City Hall
7. Paul Revere House
8. Old North Church
9. North Station &
   Boston Garden
10. Old Ironsides
11. Bunker Hill

12. Museum of Science
13. Government Center
14. General Hospital
15. Lovejoy Sq.
16. U.S.S. Constitution
17. Logan Airport
18. Logan Airport
19. South Station
20. Hatch Shell
21. Trinity Church
22. John Hancock Tower (1971)

23. Public Library
24. Copley Square
25. Christian Science Center
26. Symphony Hall
27. Colleges of the Arts
28. Fenway Park
29. Boston University
30. Harvard Business School
31. Massachusetts
    Institute of Technology
33. Harvard Yard

Take our word for it, adults have just as much fun as the kids do in this fun place where the signs say "Touch." It is set up so that kids can be on their own in a two-hour, unstructured experience, wandering randomly from one participative exhibit to another. Kids keep busy, for example, making spinning tops on a real production line; trying on old costumes from the trunks in Grandmother's House; playing games on computer terminals; exploring the subway tunnel beneath a city street; and making their own movies on a Zoetrope machine.

Museum Wharf on Congress Street, the new home of the Children's Museum (as of July 1, 1979), has an unmistakable landmark—a 40-foot wooden milk bottle that sits outside the building in a waterfront park. To reach it, take the Red line to South Station and walk one block toward the waterfront on Atlantic Avenue, then turn right on Congress Street. By car: from the north take the expressway south to the High Street–Congress Street exit; from the south, take the expressway north to the Atlantic Avenue exit, right on Northern Avenue, then right on Sleeper Street.

Admission is $3 for adults, $2 for children (3 to 15) and senior citizens. For a listing of hours and special activities, call 426-6500.

MUSEUM OF TRANSPORTATION: Also at Museum Wharf is the **Museum of Transportation**, a hands-on activity center, where you can ride a trolley, harness a horse, climb in a fire engine, or visit a railroad depot. For more passive activities, view the slide tape shows about transit history. Admission: adults, $2.25; children 6 to 15 and students with IDs, $1.50; tots, 50¢; senior citizens, $1. For movie buffs, the museum also shows old-time silent films, featuring Laurel and Hardy and others on weekends. Free with admission. For hours and programs call 426-6500.

ZOO: Did you ever feel a lion's whiskers? Try it at **Franklin Park Children's Zoo**, Dorchester (tel. 442-2002), another center that encourages visitors to use their five senses to explore. Don't worry about the lion's appetite. Although the whiskers are real, the owner is a paper lion in a "touchy-feely" box. The Children's Zoo is open from 10 a.m. to 4 p.m. daily (except during the winter months), and admission is $1 for adults and 50¢ for children.

And while at **Franklin Park,** take time to visit Bird's World in the main zoo (no admission charge here), which features a free-flight cage, waterfowl pond, and flamingo pond outdoors; and dioramas of a swamp, rain forest and desert in the indoor Chinese-style birdhouse. To reach Franklin Park, which is part of Frederick Law Olmsted's famed "Emerald Necklace," the green strip in and beyond Boston, take the Red line of the MBTA to Andrew Station. For more information on the zoo, write to the Boston Zoological Society, Franklin Park, Boston, MA 02121.

MUSEUM OF AFRO-AMERICAN HISTORY: Located in the African Meeting House, 8 Smith Court on Beacon Hill (tel. 723-8863), the museum features exhibits of the black experience in New England, including gallery talks, films, workshops, and family history. Open Tuesday to Friday, 11 a.m. to 5 p.m.; Sunday, 1 to 5 p.m. Admission is free. The museum is also the starting point for the Black Heritage Trail.

THE MUSEUM OF THE AMERICAN CHINA TRADE: In the early 19th century many Yankee fortunes were made in the American China trade, and the captains of the clipper ships that sailed this route brought home porcelains, textiles, and many beautiful wares. The Museum of the American China Trade, 215 Adams Street, Milton (tel. 696-1815), has an excellent collection of the furnishings, paintings, fancy goods, and portraiture of that period. And if you're interested in doing research, the museum has 75,000 documents, original and microfilmed, available. *Note to needlepointers:* The museum gift shop has handpainted needlepoint patterns copied from plates, porcelains, robes, and shawls. Open Tuesday through Saturday, 2 p.m. to 5 p.m. Admission, $3 adults; $1.50, children.

KENNEDY BIRTHPLACE IN BROOKLINE: Ever since John F. Kennedy's assassination, the suburb of Brookline, where the president was born, has become an important sightseeing stop. Brookline is a graceful town, one of the prettiest in the Boston area, and the short subway ride from downtown will reward you with another sightseeing attraction as well. Top of the list is the house at 83 Beals Street, Brookline (tel. 566-7937), where JFK lived as a child. (Take the Green line to Coolidge Corner at Beacon Street to get there.) It is now a National Historic Site, restored to the way it was during John's childhood and calculated to provoke nostalgia in anyone who grew up in the '20s and '30s. A tape-recorded voice of Rose Kennedy tells the story. Open daily from 9 a.m. to 4:30 p.m. Admission is 50¢. Children under 16, free.

Another influential New Englander was Mary Baker Eddy, the founder of Christian Science, whose name is preserved at the **Mary Baker Eddy Museum** (The Longyear Historical Society), 120 Seaver Street, Brookline, overlooking the Reservoir and Route 9. Portraits, manuscripts, and other memorabilia are on display at the Foundation, which is atop one of the highest hills in Brookline. For hours and fees, call 277-4893.

ART GALLERIES: The big museums are the beginning—but by no means the end—of the lively Boston art scene. There are exhibits all over Boston town: **Boston City Hall, Boston Public Library, Prudential Center,** and many of the colleges and universities. **The Boston Center for the Arts** always has lots to view. A complex of eight old buildings adjoining the Cyclorama building at 539 Tremont Street, the center is home to 60 artists and 25 arts groups who use the building for studios, exhibits, and performances. The Mills Gallery is a good place to discover new artists. Call 426-5000 for a schedule of events.

There are also clusters of little galleries along Newbury, Boylston, and Charles streets—really too many to be discussed individually. So, we suggest that you browse along these streets and enjoy the many different schools of art and sculpture you find there. The Newbury Street art galleries have put out a map which includes a brief description of each gallery. You can get a copy at most of the shops on the street. Just for a bit of a guide here and now, we're listing some galleries according to the type of work they feature. For fine prints by important 20th-century artists, visit **Graphics 1 and Graphics 2,** 168 Newbury Street; for contemporary painting, sculpture, and master graphics, **Kanegis,** 244 Newbury Street; for 18th-, 19th-, and 20th-century painting, the **Vose Galleries,** 238 Newbury Street; **Pùcker-Safrai,** 171 Newbury St., features works by leading Israeli artists, also works by Chagall and Picasso, and Eskimo and African sculpture. Paintings of Boston and sculpture are at **Judi Rotenberg Gallery,** 130 Newbury Street; archaeological and ethnic art at **Origins,** 134 Newbury Street.

Doll and Richards, the oldest gallery in America, is at 177

Newbury Street, and shows realistic art of America from the 20th century. And the oldest nonprofit craft organization-gallery in the United States, the **Society of Arts and Crafts,** is also on Newbury Street at 175. Call 266-1810 for exhibit information. The **Thomas Segal Gallery,** 73 Newbury Street, is among the newest in town and is much like the chic New York galleries. Segal has original works by contemporary artists. The **Harcus-Krakow Gallery** exhibits a variety of contemporary and modernist work at 7 Newbury Street, and **Sunne Savage,** 105 Newbury Street, features local artists and sculptors. **Nielsen Gallery,** 179 Newbury Street, shows both contemporary and historical paintings.

Rolly-Michaux, 290 Darthmouth Street in the former Hotel Vendome (just around the corner from Newbury Street), is well known for French Impressionist and Post-Impressionist collections. American and European contemporaries are also represented. At 77 North Washington Street, the **Boston Visual Arts Union** is an organization by artists for artists. A wide variety of visual art forms are included in their monthly exhibits—paintings, sculpture, prints, film, and photographs. Call 566-4791 for a schedule of gallery shows. **Stone Soup,** 313 Cambridge Street at the Charles Street Circle, gives new artists an opportunity to display their works, and in addition features readings by obscure and known poets.

Sporting Activities

Boston is very much a sports-happy town. And with four major-league teams, three of them championship winners, there's usually something to be happy about. Consider that the hockey wizards, the Boston **Bruins,** have brought home Stanley Cups; the **Celtics** boast a long string of basketball world championships; the **Red Sox** won the pennant twice in an "impossible dream"; and the **New England Patriots** keep the adrenalin high as they aim for football's top place. Fenway Park is baseball headquarters, and the Boston Garden switches from basketball court to ice rink from December to April. The Patriots reign at Schaefer Stadium in Foxboro.

And soccer has now become big time in Boston with the **Tea Men** playing at Boston University's Nickerson field on Commonwealth Avenue in Boston. The **Longwood Cricket Club,** also in Chestnut Hill, Brookline, has been host to championship tennis matches for many years; but now Boston has its own professional tennis team, **The Boston Lobsters**, which play their sets at the Walter Brown Arena, 289 Babcock Street, Brookline.

To the north in Marblehead, one of the world's leading yachting centers, **Race Week** attracts thousands each July. And if you've always wanted to watch a polo match or a fox hunt, call the **Myopia Hunt Club** in Hamilton for schedules (tel. 1/468-4433). For horseracing, the crowds head for **Suffolk Downs** in East Boston, and to **Foxboro** for harness racing. The greyhounds run at **Wonderland**, Revere, from May to September, and in the late summer and fall in **Taunton.**

If you prefer doing your own thing to watching, the Metropolitan District Commission runs swimming pools in the summer and ice skating rinks in winter. Check our section on visitor information for details. And without driving to the slopes in New Hampshire or Vermont, you can even ski at the **Blue Hill Reservation,** Route 138, Milton.

The Sights of Cambridge

You can't be in Boston for long without hearing about Cambridge, which bears about the same relationship to Boston as Berkeley does to San Francisco. It's just a short subway ride from the Park Street station of the MBTA across the Charles River, and every visitor should see it.

Cambridge is probably America's most famous college town, dominated by **Harvard University** (the country's oldest college, founded in 1636) and the prestigious Massachusetts Institute of Technology (called either M.I.T. or "Tech" by the locals), one of the leading centers for science and mathematics in the world. Both universities have scads of resident geniuses on their faculties, plenty of boys and girls from the best families (Harvard is where the Ivy League begins), and slews of abnormally bright scholarship students crowding their campuses. Many students from smaller schools and a sometimes rather large population of "street people" hang around **Harvard Square.** This is where the subway lets you off and, to us, it is one of the most stimulating places in the entire Boston area.

Your first stop here should be at the Harvard Information Center at **Holyoke Center,** across from the subway at the corner of Dunster Street and Massachusetts Avenue, where you can pick up a brochure on Cambridge's **Heritage Trail** (not to be outdone by Boston's Freedom Trail, Cambridge has its own walking tour of Harvard Yard, Radcliffe, the museums, historic homes and churches, and Cambridge Common, where George Washington took command of the Continental Army, and where the young now gather for concerts, festivals, and political demonstrations). There are also pamphlets describing Cambridge in French, German, Spanish, and Portuguese.

Do a little exploring of Harvard Square first. Here you can buy a newspaper from anywhere in the world, shop at the big **Harvard Coop** (rhymes with soup), wander through Brattle Street, with its great little bookstores and boutiques, perhaps have tea at the charming Blacksmith House near the spot where Longfellow's Village Smithy once stood. Stop in at No. 105 to inspect the **Longfellow House**, where books and furniture have remained unchanged since the poet died there in 1882. (Open daily, 9 a.m. to 4:30 p.m., except Christmas, Thanksgiving, and New Year's Day.) Admission is 50¢ for adults, children, free. No charge for senior citizens over 62. (The house was also General George Washington's headquarters, 1775 to 1776.)

On adjoining Mount Auburn Street, you might look in at the old cemetery where Longfellow, Oliver Wendell Holmes, and Mary Baker Eddy are buried. And opposite Harvard Common, north of the square, is the 18th-century **Christ Episcopal Church**, used as a barracks during the American Revolution.

You will, of course, want to explore **Harvard Yard**, which you can do by wandering about on your own, or by taking a free guided tour. Back at the Holyoke Center (tel. 495-1573), enthusiastic student volunteers conduct tours weekdays at 10 a.m., 11:15 a.m., 2 p.m., and 3:15 p.m.; Sundays, at 1:30 p.m. and 3 p.m. The 35-minute tour, highly informative, is usually tailored to the interests of whomever is taking it. Some of the highlights include the ultra-space-age **Carpenter Center**, designed by Le Corbusier, which manages to be both circular and square at the same time; **Memorial Hall**, with its breathtaking stained-glass windows and vast ceilings; the eight residential houses for undergraduates, styled in Georgian tradition with domes and bell; the imposing **Widener Library** with its 2½ million books (second in size only to the Library of Congress), built by Mrs. Widener in memory of her son who went down on the *Titanic.* You may also get to see Yamasaki's **William James Center for the Behavioral Sciences**; handsome **Lamont Library**, where you can listen to records on private earphones; the beautiful, modern **Loeb Drama Center**, or the **Gutman Library**, at the School of Education, which has won many architectural awards.

Harvard boasts several important museums, which richly reward the visitor. The **Fogg Art Museum**, 32 Quincy Street, free (contributions accepted), open Monday through Friday, 9 a.m. to 5 p.m.; Saturday, 10 a.m. to 5 p.m.; and Sunday, 2 p.m. to 5 p.m. (closed weekends, July 1 to Labor Day), is known for its collections of Oriental art, late medieval Italian painting, and French painting and drawings from the 18th century through the Impressionists. The drawing and print collections are open by appointment.

The **Harvard University Museum**, 24 Oxford Street, is actually four museums in one building: the Peabody Museum, the Museum of Comparative Zoology ("Agassiz Museum"), the Botanical Museum, and the Mineralogical and Geological Museum. A fee of $1, 50¢ for children 5 to 15, covers admission to all the buildings. There are no charges on Fridays. The **Peabody Museum** (enter at 11 Divinity Avenue) concentrates on archaeology and the art of the Mayas.

Most unusual of the museums in this complex is the **Botanical Museum**, Oxford Street, but you don't have to be a botanist to appreciate it. The highlight here is the stunning **Ware Collection** of glass flowers, the most unusual—and durable—flower garden in the world. At first glance, it's almost impossible to tell that the flowers and plants are not real; even when you *know* they're not, you still want to bend over and sniff the perfume. The flowers are considered the finest example of decorative glasswork ever done, the masterpieces of two German brothers, Leopold and Rudolf Blaschka, whom Harvard hired to work at their home near Dresden, Germany, from 1887 through 1936. Since Rudolf's death in 1939 no one has been able to duplicate the artistry of the Braschkas, who "combined the mind of naturalists and the skill of artists in glass." The museums are open 9 a.m. to 4:30 p.m., Monday through Saturday; 1 p.m. to 4:30 p.m., Sunday. Closed New Year's Day, July 4, Thanksgiving, and Christmas.

Harvard's **Busch-Reisinger Museum**, 29 Kirkland Street, has a major collection of Central European art, from the Middle Ages to the present. A delightful bonus is a small courtyard garden where you may enjoy lunch or a snack. Bring your own or buy food at the nearby canteen. The garden is open 9 to 4:30. The museum is open Monday through Saturday from 9 a.m. to 4:45 p.m., and closed Sundays, holidays, and Saturdays during the summer. Admission free. From September through May, there are free Thursday noon concerts in the Romanesque Hall.

If you'd like to visit the **M.I.T.** campus on the Cambridge side

of the Charles River, facing Boston, you're also perfectly welcome to wander around on your own. Ask for the "Walk Around
MIT" map-brochure at the Information Center, 77 Massachusetts Avenue, Cambridge (tel. 253-4795), which describes the
environmental sculpture collection and outstanding architecture. And, if you have time, take one of the student-guided tours
of the campus (85 minutes long, at 10 a.m. and 2 p.m.). You'll
see the two Saarinen buildings on the Kresge Plaza, the Nautical
Museum, Hayden Library, and several new buildings designed
by I. M. Pei. Stop to look at the exhibits of contemporary art,
graphics, and photography in the Hayden Gallery, open free to
the public on weekdays from 9 a.m. to 4 p.m. Since the total
enrollment at M.I.T. is about 8,500, almost evenly divided between undergraduate and graduate students, there is always
something interesting going on—art and photography shows,
musical and theatrical productions, and varied exhibits to which
the public is invited.

Harvard and the Harvard Museums are reached by taking the
MBTA Red line subway at Park Street and riding to the end of
the line. Take the same line to M.I.T., but get off at Kendall
station. If you're driving, just cross the Longfellow Bridge at
Massachusetts Avenue and you're at M.I.T. on Memorial Drive.
Continue along the drive to your left for the scenic approach to
Harvard, or drive straight ahead from the bridge through the
traffic of Massachusetts Avenue for the stores-restaurants-the-
ater approach.

As you wander about Cambridge, you'll note that dotted here
and there throughout the city are houses with black bands on
their chimneys. The band indicated the home of a British sympa-
thizer during Colonial days: a Tory. So many of them, in fact,
once lived on Brattle Street that it came to be known as Tory
Row. You'll note, too, that many of the houses in this area are
just 2½ stories high, since taxes were once levied according to
the number of floor—and fractions weren't counted.

But Harvard Square isn't all there is to Cambridge. There's
much more to this city of 100,000 than the universities. It is a
"Model Cities" community with many small "communities" of
people melded together by a common interest—feminism, civil
liberties, a religious cult, or a political group. If you have time,
go beyond Harvard Square to Inman Square, Central Square, or
North Cambridge, and explore the rest of the city.

Some Useful Phone Numbers

Time: dial NER-VOUS (637-8687)
Weather: WE 6-1212
Dow Jones Averages: 523-6606
Audubon Society: 1-259-8805
Artsline (citywide cultural activities and programs): 261-1660
Museum of Fine Arts: 267-9377
Boston Police: 338-1212
State Police: 566-4500
Boston Fire Department: 232-4646
Emergency Physicians Service: 482-5252
Poison Information Center: 232-2120
Boston Evening Clinic (medical care): 267-7171
Massachusetts Lawyers Guide: 661-8898
Fenway Park (Red Sox): 267-2525
Boston Garden (for Bruins and Braves hockey and Celtics basket-ball information): 237-3200
Traveler's Aid Society: 542-7286
Medical Hot Line at Beth Israel Hospital: 735-3300
Hotline for Handicapped: 1-800/392-6077
National Park Service: 242-1913

Public gardens and swan boat

Chapter VI

SHOPPING IN BOSTON

THE QUALITY OF Boston shopping can be summed up in just one word: great. For when you shop in this town, you're benefiting from two of the secrets of Boston's success: its very chic, very contemporary sophistication, and its centuries-old heritage of shrewd Yankee trading. As a result, Boston has some of the finest specialty and department stores, some of the most imaginative boutiques, and—in particular—some of the sweetest bargains to found anywhere. The only problem, for serious shoppers, is that once you've surveyed the situation and started digging in, you may never have time to get back to—the Old North Church.

There are, roughly, four major shopping areas in Boston, and others close by. The first is the big **downtown area along Washington and Summer streets,** where the major department stores and bargain emporiums are; the second is the bevy of boutiques, art galleries, and Boston-sized branches of New York specialty shops along **Newbury and Boylston streets** and near the **Prudential Center;** the third is the **Charles Street** neighborhood at the foot of Beacon Hill, Boston's Greenwich Village, with its antique stores, arts-and-crafts shops, and the like. And fourth, the **Quincy Market,** where you can find everything—from status boutiques to pushcarts.

A ten-minute subway ride to Cambridge takes you to a glamorous, boutique-filled shopping world in and around Harvard Square. And, if you're driving north to visit historic Salem and Marblehead and Gloucester, or to swim at Nahant Beach or Crane's Beach, you can conveniently detour at several remarkable discount and bargain establishments for women's clothing and a variety of fascinating items.

Note: Massachusetts has no sales tax on clothing and food. All other items are taxed at 5%. Restaurant meals and food prepared for takeout are also taxed at 5%.

And so—to work. Let's begin at the place where society matrons and secretaries and local housewives meet and compete for the most remarkable bargains in town—at **Filene's Basement.**

The Downtown Bargains

To look at the upper floors of **Filene's,** a calm, pleasant department store at 426 Washington Street, you would never have any idea of what goes on beneath the first floor. But walk downstairs to the basement level and pow! it seems as if every other shopper within a 500-mile radius of Boston has also descended on the area. The reason, of course, is that "The Basement," as Bostonians affectionately call it, is a unique institution that has never really been duplicated anywhere else. When the most fashionable stores in the country—Nieman-Marcus, Bergdorf Goodman, Saks Fifth Avenue, to name a few—need to clear out their overstock, when a store goes out of business, when manufacturers have extra merchandise, they sell the lot to Filene's. The result is one of Filene's famous specials, advertised in advance in the Boston papers. There they are, scads of Nieman-Marcus $200 and up women's dresses—each about $50. $150 pants suits from SFA: $80. $36 name-brand bathing suits: $15. Men's quality shoes: $12 a pair. Children's $8 slacks: $2.49. Wedding and evening gowns are especially good buys. And so it goes: clothing for everybody, luggage, pocketbooks, lingerie, cosmetics, linens, a miscellany of items at phenomenal savings, much of it beautiful, plenty of it junk. The crowds are fierce, the competition keen, and the race is not for the faint-hearted. Get there early, sharpen your elbows, and good luck. We should explain that you won't *always* make a killing—some days are better than others—but it's always worth a look. There are no dressing rooms, by the way, but nobody minds if you slip things on over your clothes and—an unusual policy for a discount operation—everything is returnable.

Filene's is at one corner of Boston's new pedestrian mall—a section of Washington, Summer, and Winter streets—which has been closed to private automobiles. The MBTA has arranged special shuttles to take shoppers around the district. Taxis are permitted after 7 p.m.

Across the street from Filene's, at the corner of Summer and Washington streets, is **Jordan Marsh Company,** New England's biggest store, which recently had a "facelift" to enlarge and modernize its many departments. Inside the handsome new facade you can find family clothing and designer apparel, gift boutiques, housewares, furniture, needlework and fabric departments, and a bargain basement, too. Plus a bakery that has a secret recipe for blueberry cupcakes that are famous throughout the area.

Filene's and Jordan Marsh are on one side of Washington Street. On the other side is a new vertical shopping mall, "The Corner," and several small stores joined with a Victorian-style canopy that has been called beautiful by some observers and "tacky" by others. But it does keep out the rain and the hot sun. In the middle of that block is *the* bargain bookstore, **Barnes & Noble,** 395 Washington Street. It's big and crowded, and you check out supermarket style, but you can save $1 and more on many current books and quite a bit on publisher's overstocks. And if you have any money left, proceed to the world's biggest **Woolworth's,** next to the little park alongside Filene's at 350 Washington Street, which has huge souvenir sections as well as clothing, housewares, and—very important in Boston—a parking garage.

For the best cutlery in Boston—or perhaps anywhere—we always go to **Stoddard's,** 50 Temple Place between Washington and Tremont streets (just follow the display windows at Jordan Marsh to Temple Place). The variety of items is amazing and the quality is always excellent. You can choose from about 100 kinds of sewing scissors and 25 styles of nail scissors. (We have given their Swiss army knives for Christmas gifts for many years.) Stoddard's also has fine fishing tackle and fly rods. Open 9 a.m. to 5:30 p.m., Monday through Saturday.

Tired and hungry? Relax and refresh yourself at **Yogurt, Yes,** 367 Washington Street, corner of Bromfield, with a delicious yogurt concoction. Or take a dish of yogurt to the Boston Common where you can sit on the benches or the grass and plan the rest of your shopping spree. We also like the fresh-fruit drinks and heavenly "Blondie" (butterscotch brownies) at **The Mulberry Bush,** just across the street at 324 Washington Street. And for the pause that adds calories, treat yourself to the most delicious hot-fudge sundae anywhere at **Bailey's,** 26 Temple Place or 74 Franklin Street. They also gift-pack candies for you to send home—or keep. (Ask for a folder with mail-order prices.)

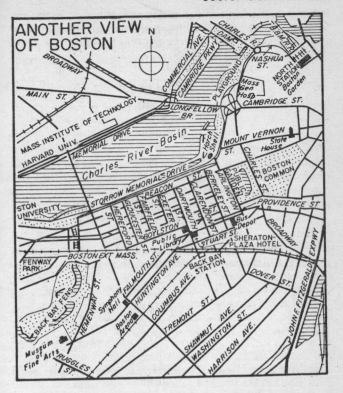

Prudential Center and the Boutiques and Art Galleries of Newbury Street

You can start your next shopping excursion in Boston at the **Prudential Center.** Many of the stores in this area are smaller, more relaxed, and less crowded versions of some of New York's best specialty shops: **Lord & Taylor, Saks Fifth Avenue,** and **Bonwit Teller's,** a few blocks closer to the center of town, on Boylston Street (housed in a handsome brick building that was once the Museum of Natural History). **F. A. O. Schwarz** for children's things and **Brooks Brothers** for perfectly tailored clothes are around the corner from Bonwit's on Newbury Street. In the enclosed mall opening onto the plaza at Prudential Center are more shopping treats: **Brentano's,** where you can buy small sculptures, prints, paintings, and jewelry as well as books; and **Pine and Print,** with a fascinating array of gifts, prints, needlework, and cards. Have lunch or dinner at any of the restaurants in the **Sheraton Boston Hotel.**

Newbury Street runs parallel to Boylston, so, from the Prudential complex, take any of the streets at right angles to Boylston (Hereford, Gloucester, Fairfield) and walk along Newbury, in the direction of the Public Garden. Up at this end are bookstores, craft shops, natural-food stores, and restaurants—macrobiotic, French, Italian, and Japanese. The blocks nearer the Public Garden have the expensive stores and art galleries (some of the smaller galleries come and go as the rent is due, so you might pick up some bargains). The Newbury Street that most shoppers know begins at the **Ritz-Carlton Hotel.** And that says it all. The boutiques are lovely, the galleries (discussed in Chapter V) excellent. Herewith a boutique sampling.

THE BOUTIQUES: A great place to begin your boutique hopping is at **The Artisans,** 165 Newbury Street (tel. 266-6300), an imaginative "league of nations" shop stocked with a wide array of handcrafted gift items that are reasonably priced and easily packed into your suitcases, among them: Nepalese moustache combs at 35¢; scented soaps from Switzerland; all kinds of marvelous beads, like "evil eye" beads from Turkey at 15¢; as well as all sizes and shapes of kites. Hundreds of kitchen items, too, as well as collectibles like Japanese prints, folk art, Russian lacquered boxes, Japanese procelain, and Eskimo art, sculpture, and prints in the upstairs gallery.

If you're in the market for a magic carpet, or just a tapestry or handwoven rug, stop in at **Decor International,** 171 Newbury Street, for the finest collection of unique handwoven rugs in the city—tribals, Orientals, and kilims. Wall hangings are priced from $10, and there are quilts, bedspreads, pillows, folk art, and ethnic jewelry, too. But mostly it's rugs, rugs, rugs—in all sizes and shapes from the far corners of the earth. One of the most delightful and unusual Newbury Street shops.

For the ultimate in bathroom accessories, stop in at the fabulous **Bath & Closet,** 139A Newbury Street (tel. 267-6564). Collected from every part of the United States and Europe, the merchandise is wide-ranging, from French-designed bowls with faucets to antique wooden shelves for perfumes and bath salts. Gilt and glass containers, rare and oddly shaped soaps, plus handsome patchwork bed throws (very expensive, but lovingly done by hand)—all are to be found here.

Alianza, 140 Newbury Street (tel. 262-2385), a North and Latin American crafts center, features piñatas, tile trivets, brass and copper mugs and goblets, silver jewelry, and kinetic sculptures, all reasonably priced!

Carol Cravats, 144 Newbury Street (tel. KE 6-9214), was created by a charming lady—thoroughly Back Bay—who is used to clients coming in just to buy neckties. And why not, when all the ties are handmade, of pure materials (no synthetics) like imported silk, wool, or cotton. They are superb, unique, and realistically priced from $8.50 to $25. In addition, she offers European men's jackets; impressive one-of-a-kind cuff links made from old coins, buttons, enamels, etc.; and stunning men's shirts, sweaters, and Swiss velours. Those hard-to-find bowties that are coming back into style are here, too—a large and beautiful selection—as well as gorgeous pure silk scarves with all handrolled edges.

Also on Newbury Street: **Peking Oriental Imports,** at 159, features imports from the People's Republic of China, including the ever-useful straw baskets.

Take a few minutes or longer to stop at one of Newbury Street's sidewalk cafes (see Restaurants), and refresh yourself with iced drinks and pastries or sandwiches while you people-watch. Then perhaps you might like to try your hand at weaving your own sheepskin rug. **Antartex,** at 18 Arlington Street (between Newbury and Boylston), gives you materials, instructions, and use of a loom; and for approximately $25 you can make a three- by five-foot rug. Or you might take a lesson in sewing sheepskin mitts, slippers, hats, or muffs. This is also a retail store, featuring beautiful, warm sheepskin coats from Scotland, jackets, sweaters, and other fine apparel. Workshop hours, 10 a.m. to 5 p.m., Monday through Saturday.

One more stop before you leave the area should be the **Women's Educational and Industrial Union,** 356 Boylston Street. We've found lovely handmade children's clothes there as well as needlepoint designs, yarns, antiques, and gourmet foods. This nonprofit educational and social service organization has been part of the Boston scene since 1877.

Charles Street

Charles Street, which begins at the Boston Public Garden on the Beacon Hill side, is studded with specialty shops where one can buy anything from fine antiques to health foods. **Walter Dyer,** 110 Charles Street, makes and sells sandals, shoes, and leather goods; and **Helen's Leather Shop,** 91 Charles Street, has leather garments, boots, bags, and luggage.

Eric's of Boston, 38 Charles Street, is actually four shops (antiques, stationery, graphics, and imported art works) rolled into one. Stationery is the specialty, with cards from France, Germany, and Switzerland, as well as comparatively inexpensive ones handdone in old-fashioned calligraphy. Also of note are the handloomed ribbons and laces from Europe, sold by the yard, the imported lead soldiers, and the doll-house miniatures, over 6,000 of them, the largest collection in New England. Unicorn lovers take note: The unicorn is Eric's logo, and he has them in sculptures, cards, and calendars.

Both antiques and good reproductions are featured at **Period Furniture Hardware,** 123 Charles Street. Biggest items are the increasingly popular (and increasingly expensive) antique weather vanes: the selection ranges from fat old cows to prancing horses. You're likely to find chandeliers of brass and tin, perhaps a bronze reproduction of an old-fashioned penny bank, or an authentic Boston bean pot.

Don't worry about putting all your purchases in one basket. **Baskets and More,** 103 Charles Street, has hundreds of them. They're made of split bamboo, reeds, sea grass, and willow, and come from Central America, Africa, Peru, and Portugal. Prices range from about $3 to $24 for baskets; and $38 for the gorgeous tiered birdcages (for plants). The Chinese straw purses and wicker animals make fine gifts.

When you've finished your Charles Street shopping, follow the cobblestones down a few steps to **Romano's Bakery and Coffeeshop,** 89 Charles Street. Choose some fancy pastry or a plain croissant, pour yourself some coffee or tea, and enjoy. No one rushes you, and you can stay as long as you like. (We've seen students studying there.)

Quincy Market

You already know about Quincy Market as a food and entertainment center; it should also be part of your Boston shopping experience. There are three buildings in the market, separated by brick-and-stone malls. The Central Building (see Chapter V, Sightseeing) has the food stalls, pushcarts, craftsmen, little stores, and novelties. The South Market boasts of its expensive high-style boutiques and clothing stores. The North Market is geared to the young crowd—children, teens, college, and career people who want fashion, fads, games, hobbies, and sports equipment.

The Arcade in the South Market is a treasure trove of little boutiques with unusual wares. At **Have A Heart**, everything from jewelry, stationery, and gift wrappings to quilts, pillows, and baby T-shirts has a heart motif. There's even a herbal love potion for $3.75. If you ever find that little place over the rainbow, you can decorate it with pillows, quilts, wall hangings, and prints from **Rainbow Rags**, where everything is rainbows, from jewelry to jogging shorts ($10). **Folklorica** is a tiny shop that has a large selection of folk art, jewelry, and gift items from all over the world. Some of the semiprecious rings from Mexico are especially attractive. And **Bear Necessities** specializes, of course, in bears: stuffed polar bears, teddy bears, Goldilocks' bears, and even totebags and notepaper with the bear motif.

Move on to the **Celtic Weavers** for Irish knit sweaters, capes, and men's caps; or to **Artisan's Cooperative** for Appalachian patchwork skirts, or handmade pillows and quilts from New England craftsmen. For home decorations, browse through the brass planters, bookends, music stands, sun dials, and door knockers at **Brass 'n' Bounty** or the photographs made from original glass-plate negatives at **Gates & Tripp**—$8 to $15 for pure nostalgia. Buy soap, jellies, or dried petals and oils to make your own potpourri at **Crabtree and Evelyn.** And don't leave without listening to the music boxes at **La Boîte á Musique**, in plain cases or pure alabaster.

Start your shopping spree in the North Market in a flower shop, **Bloemenhuis,** and top it off with a buffet and drinks in a greenhouse, **The Landmark Inn.** Along the way, you can buy doll-house furniture at the **Enchanted Cottage,** needlepoint pillows and kits at **Pillow Talk,** or a piggy bank at **Hog Wild,** a store devoted to items with a pig motif. Choose an adult game for yourself at **The Name of the Game,** or stack up on boxes at **Boxes,** which has jewelry, tea, mail, or lunch boxes in all fabrics and materials (even dice, since a pair of sixes makes "box cars"). **White Rabbit & Co.** is a bookstore just for children. If you're into sports, **Bill Rodger's Running Center** has the best gear the marathon winner can find. And if you know you're going to jog off the calories, try **Sweet Stuff,** a candy store with "sensual" chocolates, peanut butter jellybeans, and chocolate pizzas, $7. North Market has its clothing stores, too, including **Louis for Women** and **Fiorucci,** the first American shop the Milan fashion master has opened outside of New York. Among the restaurants in this section of the market are the new **Healthworks,** with salads, soups, quiche, and yogurt; and the venerable **Durgin-Park** (see Restaurants, Chapter IV).

Pass the mustard and choose from nine varieties of imported hot mustard at the **Boston Mustard Shop and Museum** in Faneuil Hall. You can buy unusual servers and crocks and imported mustards in attractive packages. Memorabilia from the Colman Mustard Company, which has operated in Norwich, England, since 1823 are on display.

Shopping in Cambridge

Now on to Cambridge, just across the Charles River, where you can buy almost everything imaginable (and some things that you can't even imagine!). Take the Red line of the MBTA to Harvard Square where the most interesting shops are; or walk the length of Massachusetts Avenue, starting at Beacon Street in Boston, and browse in the many little stores along the way, including **Bharat Mata,** 711 Massachusetts Avenue, with its Indian saris, scarves, shirts, and jewelry. Harvard Square, as far as shopping is concerned, is the whole area surrounding the "T" kiosk—Boylston Street, Brattle Street, Massachusetts Avenue, Mt. Auburn Street, and the other streets backing onto them. The showpiece is the **Design Research** building, 48 Brattle Street, with Marimekko fabrics and clothes, beautiful glassware, dishes, and furniture. The little boutiques in the plaza level of the building carry everything from rainbow mobiles to earth shoes. **Harvest Restaurant** is there, too, for a gourmet dinner or lunch on the terrace. Explore **Truc,** the underground maze of shops at 40 Brattle Street, next to the Cambridge Center for Adult Education. At the **Soap Box** you'll find beautifully wrapped Camelia Plum & Honey soap and avocado soap among the array of bath supplies. The **Harvard Coop** (or "cooperative") at 1400 Massachusetts Avenue, across from the subway station, is a complete department store with three floors of books in the annex, including the required texts for Harvard classes. (For bargains in books, try **Wordsworth,** 30 Brattle Street—paperbacks are discounted 10%, and hardcovers, 15%.) **Sage's Grocery,** 60 Church Street, is where Julia Child shops, although she might buy her truffles at **Cardullo's Gourmet Shop,** 6 Brattle Street.

The Garage on Boylston Street *was* a garage before it became home to a complex of little shops and restaurants. Treat a special child (or yourself) to a plastic butterfly kite ($4.25) or a kit from which you can make a clipper ship that flies ($29.95) at the **Kite Shop.** If you've ever considered making your own wine, **Soft as a Grape** has all the paraphernalia, as well as pottery, chimes, greeting cards, and fascinating gifts such as the lucite cube filled with a thick colored liquid that forms surrealistic patterns when rotated (about $13). No one leaves the Garage without a cup of fresh-ground, freshly brewed coffee (55¢) at the **Coffee Connection,** where you can also buy coffee beans and coffee-makers. A hearty roast beef and boursin cheese sandwich is $1.79 at **Formaggio** next door, and **Baby Watson** has that famous cheesecake, 85¢ a slice.

Or try the cheesecake competition, **Rowinsky's** in the **Mall at 99 Mount Auburn Street,** where you can smother a slice of cheesecake with your choice of fruit topping for $1.25, or for 99¢ plain. Sample the stores in the Mall, too, especially **Nature's Body,** which sells over 200 varieties of spices, teas, and herbs by the ounce, and also carries natural cosmetics.

Another complex of stores is the **Crimson Galeria,** 57 Boylston Street, which houses a dozen shops on three levels. Our favorites are the **Museum Shop** with its assortment of cards, posters, photos, and prints with an art theme; and the **Stoned Elephant,** where we found a Mexican "worry stone" among the animal figurines and onyx chess sets. For only 59¢ we bought it, and the legend that tells how to rub away worries.

Handmade gifts from all over the world, many of them selected by graduate students of anthropology while doing their field work, are featured at the **Peabody Museum Gift Shop,** Divinity Avenue in Cambridge. The items reflect the collection of the museum with many ethnic handicrafts from Nepal, Bali, India, and Japan. Little clay doves from Guatemala are only 80¢; a unicorn stickpin in sterling silver is $13. The gift shop is open Monday through Saturday, 10 a.m. to 4:15 p.m., and Sunday, from 1 p.m. to 4 p.m.

Collector's Items

Flash Gordon and Superman are still around at the **Million Year Picnic**, a small shop at the **Mall at 99 Mt. Auburn Street**, Cambridge. Here you can find back issues (as well as current ones) of almost every comic ever printed. Hundreds and hundreds stacked away, from 25¢ to several dollars depending on rarity. **Movie Madness**, 1642 Massachusetts Avenue, will help you relive the days of Bogey and Garbo with its collection of books, posters ($5 to $20), stills, and magazines. And to prove there's a market for almost everything, **Goods**, 11 Boylston Street, Cambridge, sells old postcards, some used, some blank (mostly from the '30s through the '50s), for 25¢ apiece.

Bargains and Buys on the North Shore

Chances are you'll be driving up to Boston's North Shore area to swim or sightsee in Marblehead, Salem, Gloucester, or Rockport. If so, it's worth your time to make a few stops en route for some of the most rewarding shopping in the area. Your first such stop could well be at Vinnin Square, where Salem, Swampscott, and Marblehead merge; follow Route 1-A through Lynn and you'll come right to it. There, within steps of each other, are **Loehmann's,** a branch of the famed New York discount operation for women's high-fashion clothes, and **Marshalls,** which really lowers the prices on slightly irregular name-brand men's and women's wear, as well as kid's clothing and household goods. At the same location at the Salem Street entrance is **Dish 'n Dat,** which has terrific buys on dinnerware, cookware, and stainless steel. *(Note:* Loehmann's and Marshalls have other stores in shopping malls south and west of Boston).

Then splurge at **Deerskin Trading Post** on Route 1 in Danvers. This is a huge North Shore institution that actually does trade in deerskins (bring in a few you've bagged yourself and they'll give you credit), and specializes in scrumptious leather and suede jackets for men and women, women's leather skirts, moccasins and shoes, woolen and corduroy clothes for the whole family—as well as Indian handicrafts and gourmet items. *(Note:* If you're driving to Gloucester, make this stop on the way back to Boston; it's easier to find going in that direction. Take Route 128 to Route 114, take the loop for Route 1-A South and you'll find yourself practically in Deerskin's parking lot.)

Other North Shore bargain centers you might want to investigate: **Ann & Hope,** off Route 128 at the Liberty Tree Mall, in Danvers, has ridiculously low prices on clothing, appliances, toys, garden equipment. Also in the mall is **Lechmere Sales,** for great buys on cameras, radios, stereos, and luggage. And there's a huge, new **Sears Roebuck** at the **Northshore Shopping Center,** Routes 114 and 128.

Name Droppers at Hawthorne Square Center, Highland Avenue, in Salem, has a good selection of high-style outfits for women who need half-sizes and larger sizes. And the price is reasonable, too. From the Salem Historic area take Highland Avenue (Route 107) in the direction of Lynn. It's next to **Caldor,** another popular discount store.

And Elsewhere

The **Chestnut Hill Mall,** Route 9, has architectural buffs agog and shoppers reaching deep into their pocketbooks. It's one of the most handsome enclosed shopping centers anywhere, with its huge orange roof, benches, trees, and plenty of places for relaxation and people-watching. The stores are all expensive, from Filene's to Bloomingdale's with many smaller specialty shops in between, so plan on spending plenty of money as well as time here.

And there you have it. A shopping scene as varied, as exciting —and as rewarding—as any in the country. Take time to shop in Boston; once you start, you'll end up with a lot more than just a few souvenirs for the neighbors.

Note: But if you do want souvenirs, there's a little store at 19 Yawkey Way (across from Fenway Park) that has an incredible selection of sports souvenirs, not only baseball, but all sports. The emphasis is on the Red Sox, of course, but there are also pennants from every major-league team in every major sport. The store has no name, but every Sox fan seems to know about it, judging from the crowds there before and after games.

Chapter VII

BOSTON AFTER DARK

AFTER A HARD DAY'S sightseeing, should the sensible Boston visitor have an early dinner, watch a bit of TV in his hotel room, and get to bed early? Certainly not! There's so much to do in Boston once the sun sets that it's a shame to waste time resting (you can do that when you get back home). After dark, the city comes alive with theaters, films, sporting events, and music by some of the most prestigious groups in the country. Depending on the season, you might catch a play headed for Broadway, listen to the Boston Symphony or Boston Opera Company, catch a performance by the Boston Ballet, see the premiere of a new film or the revival of an old one. If you're a sports fan, join the local rooters of the Bruins, the Celtics, and the Red Sox. All through the year there's enough activity to keep the night owls busy, from jazz and rock clubs to romantic cocktail lounges for drinks and dancing, even dinner-theaters presenting Broadway musicals.

Boston, however, is not a particularly late town. The bars do stay open until 2 a.m. (1 a.m. on Saturday nights), but the public transportation systems shut down quite a bit before. Some of the MBTA lines start closing at midnight, and all trolleys and buses are safely tucked away for the night by 1:30 a.m. After that, you'll have to depend on your own wheels or on a cab, but Boston taxis are expensive.

In this chapter, we'll let you in on some of the highlights of the Boston night scene, including college drama and concerts, coffeehouses, and dating bars. Note that the minimum drinking age is 18. Let's begin, first, with the cultural scene.

Cultural Boston

MUSIC: The **Boston Symphony Orchestra.** A child growing up in Boston is likely to be under the impression that there is only one really great symphony orchestra in the world—the Boston Symphony, of course. Bostonians are justifiably proud of that remarkable orchestra, and they've been "going to Symphony"— i.e., to Symphony Hall, Huntington Avenue at Massachusetts Avenue (tel. 266-1492)—for something like 75 years now. No matter what season of the year you're in town, you should be able to see the Boston Symphony in one of its varied manifestations.

The winter season of the Symphony runs from September through April, and although most tickets are taken by subscription, the house is not completely sold out. For Friday-afternoon and Saturday-evening performances, "rush seats" in the balcony are available to a limited, lucky few. They cost $2 each and go on sale two hours before concert time. Your best bet might be to attend one of the "open rehearsals" on Wednesday evenings at 7:30, a big favorite with Boston music lovers. They are scheduled eight times each season (once a month) and all seats are unreserved. Tickets sell for $3.50, with proceeds going to the orchestra's pension fund.

Beginning in early May, everybody goes to "Pops"—that's the **Boston Pops Orchestra,** with Artur Fiedler conducting since the year 1. During Pops season, Symphony Hall is decorated in garden tones of green; the orchestra seats are taken out and replaced with tables and chairs; punch and light beverages are sold (the Pops name comes from the sound of popping champagne corks during concerts); and the music ranges from schmaltzy to schmaltzy. It's marvelous and you've got to go. The season continues for nine weeks and tickets are $4 to $10. When the regular Boston Symphony goes to Tanglewood for the summer season, the Pops musicians go to the Hatch Shell of the **Charles River Esplanade** and there some of the loveliest concerts under the stars are held. You can buy an inexpensive chair or sit on the grass free. They also play at other locations in the Boston area.

We mentioned Tanglewood, where the most musical Bostonians spend July and August at the **Berkshire Music Festival** in Lenox (tel. 413/637-1940). If you'd like to catch the B.S.O. at its summer headquarters, you can drive there in three hours on the Massachusetts Turnpike, or, even easier, catch the excursion bus from the Peter Pan Bus Lines in Boston, leaving from the

Continental Bus Terminal at Park Square at 9:15 a.m. It arrives one hour before the Sunday concert, and leaves half an hour after it. Tanglewood concerts run from the beginning of July through most of August and feature outstanding conductors and soloists on Fridays, Saturdays, and Sundays. Tickets run $4.50 to $9. There are open rehearsals on Saturday morning at 10:30, for which tickets are $3.

Other Music Groups

The **National Philharmonia Orchestra of Boston,** under conductor F. John Adams, is a well-known name in chamber music. The group performs frequently at National Theater, Boston Center for the Arts, 537 Tremont Street (tel. 426-2387). Ticket prices vary, but are always reasonable.

Student and faculty concerts are presented nightly at the **New England Conservatory of Music,** 290 Huntington Avenue (tel. 262-1120). Most concerts are free. **Berklee College of Music,** 1140 Boylston Street (tel. 266-1400), also presents free student and faculty concerts.

Under the current direction of Thomas Dunn, the **Handel and Haydn Society,** America's oldest performing-arts organization, is now in its 164th season! You'll be able to obtain current schedules by contacting the Society's offices at 25 Huntington Avenue (tel. 266-3605), although concerts are actually presented at Symphony Hall (tel. 266-1492). Tickets range in price from $5 to $15.50.

The glorious **Isabella Stewart Gardner Museum,** 280 The Fenway (tel. 734-1359), features soloists and chamber music in the Tapestry Room every Tuesday at 8, Thursday and Sunday at 4, except in July and August. Suggested admission $1, although lesser amounts are accepted.

The **Boston Ballet, Boston Lyric Opera, Community Music Center of Boston, Stage 1, Theater Lab,** and **Theater Workshop Boston** all perform at the Boston Center for the Arts (sometimes called "the poor man's Lincoln Center") in the old Victorian Cyclorama building, corner of Tremont and Clarendon streets. Check the newspapers for their programs, which also include exhibits by artists, sculptors, weavers, and photographers.

The **Hatch Shell** along the Charles River, near Arlington Street, is the scene of many free concerts during the summer . . . symphony, chamber music, rock groups, bands. Check the newspapers for listings. And at the Prudential Center weekly

Summer Showcase concerts feature everything from big bands to steel bands, all free. They happen at the North Plaza during July and August.

Check the local papers for programs scheduled at the **National Center of Afro-American Artists,** 122 Elm Hill Avenue, Roxbury (tel. 442-8820). This is the famed Elma Lewis School, with excellent dance groups and musical ensembles.

And if Sarah Caldwell and her eminent **Opera Company of Boston** are performing when you're in town, try very hard to get tickets. This is first-rate opera. Offices at 711 Boylston Street (tel. 267-8050).

THEATER: Theater is big in Boston and runs the gamut from professional Broadway shows to improvisational and experimental works and college productions. The name theaters which often host pre-Broadway tryouts are the **Shubert Theater,** 265 Tremont Street (tel. 426-4520); the **Wilbur Theater,** 252 Tremont Street (tel. 423-4008); and the Colonial Theater, 106 Boylston Street (tel. 426-9366). The **Charles Playhouse** (tel. 426-6912), 76 Warrenton Street, hosts some of the best shows in town, plus cabaret-style entertainment at "Stage Two" and "Stage Three," the latter featuring sandwiches and light dinners.

Now a Boston tradition after many years on the scene, **The Proposition,** 241 Hampshire Street, Inman Square, Cambridge (tel. 876-0088), offers first-rate improvisational sketches with help from the audience. The **Caravan Theater** (tel. 868-8520), 1555 Massachusetts Avenue, Cambridge, is a small avant-garde group that is very popular. The **Boston Repertory Theater** (tel. 423-6580) always has something good to offer at "the newest theater in Boston," One Boylston Place. **Publick Theater,** 1175 Soldiers Field Road, Brighton, opposite WBZ, radio and television headquarters, presents outdoor theater performances on the banks of the Charles River on summer evenings. No show if it rains. Performances are given Wednesday through Saturday evenings. Call 523-3310 for information. **The Lyric Stage,** 54 Charles Street, and **The Next Move Theater,** 955 Boylston Street (next to the Museum of Contemporary Art), are good local groups. And the Hub's "quietest ensemble," **The Pocket Mime Theater,** is worth watching whenever and wherever it performs. Interesting things happen, too, at the **Puppet Showplace,** 30 Station Street, in Brookline Village. And if you're hungry for theater at midday, **BAG Lunchtime Theater,** 367 Boylston Street (tel. 267-7196), presents interesting fare Wednesday through Friday at 12:10 and 1:10 p.m. Tickets are $2.50.

College theater is quite good in Boston, sometimes even better than professional. **Loeb Drama Center** at Harvard, **Tufts Arena Theater** in Medford, **Spingold Theater Center** at Brandeis in Waltham, **Boston University Theater,** Emerson and **M.I.T. Dramashop and Shakespeare Ensemble** can all be counted on for good offerings.

. LECTURES. Don't miss the chance to enjoy a stimulating evening courtesy of **Ford Hall Forum,** the venerable Boston institution that became a world-famed podium. Holding forth at Northeastern University's 1,300-seat Alumni Hall on Huntington Avenue (where there's free parking in a large floodlit area), the format of the programs is always the same—a 45-minute lecture and an open forum featuring authors, political figures, philosophers, and controversial in-the-news personalities. Five lectures are given in the fall and five in the spring, and have included such personalities as Ralph Nader, Germaine Greer, Ayn Rand, and Dan Rather. Programs are scheduled for 8 p.m. on Sundays. Tickets are sold on a subscription basis, but if there are any seats left at 7:45 p.m., the doors are open to the general public free of charge.

CINEMA: Cinema in Boston is alive and vigorous. Bostonians dote on film festivals and revivals of old classics, as well as avant-garde films. To catch all the goodies that you missed years ago, try the **Harvard Square Theater** (tel. 864-4580), 1434 Massachusetts Avenue, Cambridge, or the **Brattle Theater** (tel. 876-4226), 40 Brattle Street, Cambridge, which presented revivals when the current batch of oldies were new. Brattle has an annual Bogey festival. The **Orson Welles** (tel. 868-3000), 1001 Massachusetts Avenue, Cambridge, screens classic and offbeat films of every vintage, as well as foreign films and funky midnight flicks; and the **Central Square Cinema** (tel. 864-0426), 425 Massachusetts Avenue, Cambridge, features oldies, classics, and foreign films. Over in Brookline, the **Coolidge Corner Cinema** (tel. 734-2500), 290 Harvard Street, presents classic oldies and specialized revivals, and the new **Nickelodeon Cinemas** (tel. 247-2160), 600 Commonwealth Avenue, in the heart of the "youth belt," gets the jump on things by showing "tomorrow's classics today." Both the **Boston Public Library** (tel. 536-5400) and the

Museum of Fine Arts screen oldies. There's no admission charge at the library, or for the revivals of old silent films in the museum's Sculpture Court in the summer. The museum offers a film series during the year for which there is a charge. Call 267-9300 for details. The old **Exeter Theater,** once the dowager of Boston's moviehouses, at 26 Exeter Street (tel. 536-7067), features a mixed bag of films: foreign, revival, and first run, as well as some pretty offbeat midnight shows. **Off the Wall** (tel. 354-5678), 861 Main Street (Central Square), Cambridge, presents all manner of short films—everything from foreign classics to classic animations. And, of course, you can get standard Hollywood fare throughout town.

The city's colleges and campus organizations sponsor independent film programs. Most of them are open to the general public. The prices are low, and students often get special rates by showing ID cards. Some of the colleges offering film series are: Boston College, Boston University, Harvard University, the M.I.T. Film Society, Northeastern University, and Tufts University.

Boston's **Summerthing** program and Cambridge's **Poly-Arts** seem to have a festival of some kind or other every week in the summer. The schedules for the festivals and the college films are usually found in the Boston *Globe*'s "Calendar" section on Thursday, the *Boston Herald* 's "Weekend" section on Friday, and in the weekly papers, the *Phoenix* and the *Real Paper.*

Poetry Readings

Are you a poet, still unpublished and unheard? You'll find an audience at **Stone Soup Gallery**, 313 Cambridge Street, Boston, at the foot of Charles Street and near the MBTA subway station. Open readings are held every Thursday evening at 8:30 p.m. in this fascinating combination shop-gallery-lecture-hall-and-music-room. Come to read, listen to, or buy poetry. Sunday readings (8:30 p.m.) feature local and nationally known poets by invitation. Call Jack Powers at 523-9481 for current goings-on.

CONTEMPORARY SOUNDS: The big sound at the **Paradise,** 967 Commonwealth Avenue is pop-rock, but they also feature big names in jazz, folk, and blues. Ticket prices vary with the act, but run about $3.50 to $7.50. When there's a top group, all 500 seats are usually filled, but tickets can be purchased in advance. Two shows nightly, 8:30 and 10:30.

Lulu White's, 3 Appleton Street in the South End (tel. 423-3652), presents top-notch jazz artists in an ornate room reminiscent of a New Orleans bordello. Mainstream jazz of the '30s through the '50s is featured Tuesday through Thursday evenings; and on Friday and Saturday the houseband swings with Dixieland. Sunday is usually reserved for contemporary jazz artists. The music begins around 9:30, and the cover runs from $3.50 to $5.50, Tuesday through Thursday and Sunday, and goes down to $2 Friday and Saturday. Lulu's has good creole dinners, too (see Restaurants).

On the North Shore, **Sandy's Jazz Revival,** 54 Cabot Street, Beverly (tel. 922-7515), is renowned for big-name performers like Dizzy Gillespie, Joe Williams, and Charlie Byrd. It is a concert club open from March to November, 6 p.m. to 1 a.m. nightly. Sandy's serves sandwiches and drinks and has a "music charge" that varies with the performing artist.

THE HOTEL AND RESTAURANT LOUNGES—ENTERTAINMENT AND DRINKS: Many of Boston's most popular night spots are associated with the major hotels and restaurants (see Chapters III and IV). But some of them are interesting enough to be listed separately. To wit:

The Plaza Bar in the Copley Plaza Hotel (tel. 267-5300) is a splendid setting for romance. Soft lights and music and comfortable couches, sculpted and gilded ceilings, louvred windows, and swagged draperies make this the most opulent place in town. At cocktail time a waiter wheels in an hors d'oeuvres cart with a choice assortment of delicacies including smoked oysters. Drinks are pricey, with a glass of champagne from $7 to $30. But you can have a slice of Black Forest cake and coffee for $3. The Plaza Bar is open daily from 4:30 p.m. to 2 a.m. Jazz pianist Teddy Wilson is at the keyboard Monday through Saturday, 9 p.m. to 1 a.m.

Top of the Hub ("The Thai Lounge"), Prudential Center (tel. 267-1161). Here, in one of the highest cocktail lounges and restaurants in the country, you can order inexpensive drinks, and simultaneously dance to music by a contemporary trio. The twinkling lights and the panoramic view of Greater Boston make this one of the most romantic bars in town, in a setting that seeks to capture the atmosphere of the South Seas. Decorative Balinese figures, Buddhas, and dancing figures in gilt set a mystical mood.

The orchestra plays for dancing every night from 8 on. Drinks usually start at $1.80, but during the weekday Happy Hours, 4 to 7, many drinks are just $1.25.

Shelley's Upstairs Pub, Sheraton Boston, Prudential Center (tel. 236-2000). It's a "Colonial" tavern with music, drinks, dart board, and varying diversions. You can dance to a live band Monday through Saturday, 9 p.m. to 1:30 a.m. The drinks are big—and very good. Open Monday through Friday, 4:30 p.m. until 2 a.m.; Saturday, 6 p.m. to 2 a.m.

Scotch 'n Sirloin, 77 No. Washington Street (tel. 723-3677). Adjacent to the popular steak house restaurant is an attractive lounge with entertainment Wednesday through Sunday, 9 p.m. to 1:30 a.m. The sound varies from traditional jazz to rock 'n roll and "oldies." Drinks start at $1.50 and there's a 23-ounce Bloody Mary. There's a $1 admission charge, Wednesday and Sunday. The lounge opens at 4:30 p.m. weekdays, 4 p.m. Sunday.

Diamond Jim's in the Hotel Lenox, Prudential Center at Copley Square. As opulent as old Diamond Jim would have liked. Brocade settees, Victorian furnishings, cocktails, and hors d'oeuvres. Entertainment nightly. Open daily 5 p.m. to 1 a.m.

In case you've wondered what happened to the five-cent mug of beer, it's right here in Boston, at the very popular **Charley's Eating and Drinking Saloon,** 344 Newbury Street (tel. 266-3000). That's the price of beer when you have dinner at this Victorian saloon with its brass-rail bar, Tiffany-type lamps, and bartenders and waiters in period costumes. A fun place to stop in after the theater or concert for late-night specials like sirloin steak and eggs at $5.95. You can eat from 11:30 a.m. until 1 a.m., and you can drink until 2 a.m. It's just around the corner from Prudential Center and is open daily.

The **Up & Up,** Howard Johnson's Motor Hotel, 575 Commonwealth Avenue at Kenmore Square (tel. 267-3100). Part of the fun is the glass elevator that takes you to the rooftop lounge. Great view of the square from the elevator and the Charles River from the lounge. Dancing nightly. No cover.

Dating Bars and Discos

The swinging singles are out in full force in Boston, too, and if you want to join the boy-meets-girl scene, it's quite easy. Where the crowd goes varies from time to time, but at the time

---

Take a Spin

The **Spinnaker**, at the Hyatt Regency, 575 Memorial Drive, Cambridge (tel. 492-1234). If you leave your table for a few minutes and it's not there when you come back—don't worry! The core of this glass-walled rooftop lounge revolves, and it will return in about 50 minutes. Catch up with your friends and enjoy the view of Boston's skyline and the Charles River over your drinks—all the regulars plus some specials like strawberry daiquiris and ice-cream cocktails. Decorated in shades of brown and beige, with soft lounges and cane-backed chairs, Spinnaker is also open for lunch 11:45 to 2:30, except Sunday. Cocktails served till 1 a.m. daily, until 2 a.m. Friday and Saturday.

---

of this writing, these were the "in-est" of the singles bars.

Some of Boston's most Beautiful People—from advertising, publishing, society, and whatever—gather around the raised oak and leather bar at **Copley's**, in the Copley Plaza Hotel (tel. 267-5300) to meet, greet, gossip, and have a drink and perhaps a sandwich. The setting is elegantly Victorian, with its potted palms and chandeliers. Drinks run $1.95 and $2.10. There's entertainment—mostly piano background music—every night from 6 to 11:30.

Friday's (from Thank God It's . . .), 26 Exeter Street (tel. 266-9040), has an interesting decor, too. Or so we've been told. But we've never been able to see through the crowd of spirited young singles sampling the spirits to find out. They start coming about 5 p.m. and in a few hours the line goes halfway around the block. The attraction? Mainly the people, but there's also a bountiful hors d'oeuvres buffet, large drinks, and music on the tapedeck.

Friday's is a restaurant, too, if you can find a table, with a big selection of snacks and appetizers, salads, omelettes, burgers, steaks, and seafood, plus desserts and ice-cream and fruit dessert drinks. Food prices range from $3 to about $7. Open from lunchtime until the bar closes. The glass-enclosed sidewalk cafe facing Newbury Street is perfect for observing the scene—or being observed.

Jason's, 131 Clarendon Street (tel. 262-9000), is a trendy restaurant-disco that gets it all together—brunch, lunch, dinner, cocktails, dancing, backgammon, bumper pool, and one of the best hors d'oeuvres tables in town (free with your drinks, Monday through Friday, 5 to 7 p.m.). There are several levels, angled around exotic aquariums and palm trees, and the young professional set keeps the place crowded till 2 a.m. Jackets required after 8 p.m.; no jeans, and no cover. (See Restaurants for a description of Jason's excellent dining room.)

Club Max, 54 Park Square (tel. 262-0750), is the movie version of the disco, a black-and-chrome multilevel complex of two dance floors, a lounge, a restaurant, and a well-heeled crowd that dresses for disco. After 9:30 p.m., a kaleidoscope of colored lights bounces off the mirrored walls and onto the jewels of the dancers. Monday through Friday, from 4 to 7 p.m., there's a free buffet (stock up) and very reasonably priced drinks. After 8 p.m. prices go up, and there's a $3 cover charge unless you're having dinner. Open 11:30 a.m. to 2 a.m. daily. **Max on the Waterfront,** 101 Atlantic Avenue, has lots of glass and chrome and a chic young crowd that meet either on the dance floor, at the hors d'oeuvres table, or in the restaurant.

The Fan Club, 77 Warrenton Street, in the Hotel Bradford (tel. 357-5050), lives a double life as a gourmet restaurant (at gourmet prices) and a swinging disco. From 5 to 10 p.m. it's dinner and mood music on the piano, and after 11 p.m. it's disco all the way, with flashing lights and gyrating dancers under the star-studded ceiling. Two real trees glittering with hundreds of tiny white lights are part of the decor, along with posters of theatrical personalities, some of whom you might meet on the dance floor if they're in town with a play. Cover is $4, Wednesday and Thursday; $5, Friday and Saturday. No cover on Tuesday, or any day if you're having dinner. The beat goes on until 2 a.m.

Future, 1194 Commonwealth Avenue (tel. 731-0271), is a fantastically decorated disco with art-deco mirrors, colored lights, and a multilevel dance floor. The snazzy crowd runs from 25 to 35 and up.

Lucifer, Celebration, and **Yesterday** are all at 533 Commonwealth Avenue (tel. 536-1950), under the same ownership but each with its own atmosphere and clientele. **Lucifer** is quite dressy and often has name acts. It's also popular with sports figures, especially football stars. **Celebration** is a classy place with modular seating, a large dance floor, and light shows. You need a jacket *and* tie here. **Yesterday** has quadriphonic sound and is a good place to find a date, especially on Tuesday when drinks are only 25¢. Thursday there's an open bar until midnight, but also a $4 admission fee. It opens at 11 a.m. for sandwiches and keeps right on going till 2 a.m. closing.

Rathskeller, 528 Commonwealth Avenue at Kenmore Square (tel. 536-2750), otherwise known as "The Rat," is the punk-rock capital of New England. Die-hard lovers of underground rock fill it nightly until 2 a.m. Cover varies with the group.

When the sun sets, the **Quincy Market** becomes one long dating bar from **Lily's** and **Crickets** at one end to **Seaside** and **Cityside** at the other, with lots of interesting little cafes in between. See our Restaurant and Sightseeing chapters for descriptions of the various establishments.

And on the waterfront there's lots of mingling going on at the **Wharf Restaurant,** 80 Atlantic Avenue, a red building that's really on a wharf; the **Winery,** at the Pilot House on Lewis Wharf; and **Smuggler's 3,** also on Lewis Wharf, a quiet little place with a view of the Boston skyline. In between the marketplace and the waterfront is **Friends & Company,** 199 State Street, which encourages you to meet new friends over drinks, lunch, or dinner, and to listen to the best jukebox in town.

AND IN CAMBRIDGE: The **Sunflower Cafe,** 22 Boylston Street in Harvard Square, has excellent live jazz every night in the downstairs bar. During the week you can hear some of the best sounds in town from 9:30 p.m. to 1 a.m. without a cover charge. Happy Hour between 5 and 7 p.m. has drinks at $1.25 and free cocktail food (not snacks) which might include spare ribs, ravioli, quiche, chow mein, or chichen pieces. The dining room has excellent values, too (see Restaurants).

Downstairs at the Casablanca, 40 Brattle Street, Cambridge (tel. 876-0999), is definitely an "in" place for entertainment in Cambridge after 9. It's located on the lower level of a maze of boutiques known as Truc, the pace is breezy, and the crowd mostly from Harvard and Radcliffe, plus a few wandering celebrities. Conversation here is among the best in Boston. The music varies, but it's usually jazz or piano. The club opens at 4 p.m., usually closes at 2 a.m. Yes, there also is an **Upstairs at the Casablanca.** It's upstairs, and here you can get lunch, supper, and drinks.

Coffeehouses

The best place to make the coffeehouse scene is definitely in Cambridge. Here's where the capuccino set hangs out to talk, to listen (entertainment on and off), to look, to meet. Here are the best choices, all within walking distance of Harvard Square.

Passim Coffeeshop, 47 Palmer Street, Harvard Square (tel. 492-7679). Besides being one of the leading folk clubs in the Boston area, Passim is one of the most charming, cozy cafes around, with its plants, pottery, and photo exhibits, a tiny "museum shop" often selling jewelry, pottery, museum reproductions. There's some of the best live folk around, either the greats or the soon-to-be-greats, with a cover charge ranging from $2 to $3, depending on the performers. Passim has long been famous for great desserts, like chocolate rum tarts, and very good iced chocolates and mochas. Open from noon to 11 p.m.; closed Sunday. No liquor served.

The Blue Parrot, 123 Mt. Auburn Street, Cambridge, is a 20th-century coffeehouse where the conversation flows easier with a big pitcher of sangria. You can look out two large windows and keep tabs on who's in circulation while you're drinking, perhaps a cup of espresso or coffee with a cinnamon stick. Swiss cheese fondue for two and "original Czechoslovakian sauerbraten," along with many other international dishes, can be found on the menu. You can come here to sit under Tiffany-type lamps, enjoying your letters or just looking—there's no pressure. Open from 11:30 a.m. to midnight, Sunday to Thursday; until 12:30, Friday and Saturday.

Algiers, 40 Brattle Street, Cambridge (tel. 492-1557), hidden away on the lower level of Truc at Harvard Square, is the only place we know that gives you chamber music (with harpsichord) or classical guitar several evenings a week while you enjoy exotic coffees and fresh juices, sandwiches, cheeses, homemade soups, and delicious desserts. Espresso is 75¢; cappucino, $1.25; imported teas, 75 cents; sandwiches, $2.25; and delicious frapped strawberries, $1.30. Open every day, from 10 a.m. to 1:30 a.m. (sometimes later on Friday and Saturday nights). And if you're not hungry, you can just sit and read, or listen to music (on record during the day). No one bothers you.

Chapter VIII

BEYOND BOSTON

1. The Paul Revere Trail
2. The North Shore
3. Plymouth
4. Cape Cod

OUTSIDE OF BOSTON lies the rest of the Commonwealth of Massachusetts, and what a treasurehouse of sights and attractions it is! To limit your choice to manageable proportions we survey, first, three major locations: (1) The Paul Revere Trail (Lexington and Concord); (2) Boston's North Shore Resorts and Cape Ann; and (3) Plymouth. Finally, we take you on a trip to one of the most attractive vacationlands in the United States, just a few hours away from the Hub: (4) Cape Cod.

1. Riding the Paul Revere Trail

One of America's major historic routes—and one that almost all visitors want to retrace—is the journey of Paul Revere on the night of April 18, 1775: the ride westward from Boston to Lexington and Concord to warn the colonists that the British were coming. Local residents joke that if Paul Revere were to make the ride today, he'd get stuck in traffic and reach Lexington after the Revolution was over. *Be forewarned:* Avoid the rush hours as you drive through Cambridge and on to Lexington.

LEXINGTON: Lexington is now almost absorbed into Boston as a suburb, but it still has the awesome feel of history about it, and the flavor of a small country town, with narrow streets and an open common on which stands the country's oldest Revolutionary War monument. This was the spot where the growing tension between the British occupiers and the independence-seeking rebels first came to a head with shots being fired. Hard on the heels of Paul Revere came more than 400 British soldiers, and fewer than 100 American patriots stood their ground and returned shot for shot. Nobody knows who set off the first musket, but the result of the crossfire was eight dead and ten more wounded, and the battle continued through the day, and indeed for the next several years.

The Chamber of Commerce operates a Visitor Center (tel. 862-1450) at the corner of the Village Green, 1875 Massachusetts Avenue, from mid-April till November 1. Here you can see a diorama outlining and explaining the battle of Lexington. The **Minuteman Statue** on the Green is said to be of Captain John Parker whose words, perhaps more than any other, provided the rallying cry for the Revolution to follow: "Stand your ground, don't fire unless fired upon, but if they mean to have a war let it begin here!"

Apart from the Village Green, the major historic sights in Lexington are the **Buckman Tavern**, 1 Bedford Street, which has been restored to its original state and was the rendezvous for the Minutemen on that fateful battle day; the **Munroe Tavern**, 1332 Massachusetts Avenue, where the British troops maintained their headquarters; and the **Hancock-Clarke House,** 3 Hancock Street, where Samuel Adams and John Hancock were sleeping when Paul Revere arrived to warn them of the imminent arrival of British troops. This house, furnished in Colonial style, was originally built in 1698 and is now a museum of the Revolution.

All three buildings are operated by the Lexington Historical Society, which charges an admission fee of $1 per house or $2.25 for the three for guided tours. Under age 16, the fee is 25¢. Hours are Monday to Saturday, 10 to 5; and Sunday, 1 to 5; from April 19 to October 31.

Outside town on Route 2A are the **Battle Road Visitor's Center** and the Museum of Our National Heritage. The Visitor's Center (tel. 369-6993) is a beautifully landscaped roadside park with exhibits and films run by the National Park Service. It's open daily, 9 a.m. to 5:30 p.m., June to August; and 8:30 a.m. to 5 p.m., September to May. Free.

At the **Museum of Our National Heritage,** corner Massachusetts Avenue and Marrett Road (tel. 861-6563), the emphasis is on the development of the United States during the past 150 years, with exhibits and films on dramatic events and turning points in this country's history. Open Monday through Saturday from 9:30 a.m. to 4:30 p.m., and Sundays from noon to 5:30 p.m.

Closed Thanksgiving, Christmas, and New Year's Day. Free. There are also special exhibits on the history of Freemasonry in the United States and abroad.

Where to Stay

Visitors staying over in Lexington will want to consider the 90-room **Battle Green Inn**, 1720 Massachusetts Avenue (tel. 862-6100), right in the heart of town near the Minuteman National Park. It's an unusually pleasant two-level motel, with patio and swimming pool. Singles go from $17; doubles and twin doubles, $22 and up. Beginning in November, rates drop for the season.

Budgeteers are directed to very pleasant lodgings at the **Chalet Motor Lodge**, at the junction of Route 128 and Routes 4 and 225 (tel. 861-0850), where a room with one double bed goes at $14.88, single; and $16.88, double; and a room with two double beds goes for $19.88 (for up to four).

CONCORD: What had happened earlier in the day at Lexington was to be repeated, but greatly magnified, in the little town of Concord, and today tourists visit this town to examine the site of the first pitched battle of the Revolution.

After the Lexington affair, Minutemen from all over the countryside converged on Concord, each bearing the musket that was allowed him by English law, and by the morning of April 19 several hundred had assembled. The first flare-up occurred at one of the bridges over the Concord River, which British officers felt had to be held to cut the rebels off from town. As the Redcoats began to tear up the planks of the bridge, the Minutemen advanced on them and when fired on returned the fire, killing three British regulars. Beside the bridge there is now a statue bearing the famous ode:

> By the rude bridge that arched the flood
> Their flag to April's breeze unfurled
> Here once the embattled farmers stood
> And fired the shot heard round the world.

Worried by the growing strength of the rebel force, the British began to march back to Lexington, but this was definitely a mistake. Less than a mile out of town, as the British column was plodding along, their red uniforms making only too clear a target, the crackle of musketry opened up on them from three sides. From behind houses and trees, from behind walls and from rooftops, hidden rifles picked off the column one by one. By the end of the day the British had lost 290 men, the Americans fewer than 100.

April 19, the anniversary of Revere's ride, is today a state holiday called Patriot's Day, and is observed on the third Monday in April, whatever the date. A rider in Colonial dress leaves Boston on horseback and retraces the trip, as everyone turns out in the streets to watch and recall this important date in United States history.

If you're following the Paul Revere route which would now take you along Massachusetts Avenue in Arlington, take time out for lunch or dinner at **Jimmy's Steer House**, 1111 Massachusetts Avenue, Arlington (tel. 646-4450). The values are so terrific that Revere probably would have hitched his horse and sampled the $1.95 chopped sirloin lunch; the scallops or tenderloin tips, $2.45; or the scrod, $2.25. Dinners with salad go from $3.45 for chicken to $6.75 for sirloin steak. Open from 11:30 to 9:30, except Friday and Saturday when it's open until 10 p.m.

2. Boston's North Shore Resorts and Cape Ann

Cape Ann is a smaller Cape Cod, known mainly to Bay Staters and artists. This is New England's rock-bound coast, where the Yankee fishermen and clipper-ship captains made their homes. Now a busy resort area, its beaches, seaports, and shops attract tourists, artists, and antique hunters. You can drive there directly from Boston in about an hour by following Route 128. It takes a bit longer if you follow Route 1A, the winding scenic route, but it is worth it, since you can explore the North Shore towns of Swampscott, Marblehead, Salem, Essex, and Gloucester before reaching Rockport, the famous artist's colony on the tip of Cape Ann.

The Essex County Tourist Council (P.O. Box 1011, Peabody, MA 01960) has a free map and guidebook to the area; and you may also write directly to the Chambers of Commerce in the towns you wish to visit.

THE ROAD TO CAPE ANN: Since the trickiest part of getting to Cape Ann is finding your way out of Boston, some driving instructions are in order so you won't waste precious time getting lost. (On summer weekends, this area is incredibly crowded, by

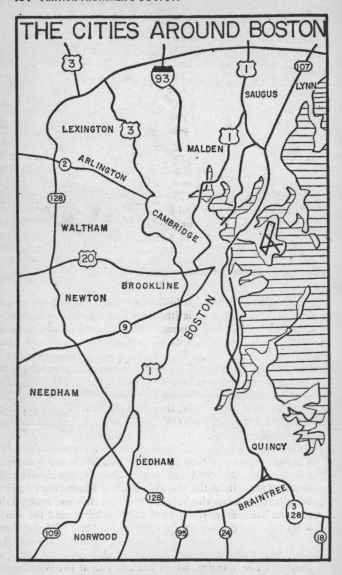

THE CITIES AROUND BOSTON

3

93

1

107

SAUGUS

LYNN

LEXINGTON

3

MALDEN

1

ARLINGTON

2

128

CAMBRIDGE

WALTHAM

20

BROOKLINE

NEWTON

9

BOSTON

1

NEEDHAM

QUINCY

DEDHAM

128

BRAINTREE

3

128

109

NORWOOD

95

24

18

the way; try to make this drive on a weekday.) First find your way to the Callahan Tunnel by following the maze through the market district. (Pay the 25¢ toll as you exit.) If you take a left at the wrong place and find yourself on the Northeast Expressway instead, don't panic. Just take the Mystic River Bridge (pay the toll as you enter) to Route 1A in Revere, where the scenic drive begins. (Take the exit marked Revere if you're on the bridge; the tunnel takes you directly to 1A.)

Revere (named after guess who?) has a long, sandy beach, crowded but good for swimming, with a sheltered harbor, and free parking along the ocean. At night the crowds block traffic for miles, heading for greyhound racing at Wonderland Dog Track. We skip all that now, though, and continue north on 1A to Lynn. Pick up Route 129 where you see the signs for Swampscott and Marblehead and follow the shoreline.

In **Swampscott,** you might visit the Mary Baker Eddy Historic House, 23 Paradise Road, which is open weekdays from 10 to 5; Sunday, from 2 to 5. Admission is 50¢ for adults; 25¢ ages 12 to 20; under 12, free. You can watch the boats in the cove at **Fisherman's Beach,** fish from the town pier, or go swimming right in Swampscott or at nearby **Nahant Beach.**

Marblehead is the next town along the coast, and we suggest you stop here for a while (there's a parking lot located behind Penni's Grocery, 118 Washington Street), and wander through "Old Marblehead," with its winding, narrow streets and 18th-century homes bordered by hollyhocks and curio shops. This is the "Yachting Capital of the World," and in summer, the boats in the inner harbor are moored together like sardines. (The Marblehead fishermen specialize in flounder, mackerel, and lobster.) In the outer harbor, there is sailboat racing all summer, and the popular "Race Week" in July attracts enthusiasts from all over the country.

Marbleheaders are very proud of their historical background. This has been a seafaring town from the time it was a colonial fishing village, deriving its name from the rock, marble-like cliffs that protect it from the sea. (Walk along Front Street to Fort Sewell, and you can climb right out on the cliffs and soak up the sun and sea breezes.) Merchant ships sailed around the world from here, and the wealthy sea captains built beautiful mansions, some of which still stand. Its citizens were active in the Revolution, and Washington and Lafayette were guests at the **Col. Jeremiah Lee Mansion,** which you can visit at 161 Washington Street. This is one of the finest examples of Georgian architecture in America, and has original Colonial furnishings and decorations. Open 9:30 to 4 except Sundays, mid-May to mid-October. Admission is $1.50 for adults; 50¢ for children 10 to 16; under 9, free (accompanied by an adult). **King Hooper Mansion,** Bank Square, now the headquarters of the **Marblehead Arts Association,** was the home of merchant prince Robert Hooper, who was known as "King" because of his generosity to the town. Splendidly decorated and furnished, it includes ballroom, slave quarters, and wine cellar (now empty). Open 1 p.m. to 4 p.m. daily, except Monday. Also closed Tuesday, November to April. Adults $1, children 50¢. The Arts Association has excellent exhibits there during the year. Another interesting house is **Lafayette Home,** at the corner of Hooper and Union Streets. One corner of the house was bizarrely chopped off—to make room for the passage of Lafayette's carriage when he visited the town in 1824.

On the hill at Washington Square is **Abbot Hall,** the town hall, where you can see the original of the famous painting, *The Spirit of '76.* It is open Monday through Friday, 8 a.m. to 9 p.m.; and Sunday, 8 a.m. to 12 noon, from October through May. Hours, June through September, are 8 a.m. to 9 p.m. daily except Sunday, when it is open 1 p.m. to 5 p.m. Free.

Dining in the Swampscott-Marblehead Area

Two of the largest and best-known restaurants on the North Shore are in Swampscott—Hawthorne by the Sea and the General Glover House, both operated by the owner of Boston's famed Pier 4, with prices in the same upper range. The Hawthorne, which perches on a cliff alongside the ocean, specializes in seafood. (We also love their fabulous strawberry ice-cream pie.) The Colonial-style **Glover,** at Vinnin Square, Route 1A, is famous for roast beef from the open charcoal hearth; and we usually feast on marinated mushrooms and popovers while waiting for the entree. A bowl of fresh fruit is served with your coffee.

Also in Swampscott, on a smaller scale is **Black Will's** seafood restaurant, across from the town pier at Fisherman's Beach (581-3300). The food is excellent and inexpensive, with weekly specials such as broiled scrod with giant salad and vegetable, $3.95. And when lobsters are in season, they pull them out of the harbor just across the street, and put them on special. Brunch is served on Sunday, and a light menu is available in the late evening.

For gourmet dining in Marblehead, it's hard to beat **Rosalie's,** 18 Sewall Avenue (tel. 631-9888), lovingly created by Rosalie and George Harrington. She is the gourmet chef whose private classes were so successful that her students asked her to open a restaurant in 1973. And that became so successful that the Harringtons purchased their own building, in which they've placed antiques, stained-glass window panels, plants against the brick walls—and, of course, a large kitchen where Rosalie creates her specialties for lunch, dinner, and Sunday brunch. Either George or Rosalie will greet you at the door, and one of their children may be waiting tables. It's all à la carte and expensive, but worth it. We find it hard to resist the veal Marsala, tender white scallops of veal, laced with wine and mushrooms, $7.95; or the filet mignon Florentine, with seasoned spinach, crabmeat and bearnaise sauce, $10.95; both served at dinner. Try the stuffed artichoke ($1.95) or the escargot in champignon ($2.75) for an appetizer, and the chocolate mousse ($1.25) for dessert. Lunch features Rosalie's famous "no crust" spinach pie ($2.95), crêpes, quiche, or a sandwich, plus daily specials. Dinner hours are 6:30 to 9:30 p.m.; lunch is served from 11:45 a.m. to 2:30 p.m.; and Sunday brunch ($2.25 to $3.95) is 10:30 a.m. to 2:30 p.m. Ask for directions when you call for reservations.

There are two entrances to **The Landing,** 81 Front Street—one by sea and one by land. Tie up at the dock if you've been sailing, or have valet service park your car. It's open daily from 11:30 a.m. to 10 p.m. (lounge stays open later) with such specialties as fisherman's platter for $5.50.

Other Marblehead favorites include the **Sail Loft** at 15 State Street, where the town's young professionals line up for great fish dinners, **Jake Cassidy's Steak House & Gin Mill,** 259 Washington Street, for beef and booze; **The Library,** a coffee and tea house at 18 Darling Street, where you can have a marvelous onion soup or quiche while you relax and play backgammon or scrabble. **Nancy's Incredible Edibles,** right opposite the town pier, is the place for light, inexpensive snacks, like broccoli-feta quiches, carrot cakes, almond cheesecake, herb teas, and the traditional Marblehead "Joe Frogger" cookies. **The Barnacle,** right on the waterfront at Front Street, has a tiny little deck that's just perfect for soaking up the salt breezes and watching the harbor boating action as you eat a hearty bowl of clam chowder—New England style, of course.

Staying in Marblehead and Swampscott

If a quick look makes you decide you'd like to spend some time in this area, very pleasant accommodations are available. **Marblehead Inn,** 52 Washington Street (tel. 631-3087), built in 1756, is one of the town's most historic structures, and conveniently situated about a block from the Public Wharf. The interior has recently been redone, and there's always an ocean breeze. There are large corner rooms with cross ventilation and fireplaces, and small efficiency apartments with private bath and studio-like setting.

Cap'n Jack's, 253 Humphrey Street, in nearby Swampscott (tel. 595-9734), describes itself as "a salty waterfront inn," and that it is. There's a tree-shaded lawn overlooking Massachusetts Bay, sailboats and rowboats available for guests, a sundeck for resting or sunbathing, and a pool. In winter, you can count on a roaring fire in the hearth and a card room for sociable activities. All rooms have a refrigerator and TV. From June through September, furnished apartments cost $185 to $225 weekly; rooms, $14 to $35 daily, or $25 to $125 weekly. In winter, rates drop to $125 weekly for apartments, $8 to $20 for rooms.

Nautilus, 68 Front Street, Marblehead (tel. 631-1703), is a guest house where you're really treated like a guest. It's located on the harbor, and some of the rooms have ocean views. And as it's right in the heart of "Old Town," you can easily browse in the little shops, go antiquing, and stroll the winding streets of the town. Rates are $20 to $22 a day for doubles, and $15 to $18 for singles. All rooms have semiprivate bathroom facilities.

In a small building adjoining the guest house, there is a unique shop with a collection of nautical antiques, navigational instruments, and old and new brass items, such as birdcages and scales, for sale.

All of these places are just 11 or 12 miles northeast of Boston, so they might even serve as headquarters for a Boston stay if you have a car. They're near public transportation, too.

When you're finally ready to leave this area, look for the signs that lead to Salem (and watch out for the one-way streets).

SALEM: Since it's not able to live down its reputation as the city where witches were hanged, Salem has capitalized on it instead. There's a **Witch House,** a **Witch Museum,** and even the **Witch Trail,** with signs showing a witch on a broomstick pointing the way. But although the witchcraft hysteria of 1692 brought Salem to the attention of the world, it is famous for much more than witches. Salem is one of the oldest of American cities, and parts of it have retained much of the former flavor. Streets are lined with 18th-century homes, some preserved with their original furnishings. Chestnut Street, with its homes of the wealthy merchants of the China Trade era, is considered one of the most architecturally beautiful streets in the country, and the residents must, by legal agreement, follow the Colonial theme in their decorating and furnishings.

Even the city's urban-renewal program is centered on the Old Salem theme: 19th-century Salem has been recreated at Derby Square; the Essex Street shopping area is now a Colonial-style brick pedestrian mall; and a new East India Square is being built in the vicinity of the Peabody Museum.

Twenty historic points are listed on Salem's Historical Trail, but there are at least twice as many attractions—cultural and recreational included—that are worth visiting. Most of them are within walking distance of each other, and you can rent a cassette **Walkingtape** at the Chamber of Commerce Office, 221 Darby Street at Pickering Wharf. The tape gives detailed backgrounds on about 30 well-known places, plus instructions on how to reach them. If you prefer driving to walking, you can get a map with directions for covering the city at an information center or the Chamber of Commerce.

We suggest beginning your tour at the wharves, from which Salem vessels set off to sail the world. They are now part of the **Salem Maritime National Historic Site**, which also includes buildings from Salem's heyday as a commercial seaport.

Derby Wharf, base for privateers in the Revolutionary War and pioneering merchant vessels in the years following the Revolution, is always open.

Custom House, topped by a cupola where customs officials watched for ships, contains restored offices and information on the Salem Maritime National Historic Site. Here Nathaniel Hawthorne labored, while composing his early literary works on the side. It is open 8:30 a.m. to 5 p.m. daily. No admission charge. (Open 8:30 to 7 p.m., July and August.)

Bonded Warehouse contains original equipment, furnishings, and cargos representative of the 1800s. Scheduled tours start from the Custom House. Open daily, 9 a.m. to 5 p.m., July and August. Check at Maritime Site for hours September to June.

Scale House is furnished with original weighing and measuring equipment which is demonstrated just as customs officials used it to determine the value of imports. Scheduled tours start from the Custom House. Open 9 a.m. to 4:30 p.m. daily in summer. Free.

Derby House was the home of Salem's most successful merchant and first millionaire, Elias Hasket Derby who owned the wharf across the street. Scheduled tours of this furnished home start from the Custom House. Admission is 50¢ for those 16 and over. All buildings in the Historic Site are closed Thanksgiving, Christmas, and New Year's Day.

Turning right two blocks farther down brings us to the famous **House of Seven Gables** on Turner Street. This impressive 1668 structure, built by Captain John Turner and the inspiration of Hawthorne's novel, has six rooms of period furniture and a secret staircase; but visitors must wait for a guide, and so popular is the house with groups of schoolchildren that you may have to wait as much as half an hour, so don't bank on a quick look. Open daily from 9:30 a.m. to 6:30 p.m., July 1 through Labor Day. Admission is $3 for adults, $1 for children 13 to 17. From Labor Day to July 1, hours are from 10 a.m. to 4:30 p.m. and the price for adults is reduced to $2; other rates remain the same.

Also on the premises: **Retire Becket House**, 1655; **Hathaway House**, 1682; and the **Nathaniel Hawthorne Birthplace**, c. 1750; which are open only in the summer and are included in the $3 admission.

Salem's next batch of landmarks is located next to each other on Essex Street at Hawthorne Boulevard. Twin jewels in Salem's crown are the **Essex Institute** and the **Peabody Museum.** The Essex Institute is open Tuesday through Saturday, 9 a.m. to 4:30 p.m.; Sunday, 1 p.m. to 5 p.m.; and on Monday from June 1 to October 15 only. Admission is $1 for adults, 50¢ for children. The institute houses an extraordinary collection of Salem memorabilia, books and manuscripts, furniture and furnishings, and period houses in a garden setting. The works of Salem artists and craftsmen of the old days, luxury objects brought back on Salem ships from the far corners of the world, reminders of the witchcraft days (nails from the old witch jail on Federal Street, a section of the tree from which some of the accused were hanged), portraits, costumes, uniforms, toys, dolls, household objects—all recreate life of this remarkable port city. The fully furnished period houses, dating from 1684 to 1804, are shown for a fee on a guided tour.

Next door to the Essex museum complex is the celebrated **Pingree House,** a classic example of the work of Samuel McIntire, probably the most celebrated architect of the early 19th century. Spacious and airy, it is decorated throughout with garlands of leaves and sheaves of wheat on the mantels and doorways, and has been carefully furnished with some of the finer examples of the period. (Open Tuesday through Saturday, 10 to 4; summer Sundays, 1 to 4:30. Fee is $1 for adults, 50¢ for children and senior citizens.)

Another classic landmark near the institute is the **Crownin-shield-Bentley House,** built in 1727 and also furnished in period style. (Open June to October 15, Tuesday through Saturday, 10 to 4; Sundays, 1 to 4:30.) Admission, $1 for adults; 50¢ for children and senior citizens.

Across the street and down the block, the building now housing the **Peabody Museum** (161 Essex Street, open daily 9 to 5; 1 to 5, Sundays and holidays) used to be headquarters for the East India Marine Society, whose one requirement for membership was to have sailed around Cape Horn or been business manager for a ship that did. The fact that the society had almost 200 members indicates how busy a seaport Salem once was. Many of the captains vied with each other to bring back esoterica from foreign ports, much of it ending up in the Peabody Museum. The place is full of fascinating items, including carved wooden figureheads and beautiful miniature ship models, plus many examples of the ancient sailor's art of scrimshaw. Large dioramas show the Salem wharves of the 1820s, natural history, and seashore scenes. There are also artifacts from the South Pacific and the Orient. The gift shop has excellent cards and reproductions. Admission is $1.50; 75¢ for children 6 to 16, senior citizens, and students with ID.

City Hall, with its interesting interior furnishings, is just to the right of Essex Street down Washington Street; and a left turn on Federal Street further down will bring you to the **Court House,** with its old deeds and documents relating to the witchcraft trials.

The **Witch House,** 310½ Essex Street (open from 10 a.m. daily, March through November; $1 for adults, 25¢ for children) was the home of Jonathan Corwin who, in 1692, conducted some of the early examinations of the accused in this house, along with John Hawthorne (a member of the same family as Nathaniel Hawthorne). It's an eerie-looking dwelling that has probably changed but little since those days.

Next door, at 318 Essex Street, is another fine old house, the **Ropes Mansion** (open 10 a.m. to 4 p.m., Monday to Saturday, May to November), also with an authentic collection of period furnishings. Adults, $1; children, 50¢. Other houses worth examining in this neighborhood are two homes built by Samuel McIntire (1757–1811), the **Pierce-Nichols House,** one of the Essex Institute houses, 80 Federal Street, open all year, Tuesday through Saturday, 2 p.m. to 4:30 p.m.; and **Hamilton Hall,** at the corner of beautiful Chestnut Street.

New to Salem is **Pickering Wharf,** a commercial and residential village on Salem's historic waterfront in the Derby Wharf district with an active shopping center and fine restaurants, including **Victoria Station.** Focal point for visitors is the theater-in-the-round presentation *The Voyage of the India Star,* recreating an 1804 voyage to Calcutta and Sumatra by a Salem schooner in search of treasure. This mixed-media presentation of Salem's maritime history is shown daily except Thanksgiving, Christmas, and New Year's from 9:30 a.m. to 6:30 p.m. in summer; and till 4:30 p.m., Labor Day to June 30. Admission is $1.75 for adults; $1.25 for children under 18; $1, senior citizens; and free for kids under 6.

Before you leave Salem, stop at the **Witch Museum,** and watch the highlights of the New England witchcraft hysteria unfold, complete with noises of rattling chains and the whistling wind. Not a museum in the traditional sense, this is a sight-and-sound presentation with 13 life-size recreated scenes of Salem's witch history. A narrator describes each event as it is shown. Located at 19½ Washington Square, opposite Salem Common, the Witch Museum is open 10 a.m. to 7 p.m. daily in the summer; and from 10 a.m. to 5 p.m. in the spring and fall. Admission to the 25-minute show is $2 for adults, $1.50 for teenagers (13 to 18), and 75¢ for children from 6 to 12. Senior citizens, $1.75.

And for a change of mood, have a picnic at **Salem Willows,** the waterfront park just a few minutes away from the center of town. There's an amusement area there with a merry-go-round and kiddie rides, miniature golf course, and dodge 'em car ride. You can relax in the tree-shaded picnic area, take a swim, or a harbor tour that sails from the pier. And you can even buy a chop suey sandwich—to go! Free admission and free parking.

Or you can head back in the direction of Marblehead to **Pioneer Village,** at **Forest River Park,** off Lafayette Street, foot of Clifton Avenue. There you'll find a model of Salem in 1630, complete with early buildings, stocks, pillory, and craft displays. Open daily, June through Labor Day, 10 a.m. to 6 p.m. After Labor Day through October, 10 a.m. to 5 p.m. Admission for adults, $1; children, 25¢.

Accommodations in Salem

Centrally located within walking distance of many of the historic sites is the **Hawthorne Inn, On the Green** (tel. 744-4080). Recently redecorated, it has antique reproductions, brass chandeliers, and Oriental carpets. Rates are $19 to $30 for singles, $28 to $36 for doubles, and $55 for suites. There's an excellent dining room and a tavern within the Inn.

Not far from Salem harbor is the charming **Coach House Inn**, 284 Lafayette Street (tel. 744-4092), a ship-captain's mansion and carriage house dating back to the middle of last century. The elegance of that time is preserved in the furnishings, high ceilings, and lavish fireplaces, many of marble or carved ebony. Rooms here run $20 to $26 in a double, $30 to $45 in suites. Efficiency apartments are also available, from $220 to $315 weekly. There's a 10% reduction on the daily rate for the weekly stays, and all rates drop 10% after Labor Day.

The **Pilgrim Motel**, 40 Bridge Street (tel. 744-9737), is an attractive motor inn which charges $16 for a single, $18 for a double in summer; $14 for a single, from $16 for a double, off-season. One-room housekeeping units go for $80 a week in-season; $50 a week, off-season.

Just across from the Libery Tree Mall shopping area in Danvers is another **Chalet Motor Lodge** with budget rates of $14.88 for a single, $16.88 for a double, and $19.88 for a room with two double beds (for up to four). Located at the junction of Route 128 and Endicott Street, Danvers (tel. 777-1030), it is a good takeoff point for your explorations of the North Shore.

And still in Danvers, **King's Grant Motor Inn**, Route 128 (tel. 774-6800), has 125 spacious rooms with color TV, phone, and in-room movies. There's also a tropical garden with a lounge and swimming pool. Prices start at $25 for a single; $28 to $30, double; and $40 to $43, twin.

Dining in Salem

Salem has many fine restaurants ranging from Chinese (**Dave Wong's** at Vinnin Square) to French (**Bistro Le bistingo**, 8 Front Street) through the steak house and fish house range. Our number-one choice is the **Lyceum**, 43 Church Street (tel. 745-7665), where Joan and John Boudreau excel at the fine art of preparing and serving good food. The building where Alexander Graham Bell made his first public demonstration of the telephone now has two dining rooms, beamed lattice-work ceilings, a glass-

enclosed patio with hanging plants, a skylight, and lots of atmosphere. The Boudreaus take great pride in their table settings—
quilted placemats and napkins, antique show plates, dishes and
platters in the shape of fish and fruit, pewter pitchers and cut-
crystal glasses. The cuisine is continental with many French
gourmet accents, such as onion soup gratinée, $1.45; veal cordon
bleu, $6.95; seafood casserole, $5.75; baked stuffed shrimp, $7.25
(and a smaller portion at $4.95). Altogether there are 120 items
on the menu, including omelettes, crêpes, salads, sandwiches,
flaming desserts, and delicious English trifle. Any selection may
be ordered any time of the day, so you can enjoy a full dinner
at noon or an inexpensive quiche or sandwich in the evening. The
upstairs dining room has an even larger menu which includes
Italian specialties. Adjacent to it is the Witches' Loft Lounge
where fashion shows, card readings, and tea-leaf readers are
featured, along with cooking demonstrations by Mrs. Boudreau.
The Lyceum is open daily, 11 a.m. to 11 p.m. On the street level,
the Pub serves an inexpensive light dining menu and is open
8 a.m. to 10 p.m.

    Stromberg's, on the bridge between Salem and Beverly, Route
1A, is one of the most popular seafood restaurants on the North
Shore. The drawing card is the combination of top-grade fish and
low-grade prices. The flounders are taken straight from the
fishing boats. On a recent visit, we had baked stuffed filet of sole,
filled with crabmeat and Newburg sauce, for $4. There are al-
ways several daily specials in addition to the regular menu and
complete dinners start at $5.50. Hours are 11 a.m. to 8:30 p.m.
daily, except Monday when the restaurant is closed. (On long
holiday weekends, they close on Tuesday.) Incidentally, Strom-
berg's is located on the spot where Roger Conant and his follow-
ers landed in 1686.

ON THE ROAD TO GLOUCESTER: You have several routes to
choose from as you head to Gloucester. If you don't have much
time, Route 128 through Danvers and Beverly (where George
Washington commissioned the schooner *Hannah,* the first vessel
to fly the Continental flag), is the fastest way. If you have time
to explore, exit from Route 128 at Route 133 to Essex, one of
the country's earliest shipbuilding centers, now known for seafood restaurants, Essex clams, and antique shops. **Old Essex
Village,** on Route 133, is a charming collection of distinctive
shops, open daily from 10 a.m. into the evening. Nearby on

Route 22 in Essex is **Misty Acres** restaurant, a family-style place with good, inexpensive food including fish, chicken, ham, and beef. Old Salem Treat, a variety of seafood "cooked in a puddle of butter" is $3.75; chicken broiled with rum, $3.25; and sirloin steak, $3.95. And these prices include potatoes, vegetables, and beverage!

Follow Route 133 to Route 127 and continue on to Gloucester.

Another scenic route is 127, which you can join just beyond 1A in Salem. The winding road goes through the picturesque towns of Prides Crossing, Manchester, and Magnolia. An outstanding restaurant in the area is the **Harbour Side,** with an ocean view and such specialties as frog legs provençale, $8.45, and roast Long-Island duckling flambé, $9.45. It's a popular spot, so call for reservations (tel. 526-1941). In Magnolia (technically part of Gloucester), the **Surf,** 56 Raymond Street (tel. 525-3313), has a menu to match your mood, and you can feast on pizzas or a superb dinner. Price range is from $6 to $10. A Sunday-evening feature in the winter and early spring is the buffet, the most bountiful we've ever sampled, with enough desserts to fill a sweet shop.

The **White House** (tel. 525-3642), a pleasant old homestead in Magnolia, has been turned into a motel offering ten rooms in the separate wing. Rates are $28 for a single, $34 for a double, and slightly less off-season.

Hammond Castle

Well worth a stop as you approach Gloucester is Hammond Castle, also known as **Hammond Museum.** You reach it by following Route 127. Two miles beyond the intersection of Route 127 and Route 133, turn left onto Hesperus Avenue, and follow the road to the castle. Financed (at a cost of over $6 million) and planned by the late inventor John Hays Hammond, Jr., the medieval castle was constructed of Rockport granite. There are towers, battlements, stained-glass windows, a great hall 60 feet high, and an enclosed "outdoor" pool lined with foliage, trees, and a marble tomb. Many 12th-, 13th-, and 14th-century furnishings, tapestries, and paintings fill the dozens of rooms, and a pipe organ with over 8,600 pipes is used for daily concerts. (See the local papers for schedules.) There are guided tours of the castle every half hour from 10 a.m. to 4 p.m. in summer; from Labor Day to Memorial Day, Tuesday through

Friday, 10 a.m. to 3 p.m.; and Saturday and Sunday, 10 a.m. to 4 p.m. Admission is $2.50 adults; $1, children. Closed during January, and on Thanksgiving and Christmas.

GLOUCESTER: Now on to the Cape Ann town of Gloucester, where the famed bronze **statue of the Gloucester Fisherman** overlooks the ocean as a memorial to the more than 10,000 fishermen who went "down to the sea in ships" and did not return. The city's history goes back to the Norsemen who skirted the coast in 1001 and to Champlain, who founded what is now Eastern Point. A more recent claim to fame is the invention here of the process for blast-freezing foods by Clarence Birdseye.

Many years ago, one historian described Gloucester as "the greatest fishing mart in the Union," adding that "at nearly all times without regard to season, the waters around it are covered with a flight of sails . . . reminding one of the restless sea gulls that circle about their rocky aerie when bringing food to their young." Gloucester is more industrialized now, but it still retains as close an association with the sea and seafarers as it did when it was founded almost 350 years ago. It has a large Italian and Portuguese fishing colony, and their annual St. Peter's Fiesta (at the end of June or beginning of July), when the boats are blessed, brings tourists from all over the country for the event. There are parades, floats, marching bands, and a 600-pound statue of St. Peter which is carried through the streets.

The **Rocky Neck Art Colony** in East Gloucester is one of the oldest established art colonies on the East Coast. Primarily a working center for artists, not just a series of shops selling their wares, it's on a tiny jetty of land connected to the mainland by a causeway. About two dozen galleries are located in its colorful alleys and piers along with fishing boats, appealing shops, and restaurants. To reach Rocky Neck, take Route 128 to East Gloucester, exit 9, and follow East Main Street to Rocky Neck Avenue. (Rudyard Kipling worked on his book *Captains Courageous* on Rocky Neck.)

Our favorite among the restaurants on "The Neck" is **Capt'n Chris'**, 77 Rocky Neck Avenue (tel. 283-9543), located practically on the edge of the pier so that when you look out the window you feel as if you're aboard ship. The accent is on seafood, of course, reasonably priced with broiled Boston scrod, $5.75; brook trout, $6.25; and a seafood pie with shrimp, crabmeat, and sea scallops baked in casserole and topped with lobster stuffing,

$7.25. Lobsters come from Capt'n Chris' own inland lobster pools, $8.95. Dinners: 3 p.m. to 9:30 p.m. weekdays, until 10:30 p.m. Saturday; Sunday, noon to 9 p.m. Luncheon: Monday through Saturday, 11:30 a.m. to 3 p.m., with entrees ranging from $3.25 for scrod or haddock to $4.45 for seafood antipasto. If you're sailing by at mealtime, you can drop anchor at the dock and climb on board.

The Sights of Gloucester

The **Beauport Museum,** East Point Boulevard (tel. 283-0800), converted by its architect-owner Henry Sleeper from a three-room cottage to a 40-room home, with each room representing a different historical period, likes to describe itself as "the most fascinating house in America." The Golden Step room with its breathtaking view of the harbor, the Pine Kitchen in the style of an old pioneer home, the Paul Revere room (its silver is now in the Boston Museum of Fine Arts), the Tower Library with an immense collection of antiquarian books, all delay the visitor longer than he had anticipated. Weekday tours, June through September. Admission charged.

Cape Ann Historical Association, 27 Pleasant Street (tel. 283-0455), consists of two buildings. In what was once the residence of Gloucester's merchant mariner, Capt. Elias Davis, dating back to 1804, there are old toys, dolls, needlework, china, costumes, brought back from all over the world. In the new museum building is an exhibit on the fisheries industry, a display of Colonial relics, and a large collection of Fitz Hugh Lane paintings and sketches. Open 11 to 4, Tuesday through Saturday; admission is $1, children under 12, free.

Sargent House Museum, operated by the Sargent-Murray-Gilman-Hough House Association, 49 Middle Street (tel. 281-2432), is a late 18th-century Georgian residence built for the sister of Governor Winthrop Sargent. It has an interesting collection of antique furniture as well as art, china, glass, silver, and needlework. Admission, $1.50 for adults; $1, children 14 and under. Open from June 1 to September 30, Tuesdays, Thursdays, and Saturdays, from 1 p.m. to 5 p.m., and year round by appointment.

Our Lady of Good Voyage Church, 142 Prospect Street, often called the Portuguese church, contains the first set of carillon bells installed in North America. **North Shore Arts Association,** 197 East Main Street (tel. 283-1857), is a free gallery of paintings, sculpture, and graphics by nationally known artists. The association also stages activities ranging from auctions to painting demonstrations. **Rafe's Chasm,** a 200-foot-deep cave, and **Norman's Woe,** a dangerous protruding ledge of rocks responsible for "The Wreck of the *Hesperus*" in Longfellow's poem, and countless other shipwrecks throughout the years, are both coastal landmarks on the way south off Hesperus Avenue near Magnolia.

Take time to visit these other points of interest, if you can: **Stage Fort Park,** the site of a historical fort with ancient cannons. It's on Hough Avenue (off Western Avenue) and has picnic areas and beaches open to the public. **Harbor Loop,** where band concerts are held. **Eastern Point Lighthouse and Breakwater,** which has a magnificent view of the ocean. In good weather you can walk to the end of the breakwater. **State Fish Pier,** Parker Street, where fishermen unload their catches every morning.

North Shore Harbor Cruises

For the cool ocean breezes, a sunset cruise, or just to sightsee, take an excursion boat through either Gloucester, Salem, or Marblehead harbors. In Gloucester an old-time paddle boat named *Dixie Bell* sails from Seven Seas Wharf and from Rocky Neck hourly seven days a week in summer. Adults, $2; children, $1. *The Stacy Star* leaves Salem Willows Pier, weekdays, 1 p.m. to 5 p.m., and weekends, 12:30 to 5:30. Adults, $2; senior citizens and children, $1.50. Also, sunset cruises Sunday through Thursday on the half hour from 7:30 to 9:30 p.m. In Marblehead, the *Delta II* sails from the State Street landing on a half-hour basis, 10 a.m. to 6 p.m.

Accommodations in Gloucester

Over in Rocky Neck is the elegant **Rockaway House,** 7 Rackliff Street (tel. 283-2592), with its yacht harbor, swimming pool, and rambling lawns overlooking the water. You can dock your boat right on the spot, and the hotel is always bustling with activity in season, when doubles go from $25 to $36. Off-season, it's $18 to $25. There's a lovely dining room overlooking the boat dock, and music on weekends. You can also rent a sailboat and take sailing instructions.

Spruce Manor Motel and Guest House, 141 Essex Avenue on Route 133 (tel. 283-0614), is, as its name foretells, a combination of a slick, modern motel and adjoining old house with spacious lawns. In the latter, double rooms range from $18 to $30; the motel charges $24 to $34, double or single. There's a price drop in each category after Labor Day and through June. (The motel is open all year.) Motel rooms have color TV, and a continental breakfast is served in the sun parlor in season.

Within walking distance to Niles Beach and the Rocky Neck Art Colony is the **Colonial Inn,** 28 Eastern Point Road (tel. 281-1953), operated by Barbara and Bob Balestraci. Here rooms cost $20 to $28 for a double in-season; $14 to $16, off-season. You get private baths, TV, and free continental breakfasts.

One of the friendliest motor inns we know is the **Atlantis** (tel. 283-5807), Atlantic Road in the Bass Rocks section of Gloucester. It has the charm and warmth of a guest house, yet it's a large up-to-date facility with Danish-modern decor, wide picture windows, private sundecks, color TVs, and landscaped swimming pool. Lunch is served on the flower-rimmed patio, and breakfast and lunch are available in the scenic coffeeshop. Rates are based on double occupancy and range from $40 to $42. There is a $5 charge for an extra person. These rates apply from June 28 through Labor Day. Lower fees are in effect from March to the end of June, and from after Labor Day through November.

Another outstanding inn directly on the oceanfront is **Bass Rocks Motor Inn** (tel. 283-7600), Atlantic Road, Gloucester. With its stately white columns and red brick walls, it has the appearance of a southern mansion transplanted to the rocky coast. A rooftop sundeck, balconies, and swimming pool all offer excellent views of the surf. In-season rates (June 21 to Labor Day) are $44 to $48, double occupancy. The inn is open April to November, and has lower rates off-season.

Dining in Gloucester

The seafood at the outstanding **Gloucester House Restaurant** (tel. 283-1812), Seven Seas Wharf, is brought directly from the fishing boats tied up at the pier to the kitchen, where specialties such as baked stuffed scrod ($7.25) and lobster stuffed with lobster (!) are prepared. You might even sample native squid or an octopus salad. There are picture windows all around giving you a panoramic view of the harbor and the fishing fleet. And after dinner, you can stroll along the wharf. Seafood entrees are in the $5 to $9 range, and steaks and chops are slightly higher. Lobster prices are seasonal. Special menu for children, $3.45. Open daily, 11:30 a.m. to 11 p.m. In the summer, clambakes are served outside on Seven Seas Wharf, $10.95. Daily luncheons start at $2.25, and you can enjoy them on the outdoor terrace, where there is also dancing under the stars on Friday and Saturday nights.

Every table at **Captains Courageous,** the excellent restaurant at 25 Rogers Street (tel. 283-0007), has a view of the harbor. On the menu are steaks, chops, and seafood with dinners going from $5.95 to $16. Open Monday through Thursday, 11:30 a.m. to 10 p.m.; Friday and Saturday, till 11 p.m.; and Sunday, noon to 10 p.m. A Sunday buffet is served from 1 p.m. to 8 p.m.

There's a romantic aura to dinner by candlelight at the **Easterly Inn,** 87 Atlantic Road (tel. 283-0140), Gloucester. Luxuriant green plants and soft background music set the mood at this charming restaurant with its window-wall overlooking the ocean. Emphasis is on New England specialties with sauteed scallops, baked stuffed filet of sole, and other native fish. Also on the menu are steak Diane and breast of chicken. Dinner prices from $5.95 to $12; luncheon specials, $2.95 to $4.25. A splendid Sunday buffet Americana is $8.95 for adults and $4.95 for children. Open for lunch and dinner, Monday through Thursday, 11:30 a.m. to 9 p.m.; Friday and Saturday, till 10 p.m. Sunday buffet served from 1 p.m. to 8 p.m.

ROCKPORT: Rockport is a few miles from Gloucester along Route 127. If you stop to do all the sightseeing we've suggested, it will probably take you three days from Boston. If you just view the scenery from the car window, it will take less than 90 minutes. Best known for its artists' colony, Rockport is also a lovely little town; and in our opinion, much more picturesque, with much more to see and do than, for instance, Sausalito outside San Francisco. Weekend parking can be a terrible hassle. (Go on a weekday if you can.) We suggest circling the square once, and if there's no place to park try the back streets, even if they're some distance from the center of town. Or you can use the parking lot on Upper Main Street, Route 127, which is sponsored by the Board of Trade. It's a short distance from the tourist information booth, and the $2 fee includes all-day parking and free round-trip shuttle service every 12 to 15 minutes from 11 a.m. to 7 p.m. daily.

You can also get to Rockport via a Boston & Maine train from North Station (phone 227-6000 for details). It's about $6 for the round trip, (45 minutes each way) through many of the North

Shore's scenic towns. A possible stop might be the **Beverly Depot,** a 19th-century station converted into an attractive restaurant.

Although Rockport is an attractive town to walk through, you might enjoy a sightseeing trip via a surrey with a fringe on top. It takes about an hour, and leaves daily from Dock Square, weather permitting, from 11 a.m. to 4:30 p.m. for the three-mile ride through downtown Rockport. It's easy to find the surrey— Kate, the old brown mare who pulls it, has her own parking space in the square.

There are also one-hour sightseeing cruises from T-Wharf, starting at about 11 a.m., and leaving almost hourly until 4:30 p.m.

Even though there are many charming areas in Rockport, the one that stands out most is the sagging wooden fish warehouse on the old wharf in the harbor, since it probably has been the subject of more paintings than anything since the Last Supper. The red shack, known as Motif #1, is a fitting symbol for this beautiful fishing town. Destroyed in the blizzard of 1978, it has been rebuilt through donations from the local community and tourists. And it stands again on the same pier, duplicated in every detail, reinforced to withstand future northeast storms.

There are more than 200 exhibiting members of the **Rockport Art Association** (you can see their regular exhibitions at the Old Tavern Gallery, just off Dock Square on Main Street), and every year their output is supplemented by the scores of entries received from all over America for the town's **Amateur Art Festival** (early October), for which the first prize is an expense-paid weekend in Rockport. Well over two dozen galleries display the work of artists both local and otherwise, and more than one first-time visitor, intoxicated by the sea air and all this creativity, has stayed on to take art lessons from the numerous instructors who offer their services.

It's easy to see why aesthetes are captivated by the town's charm: the picket-fenced Colonial houses; the narrow, winding streets; the crash of waves against the rocky shore and the ever-present squeal of swooping seagulls. Rockport's pride and joy is **Bearskin Neck,** a narrow peninsula of one-way alleys lined with galleries, antique stores, and ancient houses, set so near together that neighbors could almost lean out of their upstairs windows and shake hands across the street. Bearskin Neck was supposedly named after an unfortunate bear which drowned and was washed ashore here almost 200 years ago.

Bearskin Neck runs off Dock Square, the main center of town, where you'll find the Board of Trade's Information Shack carrying lists of accommodations and things to do around town. First, of course, after the window-shopping, are the beaches. There are several up and down this coastline of harbors, extending to Pigeon Cove almost two miles to the north, and Gloucester about the same distance to the south.

Numerous 18th-century historic homes bear inspection, a trio of them—nos. 6, 8, and 25 Dock Square—in Rockport itself; many more—nos. 7, 96, 141, 159, 188, and 281 Granite Street (the main road)—on the way to Pigeon Cove. One of the oldest houses in the region, the Old Castle at the junction of Granite and Curtis, in Pigeon Cove, dates from 1712 and has never been remodeled or changed. It can be visited 2:30 p.m. to 5 p.m. Saturdays and Sundays, July through August.

Also on the way to Pigeon Cove, take a look at the massive stone quarries which gave Rockport its name and provided industry for the region for at least a century, during which Rockport granite produced paving stones for many American cities, including New Orleans and San Francisco. Rockport granite also provided the foundation for the bandstand at the town's Front Beach, where every Sunday night open-air concerts are still held under the stars.

One of the country's oddest museums must be the **Rockport Paper House**, 50A Pigeon Hill Street, Pigeon Cove (admission: 25¢), which was built in 1922 by Elis Stenman entirely out of 100,000 newspapers. Talk about recycling! The house walls are constructed from 215 folded layers of papers, the fireplace mantel made out of rotogravure sections, and every item of furniture made from papers of a different period—a desk from papers about Charles Lindbergh's flight, for example, and a bed from newspapers reporting on the progress of World War I.

Be sure to ask the Board of Trade Information Office for one of its colorful maps of the town. In the bottom right-hand corner it bears the warning: "Our sea serpent visits only every 25 years." How reassuring!

Picnic Areas

You really have to know about **Halibut Point Reservation** to find it. It's off Gott Street, and you follow a dirt path meandering through blueberry bushes to these flat coastal rocks where you can picnic or just enjoy the sun and the view. A long jetty of

Rockport granite, known as **Granite Pier Wharf,** off Granite Street, is popular for picnics, sailboat-watching, and fishing.

Staying in Rockport

Just north of town on the road to Pigeon Cove is the luxurious **Yankee Clipper,** Route 127 (tel. 546-3407), on extensive lawns overlooking the sea. There are actually three different buildings, of which the inn is the most attractive. Georgian architecture, saltwater swimming pool, and rooms with private balconies. From almost all parts of the property there are excellent views of the sea, especially from the extensive and attractive dining room. Rates begin at about $33 for a double, European Plan, about $65 per day American Plan, with various prices according to season, type of room, etc. The Clipper is closed in winter.

Back in town is the delightful **Seven South Street Inn,** 7 South Street (tel. 546-6708), a gracious New England frame house, furnished in a pleasant style, plus motel units, cottages, and an outdoor pool. There is a comfortable dining room and sitting room in the Inn in Colonial decor, and hosts Helene and George Waldschlagel are friendly and helpful. Single rooms, with shared bath, rent for $10 to $14 daily; doubles with private bath are $28 to $30. Doubles with shared bath are $18 to $22. Breakfast is served on the house. Efficiency units and cottages are available for $190 to $275 per week, considerably reduced off-season. Open March to November 1.

For those who want modern hotel comfort and a beachfront location, **Captain's Bounty Motor Inn,** 1 Beach Street (tel. 546-9494), is the place. Ocean breezes provide natural air conditioning, since each room overlooks the ocean and has its own balcony and sliding glass wall. TV, soundproofing, wall-to-wall carpeting, ceramic tile baths, and all the comforts are provided. Kitchenette units available. In-season doubles are $36 to $38; kitchenettes, $38 to $42.

There are two "Peg Legs" in town. One is **Peg Leg Motel,** 10 Beach Street, Rockport (tel. 546-6945), operated by Jim and Polly Erwin. This attractive motel is on a quiet knoll overlooking Rockport Harbor and directly across the street from the public beach. The rooms are decorated with Ethan Allen furniture, some with rocking chairs or "overstuffed" comfortable chairs. All have double beds, TV, and ceramic tile bath with tub and shower. In-season rates are $35 to $45, double; and off-season, $25 to $35, double. There is plenty of free parking at the motel;

and arrangements can be made for free tennis and golf in town. Open April 1 to mid-November. If you prefer Colonial atmosphere, **Peg Leg Inn,** is just down the street at 18 Beach Street (tel. 546-2352), a group of five Early American houses with front porches, attractive living rooms, and well-kept flower-bordered lawns. Rates are $22 to $40, double, in-season; and an efficiency unit for four with kitchen is $45. All rooms have private baths and TV, and some have excellent ocean views.

Shopping in Rockport

Part of the fun in Rockport is shopping along Bearskin Neck and Dock Square. There are the art galleries, of course, where you can buy originals for up to $20,000 or inexpensive prints for much less. And then there are the over 100 shops squeezed into Bearskin Neck. Lovely little places such as **The Happy Whale,** with puppets, doll-house furniture, and handcrafted wooden toys; **The Dancing Bear,** brimming over with stuffed animals; **Serendipity,** a lovely shop for gifts in all price ranges; and **The Country Store,** which has the little novelties, candies, and jellies typical of country stores. And there are plenty of places to snack on Bearskin Neck, too; take your choices from lobster in the rough to Austrian-style strudel in four delicious flavors.

Once the summer crush is over, peace descends on Rockport. You might want to come in October for the Amateur Art Festival; at Christmas to join a live Christmas pageant sponsored yearly by the Rockport Art Association; or to artists' workshops in spring, fall, and winter at the Seven South Street Inn. Write to the Rockport Board of Trade, Route 127, Rockport, MA 01966, for dates.

Dining in Rockport

Although most visitors to Rockport go to the Blacksmith Shop, 23 Mount Pleasant Street (tel. 546-6301), primarily for the excellent food, some connoisseurs choose this fine restaurant overlooking Rockport Harbor for the atmosphere—the antique furnishings, chairs from Italy, lights from Spain, paintings in the gallery, and the old forge, anvil, and bellows, preserved from the shop where Rockport's village smithy stood. The main dining room, resting on stilts in the harbor, has been enlarged many times since its establishment in 1927, and now accommodates 200. Seafood is the specialty, and owner Larry Bershad goes to the docks every morning to select the best of the local catch. You can't go wrong with broiled yellow-tailed flounder at $6.95; Gloucester scrod with lobster sauce, $7.25; or baked stuffed Alaskan king crab, $11.95. East Coast lobster is $12 to $18; broiled chicken, $6.75; and filet mignon, $10.95. The Blacksmith Shop has its own pastry chef, who turns out cheesecake, pecan pie, and blueberry pie with berries from Gloucester's Dogtown Common. Lunches are also excellent: prices range from $3 for a sandwich to $9 for the fisherman's platter. A delicious shrimp quiche and salad is $4.50. You can also come in the afternoon just for dessert and coffee. Open seven days a week from March to December, 11:30 a.m. to 11 p.m. (Mrs. Marion Bershad also runs the Coach House guest house in Salem.)

For lunch or dinner in a greenhouse, complete with hanging baskets, five-foot geranium trees, and flowers all around, walk through town to the end of Main Street to **Pegleg's,** 18 Beach Street (tel. 546-3038), where both the food and surroundings are superior. The greenhouse, very romantic in the evening with its recessed spotlights and candles, is behind the cozy and attractive main restaurant. Pegleg's is open for breakfast, lunch, and dinner, serving from 8 a.m. to 9 p.m. weekdays, and from noon to 9 p.m. on Sunday. Dinners run from $4.25 for chicken pie to $8.95 for Maryland soft-shelled crabs. Steaks are $9 to $10 and lobsters are priced according to availability. Luncheon prices range from $2.25 for chicken or beef croquettes to $4.95 for baked stuffed shrimp. Baking is done on the premises, and breadbaskets always have sweet rolls and treats such as fresh cranberry bread or blueberry muffins. The service is excellent; owner Robert H. Welcome exemplifies his name.

It looks like a coffeeshop in front, but don't let that fool you. **Oleana** (tel. 546-9447) is a Rockport institution with excellent food and a magnificent harbor view from the windows in the rear of the restaurant at 23 Main Street. Choose from the à la carte menu with items from $2.65 to $9.50, or just have a sandwich and Norwegian rosette pastry topped with strawberry sauce, 65¢. Oleana serves luncheon and dinner every day from 11 a.m. to 7:30 p.m. Closed November through February, and on Monday in the months of March and April. Smorgasbord is served Friday night from 5 p.m. to 7 p.m., and Saturday and Sunday from 11 a.m. to 2 p.m. And while you're there, look at the beautiful stained-glass window designs.

A short distance from Rockport at the tip of Pigeon Cove is the charming **Old Farm Inn** (tel. 546-3237), 291 Granite Street on Route 127. Lunch and dinner are served in the dining room of this old home, and during the summer, on the open terrace. Crabmeat-mushroom pie ($7.50) and finnan haddie ($5.95) are among the specialties. Entrees go from $5.95 to $11.95. And while you're there, forget the calories and feast on Old Farm Indian pudding, baked in a black iron stove, and served hot, topped with ice cream, 85¢. Open 11:30 a.m. to 2 p.m., Tuesday through Friday for lunch; and from 5 to 9 p.m. for dinner. On Sunday, brunch is served from 9:00 a.m. to 1:30 p.m., and dinner from 4 to 9 p.m.

Note: Rockport is a "dry" community and restaurants are forbidden by law from serving alcoholic beverages, but you can brown-bag it with your own bottle.

If you'd like to do some more exploring after leaving Rockport, take Route 128 to Route 1A to Ipswich, another historical town, probably best known for magnificent Crane's Beach, and then on to Newburyport, with elegant 19th-century homes, and a history of waterfront shipyards. Or you can take Route 128 back to Boston. Just follow the signs.

3. The Road to Plymouth

A visit to the South Shore resorts usually ends in a trip to historic Plymouth, where the *Mayflower* Pilgrims took up residence at the close of 1620; but there are worthwhile stops along the way, the first being Quincy, about eight miles to the southeast of Boston.

Quincy is notable as the birthplace of two presidents—John Adams (1796–1800) and his son John Quincy Adams (1824–1828)—the second and sixth persons, respectively, to hold that office. John's wife Abigail, the only woman in American history to be married to one president and mother of another (although she died before her son took office), kept a neat and tidy household in what was then a pitifully inadequate house, but which has since been added to by one generation of the family after another.

The house, the **Adams Mansion,** 135 Adams Street, has been maintained much as it was in those days, and is open to the public from 9 to 5 from April 19 to November 10, and admission is 50¢. Filled with period antiques and surrounded by a lovely garden, it is well worth a visit.

Hingham, with its 17th-century church (open noon to 5 p.m. Tuesday through Sunday, July and August), and neighboring **Cohasset,** whose extensive fortifications in 1814 frightened away a British warship which had been bent on attacking the community, are steeped in history, and Cohasset's contemporary claim to fame is its nightly **Music Circus** (summer only).

Duxbury, on Route 3A, 30 miles southeast of Boston, was settled by Myles Standish, John Alden, and some of the other original Pilgrims two or three years after the founding of the Plymouth colony. Among the remembrances of them that can be inspected today are the **Myles Standish Homestead** and the nearby monument at a picnic site; the **Old Burying Ground** where Standish and Alden are buried; and the **Alden House,** built by the Pilgrim's son. All are open to public during the summer months.

PLYMOUTH: The historic town of Plymouth (pop. 16,000) is where the United States began, and it's impossible not to be awed by reminders of the 3½ centuries of history which have accumulated there. When the Pilgrims first set up their encampment at this site in December 1620 (after a preliminary but unsatisfactory landing at Provincetown), all was bleak and uninviting. But the hardy adventurers built homes, planted crops, and established friendly relations with the natives; and the seeds they planted have, in more ways than one, endured to this day. (To reach Plymouth by car, follow the Southeast Expressway to Route 3. Take exit 38 to Plymouth Center, turn right on to Route 44, and follow signs to the historic attractions. Plymouth is about 40 miles from Boston. Buses operated by the Plymouth and Brockton Street Railway leave the Greyhound Terminal every hour; tel. 749-5067.)

The Plymouth of today is an attractive seafaring town with much to occupy your attention. Even if you're just passing through, you'll at least want to inspect the famous **Plymouth Rock** on which the first Pilgrims made their initial contact with the land. You should also find time to examine **Mayflower II,** a reproduction of the ship that brought them to this country, and **Plimoth Plantation,** which gives an idea of what life was like in those rugged days. Possibly your first stop should be the town's **Information Booth,** just below the intersection of Route 44 and Court Street (tel. 746-4734), where hotel and motel reservations can be made and all your questions answered. Open daily, 8 a.m. to 9 p.m. Parking at Plymouth Rock parking area is $1; metered parking along the waterfront, 50¢ for 2½ hours.

The most logical place to begin your tour of Plymouth is

where the Pilgrims began—at **Plymouth Rock.** The Rock, accepted as the landing place of the *Mayflower* passengers, was originally fifteen feet long and three feet wide. It was moved on the eve of the Revolution and several times thereafter, before acquiring its present permanent position at tide level, where the winter storms still break over it as they did in Pilgrim days. The present portico which enshrines the Rock was a gift in 1920 of the Colonial Dames of America.

Cape Cod was named in 1602 by Captain Bartholomew Gosnold, and 12 years later Captain John Smith sailed along the coast of what he named "New England" and designated "Plymouth" as the mainland opposite Cape Cod.

The passengers on the *Mayflower* had contracted with the London Virginia Company for a tract of land near the mouth of the Hudson River in "Northern Virginia"; in exchange for their passage to the New World, they would work the land for the company for seven years. However, on November 11, 1620, falling among perilous shoals and roaring breakers, with the wind howling, they had to make for Cape Cod Bay and anchor there. Subsequently, their captain announced that they had found a safe harbor and refused to continue the voyage farther south to their original destination. They had no option but to settle in New England, and with no one to command them, their patent from the London Virginia Company became void and they were on their own to begin a new world.

The **Mayflower II,** berthed at State Pier in Plymouth, only steps from Plymouth Rock, is a full-scale reproduction of the ship which brought the Pilgrims from England to America. Though there is little technical information known about the original *Mayflower,* designer of *Mayflower II* William A. Baker incorporated the few references in Governor Bradford's account of the voyage with other researches to recreate as closely as possible the actual ship. Exhibits on board show what life was like during that 66-day voyage in 1620 on a vessel crowded with 102 passengers, 25 crewmen, and all the supplies needed to sustain the colony until the first crops were harvested. Trying to imagine the hardships of that voyage, when one sees how little room there was for so many people, boggles the mind.

Men and women in period costumes on board the ship talk about the crossing of the *Mayflower,* answer questions, and dispatch little-known but interesting pieces of information (such as the fact that the first two Indians to greet the Pilgrims upon their landing spoke pretty good English—taught to them by British sailors and fishermen who had earlier sailed up the coast, and that John Alden was the ship's carpenter). Below deck is a life-size tableau (with mannequins) of the signing of the *Mayflower* Compact.

You will not want to miss a tour of the ship. The *Mayflower II*, is open to the public from April 1 to November 30, 9 a.m. to 5 p.m. daily. During July and August, tickets are sold until 8 p.m. every night. Admission is $1.25 for adults; 75¢ for children 5 to 13; under 5, free. The vessel is owned and maintained by Plimoth Plantation which is three miles south of the ship.

Right alongside the *Mayflower II*, there is a replica of an early Pilgrim dwelling, one of the first houses built in that winter of 1620–21. Open daily from 9 a.m. to 4:30 p.m., admission is 10¢, and again costumed guides explain the details.

Apart from the *Mayflower* and the Plimoth Plantation, possibly the town's major attraction is **Pilgrim Hall**, Court Street, open all year from 9 a.m. to 4:30 p.m. Admission is $1 for adults; children, 25¢. The oldest public museum in the United States, and a registered Massachusetts Historic Landmark, it is replete with original possessions of the early Pilgrims and their descendants. The building itself dates from 1824. Among the exhibits is the skeleton of the *Sparrowhawk*, a ship wrecked on Cape Cod in 1627, which lay buried in the sand and undiscovered for more than 200 years.

Plimoth Plantation

At this oddly spelled establishment, a 1627 Pilgrim village has been recreated with great authenticity. In Plimoth Plantation, you can wander around thatched houses, herb gardens, and the primitive early fort, all the time within sight of "residents" who in speech, dress, manner, and attitude have assumed the personality of a known member of the community in 1627. Daily activities in the village and responses to questions are based entirely on these assumed 17th-century personalities. Whether they are thatching a roof, tending gardens, shearing sheep, harvesting crops, or preserving foodstuffs, the villagers are friendly and eager to answer your queries. Sometimes you can even join in the activities.

The community is as accurate as research can make it; eyewitness accounts of visitors to the original Pilgrim colony were combined with archaeological research, old records, and the 17th-century history written by the Pilgrims' leader, William

Bradford. The village is set in what purports to be the year 1627, and all the tasks and duties are carried out with the implements available at that time. There are daily militia drills with matchlock muskets laboriously filled with powder and fired to demonstrate the community's defense system. In actual fact, very little defense was needed because of the unexpected friendship of the local Indians.

Not far from the village, the **Wampanoag Summer Settlement** with wigwam, firepit, and corn fields, recreates the summer residence and activities of a Wampanoag family in the early 1600s.

To reach Plimoth Plantation (tel. 746-1622), from Route 3 take the exit marked Plimoth Plantation Highway. The village is open daily from April 1 through November 30, 9 a.m. to 5 p.m. The Wampanoag Settlement is open May 15 to October 15. Admission for both exhibits is $2.50 for adults; $1, children 5 to 13; under 5, free. *(Note:* Wear comfortable shoes. There's lots to see and do.)

The Mayflower Experience, a unique sound, light, and animation presentation, recreates the Pilgrims voyage on the *Mayflower.* Located at 114 Water Street, next to the Governor Bradford Motel, it is open from 9 a.m. to 5 p.m. in the spring and fall; and from 9 to 9:30 p.m. in the summer.

If you like cranberries—cranberry sauce, cranberry bread, or even cranberry sherbet—you'll be fascinated by the exhibits at **Cranberry World,** Water Street (tel. 747-1000), where there are outdoor working bogs, antique harvesting tools, and a scale model of a cranberry farm. In addition there are daily cooking demonstrations at 11:30 a.m. and free refreshments. Hours are 10 a.m. to 5 p.m. daily, June through September; and Wednesday through Sunday in April, May, October, and November. Admission free. The Cranberry World Visitor's Center is about a ten-minute walk from Plymouth Rock.

Staying in Plymouth

One of the most luxurious hotels in Plymouth, the **Governor Bradford Motor Inn,** Water Street (tel. 746-6200), is beautifully situated right on the waterfront and only one block's walk from Plymouth Rock, the *Mayflower,* and the center of town. The 94 rooms, each with two double beds, are attractive in the modern style, colorful, with wall-to-wall carpeting, TV, individually controlled air conditioning and heating. A game room, outdoor pool, and terraced rooms overlooking Plymouth Bay are added attractions. Rates vary according to the season, the highest being from June 15 to September 14: $32 to $45 for a single, $36 to $48 for a double. During the winter, they go down to $25 for a single, $26 to $32 for a double, with varying scales in spring and fall. Children under 14 are free.

A sister hotel to the Governor Bradford, the **Governor Carver Motor Inn,** 25 Summer Street at Town Square (tel. 746-7100), is a fine Colonial-style building, with excellent modern accommodations, heated pool, color TV, free cribs, and all the amenities. It is also within walking distance to the main attractions, and in-season rates run $32 to $45 in a single, $36 to $48 in a double. The Hungry Pilgrim Restaurant and Thirsty Pilgrim Lounge are right on the premises. Again, open all year and very comfortable. Pick your Governor.

The **Loremar Guest House,** Route 3A, 126 Warren Avenue (tel. 746-9455), is situated two miles out of town, right on Plymouth Beach and a short distance from Plimoth Plantation. Loremar has a quiet and restful atmosphere with beautiful lawns and a view of the ocean. Air-conditioned rooms with showers are $20 a day, $125 per week; a two-bedroom suite is $25 daily, $160 per week; double bedrooms, $14 a day, $88 weekly. Season is July 1 through Labor Day.

Located midway between Plymouth Rock and Plimoth Plantation is the **Colonial House Inn,** 207 Sandwich Street (tel. 746-2087), whose quiet, secluded grounds offer a picturesque view of Plymouth Bay plus a swimming pool. All rooms have Early American decor, private baths, TV, and air conditioning, and are quite pleasant and home-like. In season, double rooms are $20 to $29; off-season, $18; and you may have an extra cot put in your room for $2 extra daily.

The **Cold Spring Motel,** 188 Court Street, Route 3A (tel. 746-2222), is small and quiet, with only 15 rooms in all. Modern and air-conditioned, with color TV in all units, this is not the most elegant hostelry around, but it is clean and pleasant. Summer rates run from $18 to $30 in a double and twin.

The most attractive vacation spot outside town, yet within walking distance of the Plimoth Plantation, is the **Pilgrim Sands Motel,** Route 3A, Warren Avenue (tel. 746-4360). Here, there are 42 ultramodern units, located right on the ocean, all with tile bath and shower, individually controlled heating and air conditioning, TV, wall-to-wall carpeting, and tasteful furnishings. In summertime you can enjoy the private beach and terraces and a lovely heated swimming pool, too. All rooms have two double beds, and double occupancy rates in season are $32 to $38 (the higher rate for oceanfront rooms). In spring and fall, the tariff goes down to $20 and $28.

Dining in Plymouth

Seafood is, of course, the specialty at almost all Plymouth restaurants, and we can't think of a better place to sample it than at **Bert's Restaurant,** Warren Street, Route 3A (tel. 746-3422), located three miles out of town and directly opposite Plimoth Plantation. Two large elegant rooms, newly decorated in tones of orange and brown with Tiffany-style lamps and hanging plants in rope baskets, look out on the ocean. Service is fast and efficient, and the portions are generous. Fried or broiled filets of sole or scrod are $5.95; sauteed jumbo shrimp is $7.25; and boneless breast of chicken is $4.95. Steaks and prime rib run from $7.95 to $8.95. Bert's also has two lounges and a disco. And if you should come during the month of your birthday, any day from Monday to Friday, your meal is free, providing you have at least one other paying customer with you.

Seafood is also the raison d'être at **McGrath's Harbour Restaurant** on the waterfront (tel. 746-9751), with an excellent view of the harbor. The deluxe seafood plate is $6.90; baked stuffed filet of sole, $5.45; and a delicious baked stuffed lobster is around $9.95 (depending on the day's catch). McGrath's also serves chicken, sandwiches, and steak, with a complete steak dinner at $9.95, and their special open crabmeat sandwich at $5.50. Open daily from 11:30 a.m. to 9:30 p.m., Monday through Saturday; and till 9 p.m. on Sunday in the summer. Closed Tuesdays during the winter months.

Right by the town wharf is **Mayflower Seafoods** (tel. 746-1704), with two attractive dining rooms serving fish and chicken dinners, casseroles, and a large selection of appetizers. An excellent baked stuffed lobster is $9; boiled lobster, $7.90; fried filet of sole, $4.65. Chicken dinners are $4.90 and creamed finnan haddie is $4.95. Luncheons go from $1.75 for hamburger and $2.90 for fried clam roll to $3.50 for coquilles St. Jacques or king crab casserole. Open 11:30 a.m. to 9 p.m. daily in the summer, but closed on Monday in the winter.

The Mayflower Seafoods Fish Market in the same building is self-service, no tipping. You place your order by number with the cashier; when your number is called, your order is ready. Choices range from fish and chips, $1.75; steamed clams, $2.95;

or butterfly shrimp at $4.95; all the way up to baked stuffed
lobster, $9; with all kinds of fish and chicken in between. To eat
while sitting on the wharf, just ask that your order be prepared
for take out.

Note: Before you leave Plymouth County to see Cape Cod,
take a ride on the **Edaville R.R.** on Route 58, South Carver,
where a restored two-foot-gauge railroad tours 5½ miles of an
1,800-acre cranberry plantation. In the fall you can watch the
harvesting, and all during the season (June to October 31), you
can visit the **Edaville Museum of New England Heritage** with
its collection of railroad artifacts, toy trains, fire engines, and
firefighting equipment; explore the children's petting zoo; stroll
along an authentic 1800s Main Street; or ride an antique carou-
sel. Try the famous chicken barbecue dinner, too. Open 10 a.m.
to 5:30 p.m. daily, with an admission fee of $3 for adults and
$1.50 for children. To reach Edaville, take exit 38 on Route 3
(Plymouth exit), then Route 44 west to Carver and Route 58
south to Rochester road.

4. Cape Cod

Cape Cod—pine-scented, sea-swept, cranberry-bogged—is
one of the most popular vacation lands in the Northeast and one
of the most amenable anywhere. Here, where the Pilgrims made
their first landing (at Provincetown, before they sailed to Plymouth looking for a better harbor), thousands of Bostonians now
maintain beach homes; New Yorkers and Philadelphians and
even people from the Midwest love it for summer vacations, as
do ever-increasing throngs of Canadians. And there is plenty to
attract the visitor in this bent-at-the-elbow peninsula which juts
out into the Atlantic 57 miles south of Boston to point its tip
northward to the city. This old seafaring corner of New England
(whaling ships once put out from its ports; fishing is still a big
industry) boasts a landscape that includes 300 miles of sparkling,
sandy white beaches, as well as marshlands, meadows, pine forests; quaint New England towns with their trim architecture,
their old saltbox houses and winding, tree-shaded lanes; scores
of art galleries, museums, summer theaters, historical attractions; facilities for a dozen different sports; plus some of the best
antiquing and most diversified shopping anywhere.

There are hundreds of restaurants and hotels to feed and
house the almost half-million people on the Cape any given
summer day, and accommodations run the gamut from cozy

guest houses run by old-time Cape Codders, where the landlady fixes you coffee in the kitchen in the morning, to shiny new motels complete with heated year-round pools and individually controlled air conditioning. It's a modern, bustling, heavily crowded summer resort area, but with enough salty New England flavor still left to make it a rather unique spot on this globe.

If you're in Boston in the summer, you must certainly go "down the Cape" for a few days, or, better yet, a few weeks; if you have the kids with you, it's a good place for them to let off some steam. In the spring and fall, the Cape is particularly lovely: not warm enough for swimming, but brisk and clear, uncrowded, and fine for sightseeing, shopping, sports. And there are those who also dote on it in winter, when they can sit by the fire in a quaint guest house and perhaps watch a famed New England "Nor'easter" lash the streets. A word about the weather: don't expect perfection, even in summer, but a rainy day on the Cape can have its own windy charm.

BEACHES: You can't miss them, and you have your choice of either bathtub bathing in the warm waters facing Buzzard's Bay and Nantucket Sound or the more traditionally nippy Massachusetts waters on the oceanside shore. Most Cape towns have both ocean and bay beaches, and some have lakes and freshwater ponds as well. Many of the smaller towns require resident stickers to use their beaches (you get one for your car when you check into your hotel), but there are also many beaches open to the general public, like **Craigville Beach** at Barnstable and the enormous, well-equipped **Scusset State Beach Reservation** near Bourne (access via Routes 3, 6, and South Sagamore Circle). The National Seashore maintains some of the best beaches of all: try **Head of the Meadow** in North Truro, **Coast Guard Beach** in Eastham, **Herring Cove** in Provincetown. There's a $1 parking fee, or a seasonal pass for $10.

CAMPING: Cape Cod's major camping sites are the **Shawme Crowell State Forest** at Sandwich, Scusset State Beach Sagamore; and a larger site, the **Roland C. Nickerson State Forest** at Brewster, where there are freshwater ponds stocked with trout (fishing license needed; write to Massachusetts Division of Fisheries & Wildlife, 100 Cambridge Street, Boston, MA 02202). Many fine private campgrounds are also open from Bourne to Wellfleet.

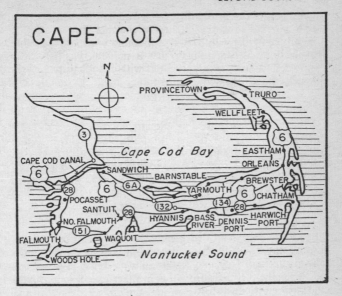

GETTING TO CAPE COD: Here you have several choices:

By Car

Take the Southeastern Expressway from Boston and follow Route 3 south through Plymouth and to Sagamore, where the Cape Cod Canal officially marks the beginning of the Cape. If you're headed directly to Provincetown or the other north Cape towns like Wellfleet or Truro (where half the psychoanalysts of New York retreat for the month of August), you can make better time by driving the fast Mid-Cape Highway (U.S. 6), but we think it's a shame to miss the charms of such graceful villages as Barnstable, Dennis, and Brewster, through which you will pass by taking the very scenic Route 6A, along the north shore.

If you're headed for Hyannis, or for Harwich with its cranberry industry; for Falmouth or for Woods Hole (where you pick up the boats to Nantucket and Martha's Vineyard), head south after you cross the Cape Cod Canal and take Route 28 eastward.

By Air

Daily flights from Boston to Provincetown, by the **Boston-Provincetown Airline**, Logan Airport, Boston (tel. 567-6090). One-way fare, $17. Flights from 7:30 a.m. to 7:30 p.m. Only one-half hour travel time.

By Bus

Almeida Bus Lines, 10 Park Square, Boston (tel. 542-7242) runs 10 buses daily to Woods Hole and 11 daily to Hyannis and Provincetown. **Greyhound** bus lines, Park Square, Boston, (tel. 423-5810) runs buses every hour on the hour from 6 a.m. to 6 p.m. Cape Cod Bus Lines runs from Hyannis to Provincetown four times daily (tel. 775-5524 in Hyannis).

By Ship

Bay State Spray and Provincetown Cruises, 20 Long Wharf, Boston (tel. 723-7800), has a round-trip boat to Provincetown daily in late June, July, and August, and weekends in early June and September. It sails from Long Wharf, next to the New England Aquarium, at 9:30 a.m. and arrives in Provincetown at about 1 p.m. The return trip leaves at about 3:15 p.m. Round-trip tickets cost $12 for adults, $8 for children. One way is $8 for adults; $6, children. There's a band on board, and sandwiches and snacks are available. Special senior citizen rates in effect Monday through Friday.

INFORMATION, PLEASE: For help, advice, driving directions, information on hotels, restaurants, sports facilities, beaches, shops, whatever, consult any of these three major information centers maintained by the Cape Cod Chamber of Commerce. They are located at: junction of Routes 6 and 132, Hyannis; South Rotary, at Bourne Bridge; Sagamore Rotary, at Sagamore Bridge. In addition, many of the smaller towns have their own information centers to care for visitors.

Or, you may write in advance for information to Cape Cod Chamber of Commerce, Jct. of Routes 6 and 132, Hyannis, MA 02601.

SANDWICH: The Cape really begins at the Cape Cod Canal, built by the army Corps of Engineers in 1914 to save southbound ships a lengthy and often dangerous journey round the tip and out to sea. (The bones of many an old ship lie deep in Cape Cod waters.) Just south of the canal, on Route 6A, is the town of **Sandwich,** a remarkably serene little village that always reminds us of the English countryside, complete with a meandering stream and several swans. The time-honored visitor attraction is the **Sandwich Glass Museum** on Route 130, a repository of the world-renowned Sandwich glassware that was made here from 1825 to 1888. (Open April 1 to November 1, 9:30 am. to 4:30 p.m. daily. Admission for adults is $1.50; children, 25¢.)

A newer attraction and also an outstanding one is the absorbing museum of Americana called **Heritage Plantation of Sandwich,** at Grove and Pine Streets, three miles from the Cape Cod Sagamore Bridge (tel. 888-3300). (Open May to mid-October, 10 a.m. to 5 p.m. daily. Admission for adults is $2.50; children 11 and under, 75¢.)

Other historical sites to note include the 300-year-old **Hoxie House** (open mid-June through September, 10 a.m. to 5 p.m.; adults, 50¢; children, 35¢), an early saltbox furnished in period style by Boston's Museum of Fine Arts; **Thomas Dexter's Grist Mill** (open mid-June through September, daily; adults, 75¢, and children, 50¢), restored to 17th-century style and offering cornmeal for sale; **Yesteryear's Doll and Miniature Museum,** Main and River streets (open 10 a.m. to 5 p.m. daily; Sunday, 1 p.m. to 5 p.m.; admission is $1.50 for adults, $1 for children) situated in the First Parish Meeting House, established by the Pilgrims in 1638.

For accommodations, **The Earl of Sandwich Motor Manor,** East Sandwich, just north of town on Route 6A (tel. 888-1415), is a very comfortable, Tudor-designed motel, complete with all the comforts, including soundproofed rooms, TV, electric heat. Doubles go from $28 to $32, with complimentary continental breakfast. Lower rates off-season.

Dining Along Route 6A

One of the pleasures of driving along Route 6A is discovering some of the finest restaurants on the Cape. Starting at Sandwich and continuing along the scenic route to East Brewster, you can enjoy everything from dinner "in the rough" to the finest haute cuisine.

Anthony's on the Canal, Coast Guard Road, P.O. Box 454, Sandwich (tel. 888-4629), serves the biggest seafood plates on the Cape to about 1,500 customers a day. Stop here if you're hungry for good food, huge portions, informality (paper plates and styrofoam cups), and low, low prices: from $3.25 for deep-fried fish to $4.95 for sirloin steak and baked stuffed haddock, to $6.95 for lobster salad plate. Lobster prices fluctuate around the $9 range. Open May through October from 4:30 on Monday to Saturday, and from 2 p.m. on Sunday and holidays.

Down the road a way in Yarmouth Port is **Cummaquid Inn** (tel. 362-4501), one of the galaxy of fine restaurants run by Anthony Athanas (of Pier 4 in Boston fame). Even if you're not hungry enough for whole Dover sole, bouillabaisse, baked stuffed lobster, or prime ribs, the view across the marshes to Mill Pond is worth stopping by for. Dinner is served from 5 p.m. on weekdays and from noon on Sunday in the dining room and garden room. Price range is from $6.95 for broiled scrod to about $16 for the large stuffed lobster. There are also lodgings at the Inn from $50 to $60.

Whenever we're on the Cape we keep coming back to the **Cranberry Goose,** a charming restaurant in a 200-year-old country inn set amid giant elms. Dinner is served from 5:30 p.m. to 9:30 p.m. daily except Tuesday (mid-June to Labor Day) in several intimate dining rooms. Every step of the dinner from preparation to serving is carefully supervised by the owner, Mrs. Fiorenzo, who has been giving individual attention to patrons for almost 30 years. The menu varies, but the veal and duck are always excellent. Entrees range from about $8 to $12. On Friday an American-continental buffet is featured. Reservations—and jackets—are required. Cranberry Goose (tel. 362-3501) is on Route 6A in the historic district of Yarmouth Port.

We know some people who make the trip from Boston to the Cape just to dine at **Chillingsworth,** in East Brewster. This award-winning French restaurant has five candlelit dining rooms with fresh flowers at each table and a view of a carefully tended garden. Dinner is *table d'hote* from $15 to $20 with five full courses prepared from top-quality ingredients and served by attentive personnel. The menu changes nightly but usually includes filet of beef Kempinski, $20; rack of lamb, $20: and several fish, chicken, and meat selections. There is usually a hot and a cold soup (we can recommend carrot and leek and the melon soup), well-prepared fresh vegetables and salads, and a splendid array of desserts including cake, sherbet, and several mousses laced with liqueur. There are two dinner seatings, 6:30 p.m. and 9 p.m. Lunch is served in the garden in fine weather, or indoors in the cocktail lounge or one of the small parlors (when the weather is not so fine) from 11:30 a.m. to 2:30 p.m. The luncheon menu features salads, crêpes, and quiches in the $4 range, and a hot meat or fish selection for about $5. Sunday brunch is 11:30 a.m. to 2:30 p.m. Chillingsworth, which is located on Main Street, Route 6A (tel. 896-3640), is closed on Mondays.

Capt. Linnell House (tel. 255-3400), in the town of Orleans where Route 6A joins Route 6, is an excellent restaurant in a restored, clapboarded ante-bellum mansion with old-fashioned gardens and wisteria-covered columns. The menu is continental with about two dozen entrees priced from about $7 to $12. Roast quail at $10.50 is a favorite selection, and so is the chicken provençale, $6.75 (baked with fresh vegetables, seasoned with herbs, and topped with Swiss cheese). We found it especially delightful at lunch (Monday through Saturday, 11 a.m. to 3 p.m.) when we could also enjoy the gardens. Located on Skaket Road, Capt. Linnell is open for dinner from 5 p.m. to 10 p.m. weekdays, and from 11:30 a.m. to 9:30 p.m. on Sundays.

HYANNIS: Hyannis became famous because it once housed what, in effect, became the summer White House, the Kennedy home. Crowds would throng the streets of the little south-shore town content to bask, however tenuously, in the glamor of the region.

Today, though much of the summer tourist boom remains, Hyannis evokes sadness for those who revered the Kennedy legend. Many visitors drive down Ocean Street to pay a brief tribute to its memory by observing the JFK memorial, a plaque on a stone wall looking over the Atlantic.

To reach Hyannis take the Mid-Cape highway, Route 6, to exit 132, which passes the airport on the way into the town. Traffic usually backs up on this road, so if you can, ask at one of the service stations for directions to the bypass roads used by the local residents.

The town itself, though small, boasts two harbors and six public beaches for which you must pay a $2.50 parking fee unless you receive a sticker from your motel or apply at the town hall for special discount stickers. There are also many fine beaches in Yarmouth, just a few miles from Hyannis where parking is $3 a day with special weekly rates.

Hour-long harbor cruises leave from the Ocean Dock in Hyannis Port starting at 9 a.m. and every 30 minutes thereafter from May through October; $2.50 for adults; $1, children. (Call

Hy-Line, 775-7185.) In addition to passing neighboring islands, these cruises offer what is probably the best view of the Kennedy estate compound (on land, guards discourage visitors from approaching too closely). At the same dock there are several daily sailings (June to September) to Nantucket and Martha's Vineyard which allow about four hours ashore on either island. Sailing time to Nantucket is two hours; to the Vineyard, 15 minutes less. For exact times and spring and fall schedules, call 775-7185. Rates are $9 for adults; $4.50 for children under 15.

Note: There is also a Jazz Boat featuring a Dixieland band which leaves from the Ocean Street Pier on Tuesdays, Thursdays, and Sundays at 9 p.m. and returns at midnight. Fare is $6.

Shopping in Hyannis

There are three major shopping areas in Hyannis: the Cape Cod Mall, Main Street, and the area near the West End Rotary. The Mall, located on the outskirts of Hyannis near the airport, is a large complex of some 100 shops following the pattern of a typical suburban mall. Main Street is touristy with many little shops and boutiques, gift stores and eating places—some of them open until 10 or 11 each night. Buy taffy there, or fudge or peanuts. Treat yourself to a gift at **Soft as a Grape,** and discover terrific buys in men's shirts at **Casual Male.**

Just up from the West End Rotary at 187 West Main Street is our favorite place for buying china, crystal, tableware, and pottery at discounts that go as high as 60%. **Cape Pottery House** (tel. 775-1112) is the domain of Harold Gordon, who "retired" to the Cape a few years ago and now works seven days a week (six in the winter) managing this attractive shop with its designer closeouts, select seconds, and Italian and Scandinavian imports.

And in downtown Hyannis at Stevens and North streets, also near the West End Rotary, is the new **ChartHouse Village Marketplace,** a cluster of brick buildings grouped around brick walks to resemble an 18th-century market. It's very up-to-date, though, with a Scandinavian design furniture store; an Eastern Mountain Sports shop; plus galleries, restaurants, and food stores, including Cardoos international foods and Baskin-Robbins ice cream; and a delightful florist shop, **Daffodils,** which has exotic plants, beautiful arrangements, and quite out-of-the-ordinary paraphernalia.

Note: Visit Hyannis's candle factories for free tours, and watch candles being made from fragrant bayberries. **Colonial Candle**

Company is at 238 Main Street, and **Old Harbor Candle** is on
Route 132 across from the Sheraton Regal Inn. And at **Old
Harbor's Cracker Barrel** you can grind your own peanut butter.

Staying in Hyannis

Across the street from Pier 1, from which the boats sail for
Nantucket and Martha's Vineyard, is the huge, bustling **Hyannis
Harborview Motel,** 213 Ocean Street (tel. 775-4420), with at-
tractive, modern rooms, both indoor and outdoor pools (plus
sauna), the 213 Restaurant on the premises (entertainment
nightly in season), and a central location overlooking Hyannis
Harbor. Summer season rates go from $36 to $44 for a double.
Rates are lower in spring and fall.

Dunfey's Hyannis Resort, West End Circle (tel. 775-7775), is
a self-contained luxury motel with 224 rooms, indoor and outdoor pools, tennis courts, 18-hole, par-3 golf course, and numerous bars and restaurants. The Dunfeys also run Boston's famed
Parker House. The 70-acre complex is open year round. Seasonal
rates: July and August, $66 to $72, double. Inquire about occasional package deals.

Need something a little less spectacular? **Hills,** 530 West Main
Street (tel. 775-0344), has a charming inn alongside their restaurant, with six large, air-conditioned rooms with two double beds
in each room. We admired their flowered sheets and pillowcases
so much, we bought some just like them for ourselves. And we
still remember the continental breakfast with home-baked coffee-
cake. Rates are around $25 to $30 for two.

New in the area is the **Iyanough Hills Motor Lodge and Golf
Club** (tel. 771-4804) with large, comfortable rooms and luxuries
such as a bedside switch to turn the TV on and off, sauna, heated
indoor pool, and whirlpool. It's set well back from the road on
Route 132, and its rates range from $26 to $35 double. And the
James Stephen Motel (tel. 775-2655) on Route 28 near the
downtown area, but away from the crowds, is an attractive
Colonial-style motel on spacious grounds with pool and picnic
area. In-season rates are $22 to $26 double; off-season, $12 to
$14. Check on family and package rates.

Mrs. Margaret Goodman operates the **Yellow Door Guest
House,** 6 Main Street (tel. 775-0321), very simple and clean, with
twin, double, or triple rooms from $5 to $8 per person per day,
double occupancy. There are also many low-cost guest houses in
the region of South Street where it crosses Ocean Street.

Dining in Hyannis

Our special favorite in Hyannis is **Hill's Dining Room,** 530 West Main Street (tel. 775-0344). The owners spend the morning and early afternoon in the kitchen, cooking and baking; and open for dinner at 5 p.m., weekdays, and noon on Sunday. Complete meals are served until 8:30 p.m. and are priced from $5 to $8. Veal cutlets, with creole sauce, are excellent at $5, and include appetizer, vegetables (fresh from the garden), dessert, and beverage. The home-cooked food (chicken, shrimp, Swedish meatballs, steak) is all excellent, but what is really irresistible is the desserts. The raspberry shortcake with berries picked that morning from the garden and served with real whipped cream, the angel cake with orange glaze, and the Bavarian mocha pie are favorites with everyone except, perhaps, weight watchers. But they can indulge in the fruit cup made with fresh fruit. Open from May to October. No reservations accepted.

Mildred's Chowder House, Route 28, near the airport, has grown from a tiny shack to a famous local landmark. There's often an hour's wait for a table, but customers feel it's worthwhile when they're finally served their clam chowder, 95¢ a cup; baked stuffed jumbo shrimp, $8.75; or broiled fresh scrod, $5.45. Open daily, 11 a.m. to 10 p.m. We've found the meals at **Shirdan's Restaurant** at the airport rotary in Hyannis equal to Mildred's without the hassle of a long wait. A large bowl of clam chowder is $1.10; broiled haddock, $4.25; and a dessert of excellent apple crisp only 60¢ Shirdan's is open from 6 a.m. to 9 p.m. daily, and a dinner special is served from 5 p.m. (Try the chicken pie.)

And if you're looking for a vegetarian restaurant, there's **Our House,** 448 South Street, Hyannis (tel. 771-4815), which also sells natural foods and baked goods. Open too, for late-night snacks Friday and Saturday evenings from 11 p.m. to 2 a.m. If you like the salt air to spice your seafood, **Baxter's,** 177 Pleasant Street (tel. 775-4490), serves the fried clams and other fresh fish on the wharf or the ferry boat. It's very much a Hyannis landmark.

We found a very good breakfast deal at a small place on Route 132 next to the Rainbow Motel. The **Somethin Worth Eatin Place** has a special for $1.95 that includes two eggs, ham, bacon, or sausage, home fries, toast, juice, and coffee. Ham, cheese, and egg on an English muffin is 85¢. They also serve salads and sandwiches for lunch, and hamburgers go from 95¢ to $1.65 depending on the fixings.

Mid-Cape Museums

Brewster is a small town that's big on museums—there are three of them on Route 6A: **The Drummer Boy Museum** follows the story of the American Revolution via life-size panoramas and guided tours, daily, May to October, from 9:30 a.m. to 6 p.m.; **The Fire and History Museum** shows an 18th-century New England common as well as antique fire apparatus, from Memorial Day weekend to mid-September, 10 a.m. to 5 p.m.; and at the **Museum of Natural History,** guided tours on the marsh trails are conducted in summer and fall from 10 a.m. to 5 p.m. Call 896-3867 for details.

In Chatham there's the **Railroad Museum**—on Depot Street, of course, which has a wooden caboose "retired from service" and a trainload of memorabilia. Open 2 p.m. to 4 p.m. daily. And in Orleans, the **French Cable Museum** on Cove Road has the original equipment used to transmit Morse Code via an undersea cable that ran to Brest, France. Open Tuesday to Saturday, 2 p.m. to 4 p.m.

YARMOUTH: Continuing eastward on Route 28 from Hyannis you travel through Yarmouth, with mile after mile of motels, gift shops, and restaurants. **The Riverway Lobster House** (tel. 398-2172) on Route 28, where you can dine indoors or on the dock, and **Fred's Turkey House,** 518 Main Street (tel. 775-6783), a family restaurant with a full turkey dinner for only $5.95, are two top dining choices.

FALMOUTH: After you leave Hyannis, drive west on Route 28 to Falmouth, at the southwest tip of the Cape. If you're making Falmouth your first stop, take the Bourne Bridge over the Cape Cod Canal when you leave Route 3. This pretty town has been around long enough to have been shelled (but not too seriously) by British warships back in the early years of the 19th century. Katherine Lee Bates, author of "America the Beautiful," was born here, and a monument to her memory stands near the village green. Overlooking the green is an 18th-century church with a bell cast by Paul Revere.

Other historical sites to note are the **Saconesset Homestead,** a 300-year-old Cape Cod farmstead with exhibits, gardens, animals, and Sunday flea market; remains of the old wooden dock where trenches were built to repel a threatened British invasion in the early 19th century; and the **Falmouth Historical Society** building, with period furniture, lovely garden, and widow's walk typical of those on houses belonging to whaling skippers.

For your meals in Falmouth, the **Flying Bridge**, Scranton Avenue (tel. 548-2700), offers an excellent view of Falmouth's busy harbor and the nautical goings-on at the adjoining yacht marina, owned by the same management. Open April through October, it serves lunch from noon to 2:30 p.m. and dinner from 5:30 p.m. to 10 p.m. On Sundays and holidays it opens at noon, with brunch till 3 p.m. and dinner till 9 p.m. Every night there's music for dancing in the upstairs lounge. Lobsters, of course, are a specialty, but there's a wide range of other entrees such as duckling and steak, with dinner prices starting about $5.95. Note the whaling scene in the lobby.

Irish food (corned beef and cabbage) and such trappings as an Irish singing group are the specialties of the **Century Pub,** 29 Locust Street (tel. 548-0196), on the way to Woods Hole past where Routes 28 and 28A intersect. Open until 1 a.m., mid-May to mid-September.

For excellent roast-beef sandwiches, German-style sausage plates, delicious pastries, and other deli items, try **Elsie's Del-Lunch,** 553 Palmer Avenue, Falmouth (tel. 548-6263). Breakfast served July and August.

And for your luxury meal in Falmouth, choose the **Coonamessett Inn,** Jones Road at Gifford Street (tel. 548-2300), where the traditional New England cooking is considered the best in town. Prices are in the upper ranges ($7 to $14) but the lobsters, scallops, and chowder are worth every dollar. Luncheon specials are around $4. The dining rooms, done in Colonial decor, overlook beautifully landscaped grounds and a pond. Coonamessett Inn serves breakfast, lunch, and dinner daily throughout the year. There is entertainment in the evening, and a "coat and tie" dress code. **Coonamessett** is a complete inn, with guest rooms as well as food. In the main inn, rooms are about $20, double; and in the cottages, about $40.

One of the most charming places to stay in Falmouth is **The Elm Arch Inn,** off Main Street (tel. 548-0133). There's a swimming pool, a pleasant lawn and screened patio, and a variety of accommodations starting at $14 in a single, $18 in a double for rooms with sink; and $20 to $30 for rooms with bath. Off-season (before July and after mid-September), rates drop to as low as $14 for a single and $18 for a double. There's history, too, at the inn, which was built in 1812, and bombarded by a British frigate two years later. The dining room wall still shows the scar of the cannonball.

WOODS HOLE: From Falmouth to Woods Hole is just a short ride on Route 28. Ride down to see the Woods Hole Oceanographic Institute (though very little of it is open to the public) or to take the ferry to Nantucket or Martha's Vineyard. It's almost worth missing the ferry to dine at the **Landfall Restaurant** on the wharf (tel. 548-1758). The food is excellent, the view spectacular, and prices range from $2.65 to $3.95 for lunch; $6.95 to $12 for dinner.

And if you do miss the ferry and want to stay over in Woods Hole, the **Nautilus Motor Inn,** Route 28 (tel. 548-1525), makes a good stopoff for the night, or longer. It's comfortable, pleasantly located overlooking the harbor, and has a swimming pool and tennis courts plus award-winning formal gardens. Rates are $36 to $44 for doubles, mid-June through Labor Day. One of the Cape's finest restaurants, **The Dome,** is there, too. Steaks and native seafood are served in this circular restaurant topped by a 54-foot geodesic dome built by the architect-philosopher Buckminster Fuller. The Dome (tel. 548-0800) serves breakfast, luncheon, dinner, and Sunday brunch from May to October.

ENTERTAINMENT ON THE UPPER CAPE: You have a choice of three well-known playhouses on the Cape: **The Cape Cod Melody Tent** in Hyannis (tel. 775-9100) at the West Main Street Rotary has a season of musical theater and drama from June to September; **The Falmouth Playhouse** (tel. 563-5922) off Route 151 has established stars doing the summer circuit; and the **Cape Playhouse** (tel. 385-3911) on Route 6A in Dennis has been famous for years for its fine productions. Musical reviews are featured at the **Golden Anchor** in West Dennis and at the **Christopher Ryder House** in Chathamport (which is also known for excellent food).

The kids will love the dolphin shows in West Yarmouth and West Brewster (you will, too). In Yarmouth on Route 28 the **Aqua Circus of Cape Cod** (tel. 775-8883) is open daily, 10:30 a.m. to 8 p.m., from June to September, with ten shows daily. Admission includes a visit to the petting zoo where Bert Quackerback, the piano-playing duck, performs. Off-season, hours are from 11 a.m. to 4 p.m. At **Sealand** (tel. 385-9252), on Route 6A in West Brewster, the trained dolphins perform five times daily from 11 a.m. to 7:30 p.m. from late June to Labor Day. You can also bring a lunch to their Marine Park and watch the penguins and turtles in the outdoor pools. Open year round; call for off-season hours.

Note: An excellent booklet detailing six self-guided tours of the Cape is free at the Cape Cod Chamber of Commerce information centers in Hyannis, at the Bourne Bridge, and at the Sagamore Bridge. Small-group guided tours are given by **The New England Gallery,** 483 Main Street, Chatham (tel. 945-3898). These include luncheon or dinner and are priced from $18 to $36 (Nantucket). There is also an evening photography tour for $12 (without dinner).

CAPE COD NATIONAL SEASHORE: In a great victory for conservationists and ecological groups, many of the beaches and forestlands of the Cape have been designated part of the Cape Cod National Seashore, protected from commercial encroachment and carefully watched over by the National Park Service. If you are at all interested in nature, natural history, and the beauty and preservation of the Cape Cod area—and particularly if you have youngsters in tow—take part in the many programs offered by the Seashore. The two places to get started at are the **Salt Pond Visitor Center** in Eastham, on Route 6, and at the **Province Lands Visitor Center,** high up on Race Point Road in Provincetown. The Eastham center is the busier, with a small natural-history museum on the grounds, picnic and bicycling areas, and evening programs several times a week in the amphitheater. The Province Lands Center also has evening programs, plus an observation roof from which you'll get striking vistas of dune and forest and sea. Both centers are starting points for numerous self-guided or guided tours through the fascinating forest, swamp, and marshland trails of the Cape. (There are special paths for the blind.)

This is a great area for cyclists. The five-mile loop through sand dunes and a beach forest starting at the Province Lands Visitor Center is a good family trail as it is not too hilly for children. There is a two-mile trail at the Salt Pond Visitor's Center, and another at the Pilgrim Heights Center in Truro which follows the route taken by the Pilgrims when they explored the area in 1629. Maps are available at the information centers. Joggers compete with the cyclers for space on the trails, but the best place for jogging is at Nickerson State Park on Route 6A in Brewster.

Note: This is surfing territory, too, with special sections set aside at Coast Guard Beach, Marconi Beach, and Head of the Meadow Beach in Eastham and Truro.

PROVINCETOWN: P-town, as the regulars call it, it perhaps the best-known spot on Cape Cod. First came the Indians, camping where the town hall now stands and barbecuing the wild boar that used to roam the forests. Then came the Pilgrims, who made their first landing here; then the Portuguese fishermen, who still go down to the sea in ships (come in June, if you can, to see the festive "Blessing of the Fleet"); then in the '20s, the artists and writers and actors and assorted free souls who made it America's Left Bank on the seashore, Greenwich Village transplanted to the waterfront. Eugene O'Neill and Edna St. Vincent Millay and Edmund Wilson and Hans Hoffman and Robert Motherwell are some of the names associated with Provincetown, all attracted by its old clapboard houses, narrow, winding streets, a profusion of flowers, a salt tang to the breeze, and a laissez-faire spirit in the air.

Provincetown today still has its art colony, but at the height of the summer, there's scarcely room for an artist to take a pencil out of his pocket, let alone set up an easel. **Commercial Street,** in the center of town, is packed tight with shoppers and strollers, their erratic passage constantly interrupted by cars struggling up the one-way street to get to the beaches at the tip of the Cape. On scores of wave-lashed wharves, vacationists sit at "nautical" bars and restaurants sampling the local seafood, served by scores of college kids who relish the chance of a job in a resort where there are so many young people. If you crave peace and quiet, come to P-town before July 4 or after Labor Day, or else stay away from the middle of town (the east and west ends of town are relatively quiet). But if you want to be part of the most exciting scene on the Cape, this is your place.

Note that Provincetown is one of the few vacation areas on the Cape—or anywhere, for that matter—where you can get along perfectly well without a car. The town beach, the local grocery and drugstores, scores of restaurants, shops, whatever, can easily be reached on foot, and you won't have to hunt for those hard-to-come-by parking spaces.

Sightseeing and Shopping

You can hardly miss seeing the **Pilgrim Monument,** a 252-foot granite shaft built in 1910 to honor the first landfall of the Pilgrims in the New World and the signing here of the *Mayflower* Compact. It now houses a fascinating museum containing a miniature memorial to playwright Eugene O'Neill. There's a fine view of the Cape from the top of the tower (open daily except Thanksgiving, Christmas, and New Year's. Admission: $1 for adults; 25¢, children under 12. Be forewarned; it's a long hard climb by stairs and ramps.)

The **Provincetown Heritage Museum,** as its name suggests, records the heritage of the town from its artists to its fishermen. The paintings on display represent a cross section of artists in Provincetown since 1899. There is a recreated dune shack, a half-scale model of a fishing schooner, and many antique exhibits. The museum is open daily, 10 a.m. to 9 p.m., at 356 Commercial Street. Admission is $1 for adults; children under 12, free.

Art is part of Provincetown's raison d'être, and you'll see plenty of it here, from sidewalk portrait painters to major exhibitions. The **Provincetown Arts Association And Museum,** 460 Commercial Street, has been part of the scene since 1914, with exhibitions by established and emerging artists. **The Group Gallery** features artists who live and work in Provincetown at its second-floor loft on MacMillan Wharf. And there are many commercial galleries throughout town. (Check the *Provincetown Advocate* or the Chamber of Commerce for listings of current shows.) Among our favorites are **Long Point Gallery,** 492 Commercial Street, and **Eva de Nagy Gallery,** 427 Commercial Street.

There are so many shops in Provincetown that it would take a book to describe them all. There are shell shops, head shops, scads of boutiques for men's and women's clothing, antique and gadget emporiums, health-food shops, bookstores, and everybody's favorite browsing place: **Marine Specialties,** 235 Commercial Street, a cavernous warehouse jumbled floor to ceiling, where you emerge with backpacks, foul-weather gear, dogsled parts, government surplus, used denims, colored T-shirts, and some of the best shells anywhere. **Graphics, Etc.,** 355 Commercial Street, features a fine selection of prints, ceramics, and wood sculpture, plus pipes in all sizes and shapes for the men. Women will treasure the antique jewelry finds at **Selma Dubrin,** 423 Commercial Street, and the young at heart will love the butterflies, rainbows, and crystal at **Chrysalis,** also on Commercial Street.

Provincetown Miscellany

We doubt that you'll run out of things to do in Provincetown. During the day, you'll probably be at the town beach or else drive out to the better ocean beaches: **Race Point** and **Herring Cove** in Provincetown, or **Head of the Meadow** in nearby North Truro. Herring Cove has small waves, Race Point and Head of the Meadow have the long rolling breakers. (Parking fee is $1 a day, or you can buy a season's pass for $10.) The sports-minded can bike, sail, fish, play tennis or golf, or ride horseback through the beach forest, across the dunes, and along the ocean at designated National Seashore areas. There are several playgrounds for kiddies, too.

What to do at night? No problem, just walk along Commercial Street, looking in at the shops, perhaps sitting down in front of Town Hall to watch the bizarre, outlandish, utterly absorbing passing parade. For something more organized, catch a movie at one of the local cinemas, an art opening at a gallery, or a play at the **Provincetown Playhouse,** still continuing in the O'Neill tradition. There are plenty of bars both "gayish" and "straightish." Among the straight bars are **Ciro and Sals,** Kiley Court, and the **Cellar Bar** at Inn at the Mews, 359 Commercial Street, both of which are crowded and busy; and **Downstairs at Plain and Fancy,** 334 Commercial Street, quiet enough to carry on a conversation. **The Crown and Anchor,** 247 Commercial Street, is the most popular gay bar. Most of the hotels feature entertainment in the lounges or restaurants and there are several dance bars. **Piggy's** on Shankpainter Road, has the "Saturday Night Fever" crowd every day in the week. The local characters, including the fishermen, congregate at **The Fo'c'sle,** 335 Commercial Street, or **The Old Colony Tap,** 323 Commercial Street.

Whatever else you do, don't miss a ride on one of P-town's famous beach taxis, a gentle roller-coaster trip up and down the giant dunes. It's unique to this part of the world, and if you take it at sunset, you'll be treated to a windblown ride along the beach at Race Point, finally to watch a brilliant sun sink into the Atlantic—the only place you can see this on the East Coast.

Or, drive your own car to Race Point and join the throng of sunset buffs watching the day fade away into the ocean.

Staying in Provincetown

The "establishment" of the Provincetown hotels is the **Provincetown Inn and Motel** (tel. 487-9500), on the very tip of Cape Cod, on what it claims is the "exact spot where the Pilgrims first landed." It fronts a beautiful beach, has a rooftop sundeck overlooking Provincetown Harbor, and is completely self-contained, with two restaurants, sauna bath, a huge indoor swimming pool (*very* useful if you should hit a few rainy days), and shops. It attracts those who appreciate its warm, comfortable air and considerable charm. Dozens of little alcoves, carved staircases, spinning wheels, old ship models, figureheads and other nautical curios placed artfully about. Whether you stay here or not, you should have a look at the lobby murals, authentic scenes of "Old Provincetown and its People" of about 100 years ago; you'll recognize the streets, old houses, and landmarks. The rooms are modern and well appointed, with color TV, private phones—all the comforts. Prices range from $32 to $60 in a double in the summer season; from $26 to $36 in a double from March 1 through June 29. Open year round. Inquire about the attractive package plans available.

A few hundred yards away from the Inn and with its own 350 feet of private beach is **The Masthead,** 31-41 Commercial Street (tel. 487-0523), a neatly kept cluster of apartments, cottages, and motel units on well-tended lawns. The waterfront sundeck, the lovely plantings, and warmly furnished units make this a distinctive spot. During the season, cottages and apartments are rented on a weekly basis, $240 to $460; motel rooms are available from $22 for a single to $46 for a double; prices go down in spring and fall. *Note:* Reservations for cottages and apartments should be made well in advance. The Masthead is open all year.

A perfect hidaway is the charming **Land's End Inn,** (tel. 487-0706), 22 Commercial Street, perched atop Gull Hill at the tip of Provincetown's West End. Hidden from the street, it was once the summer "bungalow" of a wealthy Boston merchant; and the original woodcarvings and stained glass are still there, along with beautiful antiques and plants that flourish in the sunlit rooms. The panoramic view of Cape Cod is spectacular, especially from the octagonal Tower Room (often rented as a honeymoon suite). This is a place to relax, read, and listen to red-bearded innkeeper David Schoolman's collection of classical music (no TV here). It's as popular in winter as in summer, so reservations well in advance are a must. In-season, doubles are $27 to $50; efficiency apartments, $40 to $45. Lower rates in spring, fall, and winter, with singles in winter starting at $15: doubles, at $19; and efficiencies, at $25. Some rooms can accommodate up to five people, and there is a $5-a-day charge over the doubles rate for each additional person. A complimentary continental breakfast is served in the living room areas each morning (the cinnamon toast is delicious). And there is plenty of parking available for guests.

Our own "special little place" in Provincetown is **Hargood House,** 493 Commercial Street (tel. 487-1324), in the quiet East End of town. Featured in *House Beautiful* for its architecture and decor, it consists of 17 waterfront and waterview apartments, beautifully appointed with antiques, decorator accessories, and personal touches everywhere, even including dishwashers. They are really little homes away from home and could comfortably be lived in for a whole summer. Hal Goodstein and Bob Harrison, the hospitable owners, are always on hand to see that everything functions smoothly—and it does. There's a back garden right on the beach, comfortable patio furniture, a hammock to swing in as you watch the ocean lash up against the pilings—and interesting people to talk to. The regulars here consist of Boston and New York professionals who don't mind paying a little extra for the charm and convenience. The apartments rent for between $245 and $420 a week, including maid service, depending on size and location. Only weekly rentals are available from July 4 to Labor Day, but out of season (Hargood House is heated and open year round), they will take a two-day minimum. Off-season rates go from $28 to $48 a day for two persons. Christmas on the Cape, anybody? Write well in advance for reservations.

Guest Houses: Up in the East End of town is Provincetown's most attractive guest house, the **White Dory,** 616 Commercial Street (tel. 487-0224), an immaculate white mansion with manicured lawns and a private beach just across the tiny road out front. Stay here and you'll have all the comforts of a fine motel, plus the warmth and friendliness of a Cape Cod guest house. The nicest thing here is the large, beautifully appointed "front parlour," with its fireplace, cozy sofas, piano, and bar. Guests—a mixed group ranging "from 20 to 90"—get together for free continental breakfasts, for cocktails (free setups and hors d'oeuvres), and, later at night, for conversation or cards; you can play the stereo, the TV, or the grand piano. The rates, however, are more than the usual guest house tariff: there are doubles at $42 with ocean views and fireplaces (during off-season, guests can make their own fires); others rent from $27 and up for a double, from $23 and up for a single, all with private bath. There are also four two-room apartments, at $250 a week or $50 a day. Owner Ray Sparks advises advance reservations.

Close to the center of town, **Somerset House,** 378 Commercial Street (tel. 487-0383), is a long-established guest house and one of the nicest in town. It's located just across the street from the beach with a front piazza (New Englandese for porch) for people-watching, and a lovely garden carefully landscaped by owner Jon Gerrity, who also carefully choses the classical music he puts on the stereo for his guests. The century-old house is attractively maintained, filled with plants, the walls hung with paintings, some of the rooms with Victorian marble-topped furniture, others splashingly modern, all with modern tile baths and enclosed stall showers. Rates vary according to size and location, but go from $20 to $30 for singles, from $24 to $34 for doubles: prices drop, September to June, when a few attic rooms are available at $10. Advance reservations are advised for specific rooms in season, but you'll probably always be able to find something here. Limited private parking is available, and public parking is nearby.

One block away from Commercial Street, at 142 Bradford Street (tel. 487-9810), is **Sunset Inn,** a very appealing guest house with modest rates. Keith Brickel, the friendly young owner, creates a warm atmosphere here; he serves his guests coffee out in the big backyard and patio in the morning, and after the beach, he supplies setups for cocktails. Guests can use the barbecue grill. The 20-odd rooms are clean and comfortable, some with private bath, and go from about $15 to $28. Sunset Inn is heated, and off-season rates are very low: about $10 per person, anywhere in the house. The crowd runs to people in their 20s and 30s, including families, who appreciate the big porches and the sundeck upstairs, too. Reservations advised.

A Top Family Choice: If you don't mind being a few miles away from the center of town (and if you have a car it's no problem), a perfect place for a family vacation is **Kalmar Village,** Route 6A (tel. 487-0585), not far from the entrance to Provincetown. Kalmar is a cottage colony located right on its own 400-foot private beach, a cluster of 30 cottages, plus a motel. Not only is it *at* the beach, but there is also a heated pool that the kiddies love and a laundromat that makes life easy for mom. The two- and three-room cottages are furnished with everything for easy vacation living, from maid service to toasters. In high season, expect to pay around $330 to $375 a week, less in spring and fall.

We also like the **Eastwood Motor Lodge,** 324 Bradford Street (tel. 487-0743), an attractive, immaculately kept wood-shingled building with umbrella-shaded tables on the lawn, barbecues, miniature golf, and shuffleboard. It's a short walk from the warm bay waters of the Cape, but it also has its own heated pool. The rooms all have air conditioning (and heat), carpeting, color TV, and ceramic tile bath. In-season rates are $34 to $36, double; off-season, they're $24 to $28. About a 20-minute walk from the center of town.

Also Recommended: The artistically weatherbeaten **Moors Motel,** Bradford Street Extension at the tip of the Cape, over-looks the scenic moors. Best rooms are those on the second floor with balconies. Rates go from $32 to $38, double, in-season, and vary from month to month with a low of $15 to $18 in winter. **Fisherman's Cove,** 145 Commercial Street (487-1997), offers comfortable two-bedroom apartments at $270 and up a week, as well as rooms with semiprivate baths at $16 a day. Open May to November, it's right on the beach with a private deck. **Asheton House,** 3 Cook Street (tel. 487-9966), is a lovely white home with a Colonial garden and three guest rooms, $35 to $45.

Dining in Provincetown

For the full flavor of Provincetown—the ocean, the nautical atmosphere, the seafood—we like **The Flagship,** 463 Commercial Street (tel. 487-1200). Jutting out over the water and built almost entirely of driftwood and ship salvage, it's crowded with nautical trimmings—anchors, ship's bells, ropes, and wheels. The two bars up front are actually halves of old fishing dories, and they're flanked by a large fireplace and open hearth. Try to sit by the windows and watch the sun set or the moon rise while dining on the likes of paella Valenciana, $9; scallops Française, $8; or the fish of the day, always an excellent choice at $7. Lobster Louisiana, a house specialty, features a sauce of heavy cream, wine, and shrimp stock. Dinner is served from 5:30 p.m. every evening; and lunch, Friday, Saturday, and Sunday at noon.

Cafe at the Mews, 359 Commercial Street (tel. 487-1500), part of the waterfront complex Inn at the Mews, has received high acclaim since it was remodeled and reopened under new manage-ment in 1978. The dining room, decorated in tones of burgundy and pink, is extended by a covered deck looking out onto Provincetown Harbor. The Mews features an international menu, with fresh seafood starting at $7.50; roast tarragon chicken, $6.25; medallion of beef, $8.95; and rack of lamb for two, $24. Dinner hours are 6 p.m. to 11 p.m.; and lunch is served from 11:30 to 2:30. There is an extensive wine list and a hideaway bar in the basement. Open all year.

For more than 25 years, **Ciro and Sal's**, 41 Kiley Court (off Commercial Street, about the 400 block; tel. 487-9803), has been a famous P-town landmark for excellent Italian food in intimate surroundings. Originally just a charming grotto with flickering candles atop tables and hanging Chianti bottles, it's now expanded into additional light and airy upstairs rooms. (But it's still crowded, so phone ahead for a reservation.) Pasta dishes start at $4.75 for the plainest varieties, and run to about $6 for the exotic spaghetti with walnuts, anchovies, raisins, olive oil, garlic, herbs, and pine nuts. Most other entrees—veal, chicken, fish in various manifestations—are in the $6.75 to $11.50 range. A superb 20-ounce steak with red wine is $10.95. Be sure to save room for one of the incredible desserts, such as lime pie or coeur à la crème. Open all year.

Be sure to make your reservations well in advance for dinner or lunch at the **Red Inn**, 15 Commercial Street (tel. 487-0050), because this charming restaurant is so popular that it's sold out every night. Pilots often call ahead from their planes before landing at P-town. The quaint old building has been converted into several dining rooms and our favorite is the Greenhouse Room with its flourishing plants (nourished by the classical music on the stereo, according to the owners, the Barker family). But in any room the food and the view of the harbor from the far West End are unexcelled. The cooking is "New England Country Inn" style with fresh fish, steaks and ribs, and house specialty dishes like beef stroganoff troika, $8.25; stuffed filet of sole, $8.25; and lobster of Provincetown (two pounds or better), $16. Luncheon prices start at $3.95 for baked filet of scrod, with lobster sauté going for $6.50. Desserts include such delicacies as strawberries Romanoff and grapes Pierre: marinated grapes in glasses of sparkling burgundy. Red Inn is open year round, serving dinner from 5:30 p.m. to 10 p.m. and lunch from 11:30 a.m. to 3 p.m.

Try a breakfast with enough sustenance to last until dinner in one of these restaurants (which also serve lunch/brunch and dinner): **Poor Richard's Buttery**, 432 Commercial Street (tel. 487-3825), has pancakes, omelettes, and crêpes filled with everything from fresh fruit to shrimp, from 9 a.m. to 2 p.m.; **Cookies Restaurant,** 133 Commercial Street (tel. 487-9718), favored by local fishermen and other Portuguese natives, offers homemade flippers (fried dough) with linguica, $1.85; and a breakfast special of juice, eggs, bacon, home fries, and griddle cakes for $1.75 to $2.55 from 9 to 11 a.m. Nearby at 149 Commercial Street, the **Cottage Restaurant** (tel. 487-9160) starts serving its huge three-egg omelettes at 7:30 a.m. and has breakfast available till 3 p.m. **Cafe Edwidge,** 333 Commercial Street (tel. 487-3851), features fresh-fruit bowls, whole-wheat pancakes, homemade bread, eggs, and home fries from 9 a.m. to 1 p.m. in its second-story dining room, $2 to $3.

Note: Buy lobster-in-the-rough at the **Provincetown Seafood Market,** next to Dairyland on Shank Painter Road. Open 9 a.m. to 9 p.m. daily. And if you want some "fast food", try **Mojo's** at the Ryder Street Extension at the foot of the fishing pier for french fries (60¢) and fried clams ($2.50).

Just 10 minutes from Provincetown in North Truro on Pond Road, is **Méditerranée** (tel. 487-1881), a dinner restaurant in a 200-year-old Cape Cod house which has become famous for its European food served in high style. James Beard and Craig Claiborne as well as other connoisseurs have praised the cuisine, which includes such delicacies as duck pâté with truffles and cognac. A dinner for two featuring gigot en croûte (stuffed leg of lamb in puff pastry) and steak bearnaise can run as high as $50 with wine. However, some entrees start as low as $5, and there is a three-course prix-fixe dinner at $10.50. Guests are served in formal dining rooms; and a terrace in the flower garden is the cocktail lounge. Waiters are attentive and knowledgeable, and are willing to explain the finer points of the menu. Desserts

Bunker Hill monument and model of the battle scene

are excellent, too, with rich French pastries, cakes, and unusual ice creams, such as the one we chose made with ground chestnuts. *Méditerranée* is open from 6:30 p.m. to 10 p.m., and reservations are advised.

Note: Provincetown is becoming very much a year-round vacation town, and many of the restaurants, hotels, and guest houses are open all year. It is especially beautiful in spring and fall when the beaches, dunes, and National Seashore Park are all uncrowded.

Chapter IX

A STUDENT'S GUIDE TO BOSTON

IF YOU THINK of Boston as a town for little old ladies in Queen Mary hats and tennis shoes, forget it. Boston is now a cosmopolitan and youth-oriented city. It still has its history and culture, but that's all blended now with activism and counterculture. Surrounded by universities, the Boston-Cambridge area is a combination of the Left Bank and Greenwich Village, and a magnet of such potency for the young that a recent *New York Times* article reported that Boston had outstripped New York as the city most college kids want to settle in once they get out of school.

What can you expect to find in Boston? How do you get around, and where do you go for fun and for some of Boston's culture? Where do you eat, and where do you stay? We'll try to help you make these first introductions to the city. For your part, have a student ID card and other identification with you; they may help you get special rates. And always ask if there are student discounts at theaters, hotels, and stores. The owners do not always publicize that fact.

Where to Stay

First, of course, you need a place to stay, and that will be the hardest thing to find in town, unless you can afford the hotel rates. It seems strange that there's a shortage of student housing when there are so many universities in the area. That's both the problem—and the answer. As the schools have grown, they've taken over many of the inexpensive, older hotels and rooming houses for dormitories. Visiting students get revenge by moving into the dormitories. This isn't done officially, of course, but there are ways. The best is to know a student who is willing to make room for your sleeping bag (or whose roommate is out of town). Even if you don't know anyone, it's rather easy to make friends by mingling with the crowd at Harvard's Holyoke Center in Harvard Square or Boston University's meeting places at Kenmore Square and Sherman Student Union. Someone usually knows where there is a space for a visitor. From May to August you can stay officially at **Northeast Hall,** 204 Bay State Road (tel. 267-3042). Rooms are available at $10 for a single, $14 to $16 for a double, and $18 for a triple, daily. They are immaculate and comfortable, and very near downtown Boston.

There are various ways of beating the system. One friend of ours suggests writing in advance to the college admissions office, saying you're interested in the school and would like to visit. They'll usually make dorm arrangements for you. This sounds pretty nervy to us, but it's not completely unethical; you may be so impressed with the college that you'll want to transfer there! And another friend reports that, when all else fails and you can't get a room, the Student Center Library at M.I.T. is open 24 hours. Your ID card should get you in to do "research" on the comfortable chairs. All of which is to say that the Boston campus housing situation is a pretty loose one and, with a little effort, you're almost certain to get a place to crash.

If, however, you prefer a more organized approach, there are the Ys, several youth hostels, and variety of small hotels and rooming houses in and around the university areas. Let's begin with the Ys.

THE Ys: The Huntington YMCA, 316 Huntington Avenue (tel. 536-7800), probably has the most attractive and modern accommodations to be found in a Y residence. It now accommodates both men and women. Its 350 rooms are newly redecorated, and rates include use of a wide range of Y facilities—pool, gym, and library. There is also a cafeteria on the premises. Rates start at $9.25 for a single room, $12.25 for a single with a semiprivate bath, and $13.25 for a private bath. A double room costs $14.25, and weekly rates are available at five times the daily rates. Always a bargain, the YMCA is located about ten minutes from downtown Boston.

Note: The Boston YMCA has the largest indoor track in the country.

Popular with students, the **YMCA** at 820 Massachusetts Avenue, Central Square, Cambridge (tel. 876-3860), is located about halfway between Harvard and M.I.T. It's a very old Y, but a friendly one. The rooms are just basic, clean sleeping areas, no private baths, but the sports facilities are great: a swimming pool, indoor and outdoor tracks, two squash courts, two gyms, three raquetball-handball courts. Singles and doubles run from $8 to $15. Call or write ahead for rooms.

Just up the street, off Massachusetts Avenue at Central Square, is the YWCA, 7 Temple Street, Cambridge (tel. 491-6050), which caters to college students and working women. There are two buildings, a heated pool, a cafeteria open for breakfast and dinner, and a lawn for sunbathing out back. Not too many transient rooms are available, so it's best to write in advance. Rates are $8.50 single, $16 double, in the old building; and $11 to $12.50 single and $21 double in the new building. There is a group rate of $5 a day per person for three to five people.

The **Berkeley Residence Club of the YWCA,** well located in Boston at 40 Berkeley Street (tel. 482-8850), welcomes women of all ages. It's a lovely place, with a garden, drawing room, library, sewing room, cafeteria, and laundry facilities. Transients pay $11 a night for a single room; $10.50 in a double; and $4.50 for sleeping bag and towels. Advance reservations with one night's deposit are required.

AMERICAN YOUTH HOSTELS: AYH has two youth hostels in the Greater Boston area. The **Brookline** hostel, at 45 Strathmore Road (tel. 277-2322), charges $4 a night for members and $5 for nonmembers. Check-in time is between 5 p.m. and 8 p.m.; check-out at 10 a.m. There is an 11 p.m. curfew. The **Charlestown YMCA** hostel, 32 City Square (tel. 242-2660), is a 10-minute walk from the Community College stop on the MBTA Orange line. This one is for members only, $4. Check-out time is at 11 a.m. and there is no curfew. For further information on hostels and how to become a member, write or phone American Youth Hostels, Inc., 251 Harvard Street, Brookline, MA 02146 (tel. 731-5430). **Harvard Student Agencies, 4** Holyoke Center, can get you hostel memberships, too.

SMALL HOTELS AND ROOMING HOUSES: **Anthony's Inn,** 27
College Avenue, Somerville (tel. 666-1300), is a traditional-type
New England inn near Tufts University and only ten minutes
from Harvard Square by bus. There's TV and air conditioning
and pleasant surroundings. Rates are $13 for a single without
bath; $16 with bath; and $20 for a double. Weekly rates go from
$60 to $70 depending on number of people and bath facilities.

Also in Brookline, **Longwood Inn,** 123 Longwood Avenue (tel.
566-8615), offers acceptable accommodations at modest rates.
Located in a residential area, it is near transportation on the
Beacon Street and Riverside lines, close to the colleges and medical complex. This large, old guest house has 17 rooms. Singles
with shared bath rent for $14; with private bath, $16. Doubles
are $18 with shared bath and $21 with private bath. Kitchen
privileges, laundry facilities, and parking included.

Almost hidden from the street by shrubbery, **The Kirkland,** 67
Kirkland Street, Cambridge (tel. 547-4600), has an aura of gen-
teelness about it. It's worth looking into since there are so few
inexpensive transient accommodations near Harvard Square.
Travelers must have ID cards and all guests must follow the
house rules, which include no visitors or pets in the rooms.
Depending on whether you share one of the several bathrooms
on the floor or have private facilities, singles go from $10 to $20,
doubles from $20 to $26. There are family rooms for three to five,
from $24 to $35; and apartments may be rented at rates of $20
to $35 a day, with a 12-day minimum. All apartments have
private baths, fully equipped kitchens, and linens.

Across the way at 66 Kirkland Street (tel. 547-1653) is **Toad
Hall,** two large lodging houses with an informal atmosphere.
Rates range from $25 to $35 weekly. There is a resident superin-
tendent, supervising, we suppose, the public kitchen, the coin-
operated laundry, the "pay toll baths," and the "no-stereo" rule.
Parking is available, and the office is open 10 a.m. to 4 p.m.,
Monday through Friday only. Toad Hall is within walking dis-
tance of Harvard Yard and the Divinity School.

Note: The guest house scene is a shifting one due to urban
renewal, college expansion, and the fact that it is often more
profitable to turn them into permanent rooming houses. Those
listed here will, hopefully, be around for a while. In addition,
most colleges have up-to-date listings of off-campus housing, but
you may have to show university affiliation before the housing
office lets you look at the listings. Call these numbers for information: **Boston University,** 353-3510; **Harvard,** 495-3377;

M.I.T., 253-1493; **Northeastern,** 437-2530; and **Tufts,** 628-5000, ext. 435 or ext. 300. Many of the college listings have not been checked out by the schools, so investigate before committing yourself. Some ask for security: a week's or a month's rent in advance. And some will not accept phone reservations: they'll want to look at you, even "interview" you, and you'll want to look at them. So be sure to leave yourself some extra time to look around for a room if you're interested in getting one through the schools' listings

Where to Eat

There's no shortage of inexpensive eating places in Boston and Cambridge; the challenge is to find the ones with good food. So, Alka-Seltzer in hand, we did some scouting around for you. Advice: Eat a big breakfast and a substantial lunch, when meals are cheaper; order less in the evening when they cost more. Don't be afraid to ask for a "doggie bag"—some of the best people eat doggie food the next day. Hungry students also frequent the soup and salad bars, order a bowl of soup for $1, and tuck away extra slices of bread in their backpacks. They also try the "Happy Hour" buffets in the lounges, buy a mug of beer or a glass of wine and fill up on the free food.

MARKET DISTRICT AND DOWNTOWN: That old Boston standby, **Durgin-Park,** 30 North Market Street, is still a find for inexpensive food, but only at lunchtime (evening prices have risen quite a bit lately). Get there between 11:30 a.m. and 2:30 p.m. for hearty meals. . . . And, of course, there's the **Quincy Market** for all kinds of fast foods, but they're not cheap. . . . A better deal is to check out the pushcarts in the Haymarket or walk over the North End for good, inexpensive Italian food. Have pizza at the **Galleria Umberto Rosticceria,** 289 Hanover Street, for 30¢ a slice; ham and cheese turnovers, 85¢; cold cuts and cheese in a sandwich, 60¢. Get a pasta dinner for $2.95 at **Ristorante Lucia,** 415 Hanover Street; a good meal at the **European Restaurant,** 218A Hanover Street, for as little as $2.50; or at **La Piccolo Venezia,** 63 Salem Street, where the top item, polenta and cod, is $3.95 and veal cutlet, $2.95. Buy Italian bread at **Drago and Sons,** 275 North Street, and some cheese at **Pace's,** 54 Salem Street, or **Al Capone Cheese Company,** 72 Blackstone Street, and make yourself a moveable feast. . . . Some of the government buildings at Government Center have cafeterias open to the public. You can get a meal for around $2 in pleasant surroundings. They usually don't have signs, so ask around.

Down in **Chinatown,** you'll have no trouble finding inexpensive lunches and dinners. **King Wah,** 29 Beach Street, has good specialties, and most of the places have their menus posted outside so you can check the values. . . . Fried chicken is at its inexpensive best at **Bob the Chef's,** 604 Columbus Avenue, Roxbury. Price range for great soul food is from $1.50 to $2.95 for a complete meal. . . . **Lili's Deli,** 507 Columbus Avenue, has a chitterling dinner for $3.25 and pork chops for $2.95. A generous slice of sweet-potato pie is 50¢.

In the area near the **Prudential Center, Wok In,** 845 Boylston Street, is a **Chinese** food express, with quick and inexpensive specialties. **In 'n Out,** 62 Hereford Street, is clean, open almost all day, has good food—and art displays, and a good roast-beef sandwich with Russian dressing and onions. . . . **Anthony's,** 259 Newbury Street, is open 7:30 to 7:30 and you can get a breakfast of two eggs and french toast with ham, bacon, or sausage for 99¢. For $1.29 you can add another egg, fruit juice, home fries, and tea or coffee to that. They also have subs, burgers, salads, and roast beef from 75¢ up. . . . The Japanese dish called "soba", a hearty soup filled with buckwheat noodles and beef or chicken is a meal in itself. Get a bowl for $1.95 at **Hai Hai,** a Japanese restaurant at 423 Boylston Street.

If you're on a natural-foods or vegetarian regime, you'll find

Old Corner Book Store (meeting place of Emerson, Longfellow, and Harriet Beecher Stowe)

a home at **Conscious Cookery,** 30 Massachusetts Avenue between the Prudential Center and Kenmore Square. . . . Macrobiotic devotees can be found reading their copies of *East-West Journal* at **Sanae,** 272 Newbury Street. . . . Nearby is **Erewhon,** 342 Newbury Street, one of the most popular purveyors of macrobiotic food. (They have a second store at 1731 Massachusetts Avenue in Cambridge.) You can buy grains and beans and other staples, even a macrobiotic sandwich to take out with some organic fruit or vegetables. . . . Stop in, too, at the **Organic Food Cellar,** 297A Newbury Street, for homemade bread, natural juices, homemade fudge (without sugar), sandwiches, and munchies to go. And if you're rally fending off starvation, buy an ounce of Granola to nibble on for 5¢.

If you prefer steaks, **Newbury's Steak House,** 94 Massachusetts Avenue, has them at $2.95 with salad bar, at lunch. . . . **Victoria Restaurant,** 1024 Massachusetts Avenue, has good luncheon specials under $2, and excellent inexpensive dinners. The food is American-Greek-Italian, and it's in the new wholesale meat district off the expressway. So the meat has to be good!

At 42 Charles Street, don't miss **Flourchild's** Italian pie. It's a pizza on whole-wheat bread-dough crust with a wide range of toppings to put over the tomato sauce and cheese. Prices from $1.95 up, depending on what you add. They also have sandwiches, $1.65 to $2.25. (How about sardines with Jarlsberg cheese and onion?). . . . Nearby at 280 Cambridge Street, near the Massachusetts General Hospital, you'll find **Hava Nagila,** a moderately priced Israeli restaurant. It's a Jewish mother's dream restaurant, just full of nice young doctors.

The **Cambridge area** offers just about anything you want in food. We've listed just a few of the places preferred by the local students—those we've found to give both good food and good value. (See coffeehouse listings, also later on.) Everyone's favorite is **Legal Sea Food,** 237 Hampshire Street, where the menu depends on what fresh fish comes in that day. You can even get sashimi here, Japanese style except for the french fries. Open seven days a week from 11 a.m. to 9 p.m. . . . **Elsie's,** 71A Mt. Auburn Street, is a Cambridge institution, usually open 11 a.m. to 2 a.m., where everyone goes for roast-beef sandwiches on a bulky roll with onions and Russian dressing, or TD (turkey delight). Other cholesterol nightmares include Fresser's Delight, a combination of hot pastrami, roast beef, brisket, and cole slaw. The **Rendezvous,** 24 Holyoke Street, has some great buys in Greek and Vietnamese appetizers—salad, spring rolls, spinach pie—as well as subs, pizzas, and sandwiches. And if you'd like some midnight munchies, even at 4 a.m., that's the place to go. The dinners in the downstairs dining room which serves Vietnamese and French food are both excellent and inexpensive.

Put these on your list too: **La Groceria**, 853 Main Street, near the Central Square fire station, has a small street-level room and a large upstairs dining room; **Ristorante Grotta Blue**, 18 Eliot Street, cooks all the food to order and makes a delicious pasta with pesto, plus tremendous pizza. . . . The best and most imaginative burgers in the Boston-Cambridge area can be found at **Mr. Bartley's Burger Cottage**, 1246 Massachusetts Avenue, from $1.50. Homemade soups, Greek salads, and burgers à la Sophia Loren or Greta Garbo fill up the Harvard crowd at lunch and dinner. . . . The more artsy members of the Harvard community can often be found at **Carmen's Juice Bar**, 52 Boylston Street, refreshing themselves on innovative tropical-juice drinks all made from fresh fruits, plus homemade frozen yogurts in flavors Dannon hasn't dreamed of: avocado, papaya, piña colada, and the like. All natural foods, and very good sandwiches in Syrian breads. From 60¢ for drinks, from 90¢ for yogurt.

The Hungry Persian, 14A Eliot Street, dishes up good portions of Mideastern food so that you don't leave hungry. . . . And the "Beggar's Banquet" at **Grendel's Upstairs**, 89 Winthrop Street, while not a full banquet, certainly doesn't leave you begging for more, either. Our student scroungers recommend **Sunflower Cafe** at 22 Boylston Street and **Jack's** at 925 Massachusetts Avenue for "freebies" during Happy Hour. . . . **Vienna Hofbrau**, 1314 Commonwealth Avenue, Allston, has luncheon specials from $1.95 (a great place to go in the evening, too). . . . Try some of the Portuguese restaurants, too, for good deals: **Casa Portugal**, 1200 Cambridge Street, Cambridge, or **P A Portuguese Seafood Restaurant**, 345 Somerville Avenue, Somerville. Prices are reasonable and portions are generous.

Other Suggestions: One of the best places to eat cheaply and well is at the college cafeterias, usually open for lunch only. **M.I.T.** has a huge cafeteria on the second floor of the Student Union. **Harvard's Lehman Hall** in the Yard serves from 8 a.m. to 5 p.m. in an elegant room with rich wood paneling and chandeliers. **Harvard Divinity School's Refectory**, 47 Francis Avenue, has some of the best homemade soups in the area, 35¢ and 80¢, served from 11 a.m. to 1:30 p.m. You must also sample the brownies, 40¢ (and simply divine!). Technically you should be a student to use these facilities, but if you carry an armload of books and affect a worn and harried look, you'll pass.

Check our restaurant section for additional inexpensive eating places.

Nightlife

Unless you have many months to spend in Boston, you can't begin to cover the varied Boston nighttime scene with its coffeehouses, cabarets, gallery exhibitions, cinemas, theater groups, dance groups, and lectures. So we've compiled some listings to guide you in making your choices. For more detailed selections, see the chapter on Boston Nightlife.

Some events are practically traditional and you can be sure they'll be around. Others are very fluid—the free events, dating bars, and coffeehouses come and go. Better check the weeklies or one of the daily papers.

Have your ID card with you all the time. It can help you get better rates in some places, and its a necessity if you want a drink. Legal drinking age is 18. (*Cinderella note:* The MBTA starts turning into a pumpkin after midnight, and after 1 a.m., you're strictly on your own.)

MUSIC: Try to get "rush seats" for the **Boston Symphony,** Friday afternoon and Saturday night, September through April. They're $2, on sale two hours before the 8:30 concert time, and there's always a long line. Try to attend one of the "open rehearsals" on Wednesday evenings at 7:30. Unreserved seats, $3.50 Second-balcony seats for Pops concerts (April through June) cost $4, and Esplanade concerts in July are free.

Free Concerts

Isabella Stewart Gardner Museum, 280 The Fenway, soloists and chamber music in a Venetian palazzo, Tuesday at 8 p.m., Thursday at 4 p.m. (also on Sunday at 4 p.m., when admission is charged), except July and August. Student and faculty concerts at the **New England Conservatory of Music,** 290 Huntington Avenue (tel. 262-1120), October through May, all free. **Berklee College of Music,** 1140 Boylston Street (tel. 266-1400), also at Berklee Performance Center, 150 Massachusetts Avenue. Most of the colleges have some free concerts and recitals. Sometimes you can catch rehearsals of the **Boston Lyric Opera** or the **Boston Ballet** at the **Boston Center for the Arts,** 539 Tremont

Street. Just walk through the building and peek in when you hear the music.

While there, take a peek at the glass dome of the Cyclorama, the second largest in the United States, now housing art exhibits, concerts in the round, flower shows, and flea markets. In Cambridge there are Thursday noon concerts at the **Busch-Reisinger Museum** on Kirkland Street, and Sunday concerts at 3 p.m. at the **Fogg Museum.** (These concerts are given only when classes are in session.) Both Boston and Cambridge have free summertime concerts sponsored by the city.

THEATER AND LECTURES: Tickets for the Broadway-bound shows are expensive, but there's more than enough to see at the colleges. You can count on good productions at the **Loeb Drama Center** at Harvard, **Tufts Arena Theater** in Medford, **Spingold** at Brandeis, and Boston University, M.I.T., and Emerson. The **Boston Repertory Theater** gives good performances and charges low fees. Free summer performances are given from time to time in various parts of the city, including Copley Square. Check the newspapers. You can attend a lecture free at **Ford Hall Forum,** one of America's most famous platforms, if the house has not been sold out by 7:45 of a Sunday night. Lectures are no longer given at Ford Hall, but at Northeastern University's Alumni Hall on Huntington Avenue.

FILMS: Our Boston Nightlife section has all the information, but if you want something different, try **China Cinema** in Chinatown. There are free films at the **Museum of Fine Arts,** the **Boston Public Library,** and many suburban libraries. The colleges also have film series, often as low as $1 with your ID. Since the scene changes so often, check the *Phoenix,* the *Real Paper,* or the "Calendar" section of the Boston *Globe* for current happenings.

CONTEMPORARY SOUND: Lots of good jazz at the **Sunflower Cafe,** 22 Boylston Street, Cambridge; **Pooh's** 464 Commonwealth Avenue, Boston; and **Sandy's Jazz Revival,** 54 Cabot Street, Beverly (tel. 922-7517). (Sandy's is about 40 minutes ride north of Boston, but it has the best concert offerings.) **Jonathan Swift,** 30 Boylston Street, Cambridge at Harvard Square, has rock, country, and folk entertainers. Inexpensive.

DATING BARS: In the "where-to-go" listings in the newspapers, dating bars are often dubbed "lounges." Same thing! We've listed some of the best ones in our Nightlife chapter, but here are a few that are especially student oriented: **Jack's,** 952 Massachusetts Avenue, Cambridge, (tel. 491-7800), one of the favorite dating bars of the young college crowd. About 200 people can squeeze in on a busy weekend, and it's usually busy since there's great rock, funk, or reggae music nightly. And ID card is necessary if you look too young to drink. Drinks go from 85¢ to $1.75. Admission is $1, Friday and Saturday; free the rest of the week. Open 11 a.m. to 1 a.m. daily. **The Oxford Ale House,** 36 Church Street in Harvard Square (tel. 876-5353), is almost always jammed with students, dancing or just listening to the groups that perform nightly. Dress is casual, and cover runs $1 on Thursday; $2, Friday. It's a great place to meet people—if you can squeeze your way in.

Cask 'n Flagon, 62 Brookline Avenue, near Fenway Park (tel. 536-4840), a big favorite with the singles crowd, is a very informal, very long and narrow saloon offering live entertainment Wednesday through Saturday. Good food and drink daily from 11 a.m. to 2 a.m. Drinks run 50¢ to $1.50. No cover.

COFFEEHOUSES: With over two dozen coffeehouses in the area, you can find your own style. The student-artist-writer type are mostly in Cambridge. Try **Algiers,** 40 Brattle Street, in the Truc for food and drink cum chamber music. Nobody bothers you and you can read, play backgammon, sit for hours. At the **Blue Parrot,** 123 Mt. Auburn Street, you find an international crowd under the Tiffany lamps, reading, gazing out the windows, enjoying the food. **The Idler,** also at 123 Mt. Auburn Street, has a friendly "living room"-type coffeehouse in front and "The Back Room" for beer and entertainment at night. Remember the **Passim Coffeeshop,** 47 Palmer Street, for nightly "name" entertainment.

If you're in a romantic mood, go to **Piroshka,** 24 Dunster Street, Cambridge, where you can sip Viennese coffee and foamy cappucino at candlelit tables. The **Coffee Connection** in The Garage in Cambridge, has superb coffees and teas. See our section on the North End of Boston for some of the great Italian coffeehouses.

For music and food, coffeehouse style, try **Sword-in-the-Stone,** 13 Charles Street, Boston. It's intimate and cozy with good local folk entertainment. Some of the big stars started here. The dress is casual and the setting is Old Camelot. Open 8:15 p.m. to 1 a.m.

Many of the colleges have their own coffeehouses and so do the churches. In this group is the **Nameless Coffeehouse,** one of the best, in the Unitarian Church, 3 Church Street, Harvard Square, Cambridge. Open Friday and Saturday from September to May. No charge for refreshments or entertainment, but donations are accepted.

Incidental Intelligence

It helps to know the language of the "natives" when you're ordering food. A "milk shake" is milk with flavored syrup; a frappe is made with ice cream. A "sub" is the same as a hero sandwich or a grinder, and a "bulkie" roll (pronounced bull-key rather than bulky) is a soft roll with a hard crust that you usually stuff with corned beef or some other tasty Jewish delicatessen fare. . . . You'll need exact change on the MBTA: quarters for the subways and nickels and dimes to make up the fare on the surface lines.

The best classical music station is WCRB (102.5 FM); WRKO (680 AM) plays Top 40; WBCN (101.4 FM) and WNTN (1550 AM) are rock stations; WHET (1330 AM) concentrates on jazz. WEEI (590 AM) is all news; and WITS (1510 AM) sticks to talk shows and sports.

For good values, shop the **Coop** at Harvard Square. . . . Want a good beer? Try **Jacob Wirth's,** 31 Stuart Street, a household word for about 100 years with its big draft mugs and German food, or the **Wursthaus,** 4 Boylston Street, Cambridge, which boasts the largest collection of imported beers. . . . **Frank 'N' Stein's,** 102 Massachusetts Avenue, Boston, also has imported beers, foot-long hot dogs, pinball, and free movies. . . . If you like to play chess or backgammon, there's the **Boston Chess Studio** for lessons or tournaments at 333 Newbury Street, Boston. And, if you like your moves faster than you'd get in a chess game, try the **Joy of Movement Center,** 536 Massachusetts Avenue, Cambridge, for classes in ballet, jazz, and disco, or join the joggers along the Charles River who work out even in subzero weather. And if you crave peace and relaxation, the **Integral Yoga Institute,** 129 Commonwealth Avenue, has beginners and advanced classes in hatha yoga.

HOW TO SAVE MONEY
ON ALL YOUR TRAVELS

Saving money while traveling is never a simple matter—which is why, almost 16 years ago, the **$10-a-Day Travel Club** was formed. Actually, the idea came from readers of the Arthur Frommer Publications, who felt that such an organization could bring financial benefits, continuing travel information, and a sense of community to economy-minded travelers in all parts of the world. They were right. By combining the purchasing power of thousands of our readers, we've been able to obtain a wide range of exciting travel benefits—including, on occasion, substantial discounts to members from purveyors of tourist services throughout the world.

In keeping with the money-saving concept, the membership fee is low, and it is immediately exceeded by the value of your benefits. Upon receipt of $10 (U.S. residents), $12 (Canadian and Mexican residents), or $14 (other foreign residents) to cover one year's membership, we will send all new members by return mail (book rate):

(1) The latest edition of any *two* of the books listed on the following page.

(2) A copy of ARTHUR FROMMER'S GUIDE TO NEW YORK.

(3) A copy of SURPRISING AMSTERDAM AND HAPPY HOLLAND—a 224-page pocket-size guide by Ian Keown.

(4) A one-year subscription to the quarterly Club newspaper—THE WONDERFUL WORLD OF BUDGET TRAVEL (see below).

(5) A voucher entitling you to a $5 discount on any Arthur Frommer International, Inc. tour booked by you through any travel agent in the United States and Canada.

(6) Your personal membership card, which, once received, entitles you to purchase through the Club *all* Arthur Frommer Publications for a third to a half off their regular retail prices during the term of your membership.

These are the immediate and definite benefits which we can assure to members of the Club at this time. Even more exciting, however, are the further and more substantial benefits which it has been our continuing aim to achieve for members. These are announced in the Club's newspaper, THE WONDERFUL WORLD OF BUDGET TRAVEL, a full-size, eight-page newspaper that keeps members up-to-date on fast-breaking developments in low-cost travel in all parts of the world. The newspaper also carries such continuing features as "Travelers' Directory"— a list of members all over the world who are willing to provide hospitality to other members as they pass through their home cities; "Share-a-Trip" —requests from members for travel companions who can share costs; "Readers Ask...Readers Reply"—travel-related queries from members, to which other members reply with firsthand information. It also offers advance news of individual, group, and charter programs operated by Arthur Frommer International, Inc., plus in-depth articles on special destinations (most recently, Romania, Yugoslavia, and Costa Rica).

If you would like to join this hardy bunch of international travelers and participate in its exchange of information and hospitality, simply send $10 (U.S. residents), $12 (Canadian and Mexican residents), or $14 (other foreign residents) along with your name and address to: $10-a-Day Travel Club, Inc., 380 Madison Ave., New York, NY 10017. Remember to specify which *two* of the books in section one above you wish to receive in your initial package of members' benefits. Or tear out this page, check off any two books on the opposite side, and send it to us with your membership fee.